A GUIDE TO INDEXED PERIODICALS IN RELIGION

by

John J. Regazzi

and

Theodore C. Hines

The Scarecrow Press, Inc.

Metuchen, N.J. 1975

Acknowledgment

The authors wish to express their gratitude to Mr. Edwin B. Brownrigg for his assistance and technical guidance in the writing of various computer programs for the production of this text.

A special thanks to the School of Library Service, Columbia University, for their cooperation and use of facilities in the development of this text.

Library of Congress Cataloging in Publication Data

Regazzi, John J 1948-
A guide to indexed periodicals in religion.

Includes index.
1. Theology--Periodicals--Indexes. 2. Religion--Periodicals--Indexes. 3. Theology--Periodicals--Directories. 4. Religion--Periodicals--Directories. 5. Abstracting and indexing services. I. Hines, Theodore C., ~~joint author~~. II. Title.
Z7753.R34 [BR1] 016.2'005 75-22277
ISBN 0-8108-0868-4

Printed in the United States of America

CONTENTS

Preface (Theodore C. Hines) v

Introduction (John J. Regazzi) ix

Indexing and Abstracting Services Included, with Abbreviations 1

Periodical Titles - Alphabetical List 3

Inverted Title List 59

Listing by Service 223

PREFACE

The Guide to Indexed Periodicals in Religion is the first of a new type of reference aid for librarians, teachers, and library users generally. It is intended to serve a number of purposes:

... it covers some 2700 periodicals, indexed some 3545 times, in 17 abstracting and indexing services;

... it is an aid in determining where a given periodical is indexed in the major indexing and abstracting services covered;

... it is an aid in choosing which indexing or abstracting services should be searched for a particular purpose;

... it is an aid in choosing indexing or abstracting services for purchase by a library;

... it is an aid in selecting periodicals for purchase;

... it is an aid in identifying those periodicals sometimes listed under their title and sometimes under the name of the sponsoring agency;

... it is an aid in identifying partially remembered or garbled periodical titles; and, in addition,

... it can be of some assistance in locating periodicals in various fields or subjects.

As in the case of other novel types of reference tools, we are sure that users will uncover other applications for the Guide which we have not identified here.

The basic concept of the Guide is extremely simple. It consists of four parts:

(1) A listing, by mnemonic abbreviation, of the indexing and abstracting services covered.

(2) An alphabetical list of all the periodicals covered by all the services, interfiled, with each periodical name followed by mnemonic abbreviations of the services covering it.

(3) An alphabetical listing like the above, which also includes inverted entry for each periodical under every important word in the title. This means that a title like American Church Quarterly will be listed in that form, but will also appear in the C section of the alphabet as Church Quarterly, American and in the Q's as Quarterly, American Church.

(4) A listing, by service, of the periodicals covered by each, as given in the most recent issue covering such information which could be located. Titles are given in the form given by each service.

The Guide does not, of course, replace Ulrich's or New Serial Titles, or the Union List of Serials, or any of the specialized bibliographies in the field which give fuller information about periodicals--rather, it is intended as a supplement and index to such tools. The Guide provides only the indexing or titles of periodicals and an indication of where each is indexed--the other tools provide historical information, information about locations of files of the periodicals for interlibrary loan, and ordering information.

The Guide is unique in the amount of information it gives about where each periodical is indexed, in reproducing in one place the listings of the periodicals covered by indexing or abstracting service, and in providing catchword access by each important word for every periodical title covered.

Our aim in producing this tool has been to provide as much useful information in as small a compass as possible without duplicating information readily available in other sources which libraries must have access to in any case.

This is the first edition of the first example of a new type of reference tool. We solicit comments, suggestions, and criticism to help make the next edition of this tool better, and to enable us to incorporate improvements in guides covering other areas.

Theodore C. Hines

INTRODUCTION

The evolution of this guide from a wholly different research project to this directory best explains the scope and purpose of it. While the Guide to Indexed Periodicals in Religion is a relatively simple tool, it serves to illustrate a couple of aspects involved in the development and production of such computer-based tools: a) the importance of good systems design, and b) the value of access to modular computer programs developed for handling textual and bibliographic data.

The Guide is the outgrowth of a research project which had quite a different purpose. This original study was designed to estimate the extent of duplication and overlap among existing indexing and abstracting services for the periodical literature of religion and theology. Indexes and abstracts in the fields often considered related to religion and theology, such as philosophy, philology, and classics, have not been included. Neither have those services which cover a variety of related disciplines including religion, such as the British Humanities Index, been chosen for inclusion.

For the initial research, it was necessary to prepare a consolidated listing of each journal for the latest edition of each chosen service and a comparison was made of one service to another. This, incidently, was done manually, but could have been accomplished much more easily through the use of a computer posting program available at Columbia University, School of Library Service.

Toward the end of this research and through discussion with several of the reference librarians at Union Theological Seminary, the need for a fairly comprehensive list of theological journals and where they are indexed or abstracted became apparent. The present state of indexing and abstracting in religion is such that the field is currently supporting a large number and variety of indexing services. Duplication of effort is high, and thus such a list could be used not only for purposes of verification but also in the ordering of journals and indexing services in the special and large academic library.

It was evident that the initial list of journals and indexing services could be the basis of the reference tool described above. It would have been desirable, however, to add other data which would have increased the utility of the published list, such as starting date and frequency for each journal in each service, mailing addresses for the journals, etc. The secretarial assistance and funds for such a huge clerical effort were simply unavailable.

From the onset it was obvious that the original manually key-punched list was done laboriously and uneconomically. It would have been easier to employ the program set from the beginning, precluding a great deal of keystroking and manual filing. The technique of automatic posting could have been used for each service; thus, in the recording of the list of periodicals indexed by any one service, the abbreviation for the service could have been keyed only once and assigned automatically to all of the titles on that list. By way of illustration, the data in the following format:

> IRPL
> Andover Newton Theological Quarterly
> Andrews University Studies
> Brethren Life and Thought
> Christianity and Crisis

would have produced

> Andover Newton Theological Quarterly IRPL
> Andrews University Studies IRPL
> Brethren Life and Thought IRPL
> Christianity and Crisis IRPL

IRPL was the abbreviation used for the Index to Religious Periodical Literature, and unfortunately was input after each title it included, as was done with the other services. With the list in machine-readable form, however, it offered great flexibility and advantages for saving time and keystrokes later on. It was more economical to store this data on Hollerith punched cards until we were prepared to make our final runs. It was necessary to have each title on a separate card even in those numerous cases where the same title is covered by more than one service.

Three programs from the modular set were used, and of course a sort program was also required. The latter is a routine for machine filing according to accepted library practice which was employed at a variety of points in the process. The other three programs used for this directory were modified and used in combination with each other or the sort to produce each section of this directory. These programs needed little modification for this data; they have been designed to minimize keystrokes and proofreading in each section. This was accomplished largely by developing the programs to accept variable rather than fixed field data sets. Finally, the modular programs are written so as to produce upper and lower case output, as well as accept such input if desired. This is done by routines within the program and exceptions to those routines.

The initial section of the directory was to be a single alphabetical list of the journal titles with consolidated, abbreviated references to the services including them. The basic index program was used for this list, and though the program is capable of doing much more, it did format the data to the desired specifications, handle capitalization, produce running heads at the top of each page, and consolidate entries. Entries were originally input as follows:

Bibliotheca Sacra CPI
Bibliotheca Sacra ETL
Bibliotheca Sacra IRPL
Bibliotheca Sacra NTA
Bibliotheca Sacra RTA

The program would consolidate for this listing, as follows:

Bibliotheca Sacra CPI, ETL, IRPL, NTA, RTA

To produce the title list from the keyed data, however, required some editing of the data and the program. A complete list for all words not to be capitalized in the output had to be developed for this list and inserted into the program. In addition, the data had several instances where an entire word was to be capitalized, e.g., the acronym IDOC in the journal title IDOC International. This was another permissible exception to the program, but the input was changed to ""IDOC"" International. This would alert the program to capitalize all characters between the " " and the " " sign.

The second list wanted was one of journal titles arranged by service. To produce this list, the basic run could again be used as above, and a modification of the entry development program was used to produce the desired list in one step for each service. The entry development program was rewritten so that it would search for the abbreviation of each service, one at a time. When it "matched" that service code it would output only the journal title. The running head in each case was changed to the full title of the service. This section would match input as follows for IRPL:

Andover Newton Theological Quarterly IRPL
Andrews University Studies IRPL
Brethren Life and Thought IRPL
Christianity and Crisis IRPL

and would produce:

IRPL INDEX TO RELIGIOUS PERIODICAL LITERATURE

Andover Newton Theological Quarterly
Andrews University Studies
Brethren Life and Thought
Christianity and Crisis

For the purposes of format the running heads remain entirely in upper case.

The third listing was initially suggested when it was realized that the main entry for periodicals used in most catalogs and union lists generally follows the Anglo-American cataloging rules. In some cases, this means that entry is not by title of the journal, which is traditional practice in scholarly referencing, but rather by sponsoring organization or sometimes even place. Producing entries under the organizational name or place was obviously desirable for a variety of reasons. To do it manually, however, would have been costly, time consuming, and impractical for the purposes of this publication.

A combination of factors made this feasible. First, in all instances where the organization name is the main entry, that name appears in the title, e.g., Journal of the American Academy of Religion. A list in KWIC (Keyword in Context) form would provide access to all significant words (keywords) in the title, including the name of the association. Often place would be in the title or had been added to it, though not always. The KWIC-type entry would also assist librarians and scholars in identifying titles within the library or for interlibrary loan. It could also be used in cross-checking tools such as the National Union List, New Serial Titles, and Ulrich's. It has other advantages; journal citations as they appear on interlibrary loan forms or in citations are often inaccurate or incomplete. A KWIC-type listing would be of great value in verifying and completing such citations.

While it was agreed that a significant word listing was important and necessary to the directory, the final format of the listing needed to be decided upon and developed. Most KWIC programs truncate the longer entries; the KWOC (Key-word Out of Context) type of index was also considered, but it is somewhat uneconomical of space and it usually does not subarrange on the words following the entry (significant) word.

An inverted title program was developed by modifying the existing inversion routine of the thesaurus program in the modular set. Thus modified, the inverted title program would list each significant word in the title and its context, followed by the service in which it is indexed. In addition to these features, it would also arrange by the entry word and on those words following that significant word. Thus, the entry

Brethren Life and Thought IRPL

would generate

Brethren Life and Thought IRPL
Life and Thought, Brethren IRPL
Thought, Brethren Life and IRPL.

It would not generate an entry for

and Thought, Brethren Life IRPL.

In each case the entries would be interfiled with other entries in their appropriate letter of the alphabet, in this case "B", "L", and "T". The two spaces following the comma cause the entry to subarrange as described. Thus, if there were a journal title:

Life, Brethren

it would file, as it logically should, before and not after

Life and Thought, Brethren.

Finally, there are many other pieces of information which this guide should have. To name a few, fuller bibliographic citations; inclusion of journals dealing with religion indexed in services other than those devoted only or primarily to religious materials; indication of the form of entry used in libraries where this is not the title; and, as stated earlier, the beginning date and frequency for each journal in each service.

The tool, however, should be quite useful as it is. As recently as last Fall, Palais (1974)[1] stated that a tool of this type was necessary because Ulrich's was not adequately filling the need. Though he suggested such a tool for all journals in all fields, we hope this will be the beginning of greater bibliographic control in the fields of religion and theology.

John J. Regazzi

1. Palais, Elliot S. "References to Indexes and Abstracts in Ulrich's International Periodicals Directory," RQ: 34-36, Fall, 1974.

Indexing and Abstracting Services Included with Abbreviations

B	Biblica
CPI	Christian Periodical Index
CPLI	Catholic Periodical Literature Index
ETL	Ephemerides Theologicae Lovanienses
GSSRPL	Guide to the Social Science and Religious Periodical Literature
IBHR	International Bibliography of the History of Religions
IJP	Index to Jewish Periodicals
IOB	Internationale Oekumenische Bibliographie
IRPL	Index to Religious Periodical Literature
IZBG	Internationale Zeitschriftenshau für Bibelwissenschaft und Grenzgebiete
NTA	New Testament Abstracts
RE	Revue d'Histoire Ecclesiastique
RPI	Religious Periodical Index
RTA	Religion and Theology Abstracts
SBPI	Southern Baptist Periodical Index
SISPI	Subject Index to Select Periodical Literature
UMPI	United Methodist Periodical Index

PERIODICAL TITLES - ALPHABETICAL LIST

Aachener Kunstblatter RE
Abhandlungen und Berichte des Staatlichen Museum fur Volkunde in Dresden IBHR
Abhandlungen Zur Theologie des Alten und Neuen Testaments B, IZBG
Abr-Nahrain ETL, IZBG
Academia Internazionale dei Lincei ETL
Academie Revue de Belgique. Bulletin de la Classe des Beaux Arts RE
Academie Revue de Belgique. Bulletin de la Classe des Lettres et des Sciences Morales et Politiques RE
Academie Royale de Belgique B
Accademie e Biblioteche D' Italia B
Accent SBPI, UMPI
Accent on Youth UMPI
Accion Metodista UMPI
Accrediting Association of Bible Colleges Newsletter SISPL
Acta Antiqua IZBG
Acta Antiqua Academiae Scientiarum Hungaricae IBHR
Acta Apostalicae Sedis CPLI, ETL
Acta Archaeologica Ljubliana IZBG
Acta Ethnographica Academiae Scientiarum Hungaricae IBHR
Acta Historiae Neerlandica RE
Acta Historica RE
Acta Iranica IBHR
Acta Orientalia Budapest IZBG
Acta Poloniae Historica RE
Acta Seminarii Neotestamentici Upsaliensis ETL, IZBG
Acta Universitatis Gotoburgensis IZBG
Acta Universitatis Upsaliensis IZBG
Actes du Congres International de Numismatique B
Actes du Congres International de Papyrologie B
Actes du Congres International des Etudes Byzantines B
Actes du Congres International des Orientalistes B
Actualidad Biblica ETL
A.D. RPI

Adult Bible Course UMPI
Adult Bible Studies UMPI
Adult Leader UMPI
Adult Leadership SBPI
Adult Student SBPI
Adult Teacher UMPI
Advance RPI
Advent Christian Witness RPI
Aegyptus IZBG
Aevum. Rassegna di Scienze Storiche, Linguistiche e Filologiche B, IZBG, RE
Africa (London) IOB
Africa Theological Journal SISPL
African Studies IBHR
African Studies (Johannesburg) IBHR, IOB
Afrika und Ubersee IBHR
Akkadusches Handworterbuch B
Akten des Internationale Kongresses B
Al Andalus. Revista de las Escuelas de Estudios Arabes RE
Algemeen Nederlands Tijdschrift voor Wijsbegeerte en Psychologie ETL
Al-Machriq B
Alter Orient und Altes Testament B, IZBG
Altertum ETL, IZBG
Am Tische des Wortes B
America CPLI, RPI
America Indigena IBHR
American Anthropologist IBHR
American Benedictine Review NTA, RPI
American Catholic Historical Records CPLI
American Catholic Philosophical Association Proceedings CPLI
American Church Quarterly NTA
American Ecclesiastical Review RE
American Historical Review RE
American Jewish Archives IJP
American Jewish Historical Quarterly IJP
American Journal of Archaeology B, ETI, IBHR, IZBG, SISPL
American Journal of Jurisprudence CPLI
American Journal of Legal History RE
American Journal of Philology B, IBHR
American Journal of Sociology GSSRPL
American Opinion GSSRPL
American Philological Association Transaction Proceeding B
American Quarterly IRPL

American Scholar GSSRPL
American Sciolcgical Review GSSRPL
American Studies in Papyrology B
American Zionist IJP
Ami du Clerge IZBG
Amico del Clerc ETL
Amtsblatt der Evangelischen Kirche in Deutschland IOB
Amtsblatt der Evangelisch-Lutherischen Kirche in Thuringen IOB
Amtsblatt des Evangelischen Konsistoriums in Grerfswald ICB
Anadolu Sanatu Arastermalan IBHR
Analecta Augustiniana RE
Analecta Biblica IZBG
Analecta Bcllandiana RE
Analecta Cisterciensia RE
Analecta Cracovina B
Analecta Gregcriana ETL
Analecta Lovaniensia Biblica et Orientalia B, IZBG
Analecta Ordinis Fratrum Minorum ETL
Analecta Orientalia IZBG
Analecta Praemonstratensia ETL, RE
Analecta Sacra Tarraconensia RE
Analecta Sacri Ordinis Cistercienis ETL
Analecta Sacri Ordinis Fratrum Praedicatorum ETL
Anatolian Studies Journal of the British Institute of Archaeology at Anakara B, IBHR
Anciens Pays et Assemblees D' Etats RE
Ancient Society B
Andover Newton Quarterly B, ETL, IBHR, IRPL, IZBG, NTA, RTA, SISPL
Andrews University Seminary Studies B, ETL, IBHR, IRPL, IZBG, NTA, SISPL
Angelicum IZBG, NTA, RE
Anglia. Zeitschrift fur Englische Philologie RE
Anglican Theological Review B, ETL, IBHR, IRPL, IZBG, NTA, SISPL
Anima IOB
Annalen der Historischen Vereins fur der Niererrhein RE
Annalen van het Thijmgenootschap B, ICB, RE
Annales Academiae Scientiarum Fennicae IZBG
Annales Archeologiques Arabe Syriennes B, IBHR
Annales de Bourgogne RE
Annales de Bretagne RE
Annales de Demographie Historique RE
Annales de Ethicpie B

Annales de l' Est RE
Annales de l' Institut Archeclogique du Luxembourg RE
Annales de l' Ordre Souverain Militaire de Malte RE
Annales de l' Universite de Paris RE
Annales de la Societe Archeologique de Namur RE
Annales de Sociologie IBHR
Annales du Centre D' Etude des Religiones B
Annales du Midi RE
Annales du Service des Antiquites de l' Egypte B
Annales. Economies, Societes, Civilisations B, RE
Annales Historiques de la Revolution Francaise RE
Annales Islamclogiques IBHR
Annali del Facolta di Filosofia e Letter di UN-Versita Statale de Milano RE
Annali del' Istituto Orientale di Napoli B, ETL, IBHR, IZBG
Annali della Fondazione Italiana per la Storia Amministrativa RE
Annali della Scuola Normale Superiore di Pisa B, RE
Annali di Sociologia IBHR
Annali di Storia del Diritto RE
Annali di Storia Economica e Sociale RE
Annals GSSRPL
Annee Canonique ETL, RE
Annee Philclogique B
Annoli della Facalta di Letare e Filosafia dell' Universita degli Studi di Trieste IBHR
Annuaire D' Histoire Liegeoise RE
Annuaire de l' Academie Theclogie B
Annuaire de l' Institut de Philologie et D' Historie Orientales et Slaves B, IBHR
Annuaire de la Societe D' Histoire et D' Archeologie de la Lorraine RE
Annual Egyptolcgical Bibliography B
Annual of the American School of Oriental Research IZBG
Annual of the Department of Antiquities of Jordan B
Annual of the Swedish Theological Institute B IBHR, IZBG, NTA
Annuale Mediaevale RE
Annuario di Studi Ebraici B
Annuarium Historiae Conciliorum ETL, RE
Antemurale RE
Anthologica Annua RE
Anthropological Quarterly CPLI, IBHR
Anthropos ETL, IOB, IZBG
Anti-Defamation League Bulletin IJP

Antik Tanulmanyck IBHR
Antike Welt B
Antiquaries Journal B, RE
Antiquite Classique B, ETL, IBHR, RE
Antiquites Africaines B, IBHR
Antiquity B, SISPL
Antonianum ETL, IZBG, NTA, RE
Antropologica IBHR
Anuario de Estudios Medievales RE
Anuario de Historia del Derecho Espanol RE
Anzeiger der Oestereichischen Akademie der Wissenschaften RE
Anzeiger fur die Altertumswissenschaft B, IBHR
Apollinaris ETL, RE
Apostolado Sacerdotal IZBG
Aquinas RE
Aquinas Ephemerides Thomisticae ETL
Arbeiten Zur Geschichte des Antiken Judentums und des Urchristentums B
Arbeiten Zur Neutestamentlichen Textforschung IZBG
Arbeiten Zur Theologie IZBG
Arbor RE
Archaeologia Cantiana RE
Archaeological Journal RE
Archaeologische Bibliographie B
Archaeologische Mitteilungen aus Iran B
Archaeologischer Anzeiger B, IZBG
Archaeology B, IZBG
Archeologia RE
Archeologia Classica B
Archeologie Vivante B
Archief voor de Geschiedenis van de Katholieke Kerk in Nederland ETL, IOB, RE
Archiv fur Begriffsgeschichte B
Archiv fur das Studium der Neueren Sprachen und Literaturen RE
Archiv fur Diplomatik Schriftgeschichte, Siegel und Wappenkunde RE
Archiv fur Geschichte der Philosophie B, RE
Archiv fur Katholisches Kirchenrecht ETL, IBHR, RE
Archiv fur Kulturgeschichte B, IOB, RE
Archiv fur Liturgiewissenschaft B, ETL, IBHR, IZBG, RE
Archiv fur Mittelrheinische Kirchengeschichte IOB, RE
Archiv fur Orientforschung B, ETL, IZBG
Archiv fur Osterreichische Geschichte RE
Archiv fur Papyrusforschung B

Archiv fur Rechts und Sozialphilosophie ETL
Archiv fur Reformationsgeschichte ETL, IRPL, RE, RTA
Archiv fur Schlesische Kirchengeschichte RE
Archiv Orientalni B, ETL, IBHR, IZBG, RE
Archiva Ecclesiae ETL, RE
Archivalische Zeitschrift RE
Archivar RE
Archives D' Histoire Doctrinale et Litteraire du Paris RE
Archives D' Historie Doctrinale et Litteraire du Moyen Age B
Archives de l' Eglise D' Alsace RE
Archives de l' Historie des Sciences B
Archives de Philosophie ETL, RE
Archives de Philosophie du Droit RE
Archives de Sociologie de Religions B, ETL, IBHR, RE
Archives et Bibliotheques de Belgique RE
Archives Internationales D' Histoire des Sciences RE
Archivio di Societa Romana di Storia Patria RE
Archivio Giuridico "Filippo Serafini" ETL, RE
Archivio Glottologico Italiano B
Archivio Italiano per la Storia della Pieta RE
Archivio Storico Italiano RE
Archivio Storico Lombardo RE
Archivio Storico per la Sicilia Orientale RE
Archivio Storico per Le Province Napoletane RE
Archivio Storico per Le Province Parmensi RE
Archivio Veneto RE
Archivium Hibernicum RE
Archivo Espanol de Arqueologia B
Archivo Espanol de Arte RE
Archivo Hispalense IZBG
Archivo Ibero Americano RE
Archivo Teologico Agustiniano ETL
Archivo Teologico Granadino IZBG, RE
Archivos Leoneses RE
Archivum Franciscanum Historicum ETL, RE
Archivum Fratrum Praedicatorum ETL, RE
Archivum Historicum Societatis Iesu ETL, RE
Archivum Latinitatis Medii Aevi. Bulletin du Cange RE
Archivum Linguisticum IZBG
Archivum. Revue Internationale des Archives RE
Archiwa, Biblioteki Muzea Koscielne RE
Arctic Anthropology IBHR

Argentina (Revista Biblica) B
Arhivio Veneto RE
Ariel IJP
Armenian Church IBHR
Ars Orientalis IBHR
Arsbok for Kristen Humanism IOB
Art Bulletin RE
Art Journal RE
Arte Antica e Moderna RE
Arte Lombarda RE
Artistiques du Lot Bulletin de la Societe des Etudes Litteraires, Scientifiques et RE
Arts Asiatiques IBHR
Arts, du Departement de la Marne Memoires de la Societe D' Agriculture, Commerce, Sciences et RE
Arts et Traditions Populaires RE
Artz und Christ IOB
Asian Folklore Studies IBHR
Asiatische Studien ETL, IZBG
Asprenas ETL, IZBG, RE
Assemblees die Seigneur B
Associazione Biblica Italiana, Esegesi Biblica ETL
Attempto ETL
Atti dell' Istituto Veneto di Scienze, Lettere di Arte RE
Atti della Pontificia Accademia Romana di Archeologia B
Atti della Settimana Biblica B
Atti di Societa Ligure di Storia Patria RE
Atti e Memorie de Deputazione di Storia Patria per Le Antiche Provincie Modenesi RE
Atti e Memorie de Deputazione di Storia Patria per Le Province di Romagna RE
Atti e Memorie de Societa Istriana di Archeologia e Storia Patria RE
Auchland (Colloquium) NTA
Augustinian Studies RE
Augustiniana IBHR, RE
Augustinianum B, ETL, IBHR, IZBG, NTA
Augustinus (Madrid) B, IOB
Australasian Catholic Record ETL, NTA, RTA
Australian Biblical Review ETL, IZBG, NTA
Australian Journal of Biblical Archaeology IZBG
Ave Maria CPLI, RPI
Avhandlinger Utgitt Av Det Norsk Videnskaps Akademi i Oslo IZBG
Aware SBPI

Background Information IOB
Baghader Mitteilungen B, IBHR
Banner GSSRPL, RPI
Baptist Bulletin GSSRPL, RPI
Baptist Herald RPI
Baptist History and Heritage SBPI
Baptist Leader RPI
Baptist Men's Journal SBPI
Baptist Quarterly IRPL, IZBG, RTA
Baptist World IOB, SBPL
Basler Zeitschrift fur Geschichte und
 Altertumskunde RE
Bausteine NTA
Bazmaveb B
Beihefte Zur Zeitschrift fur die Altestamentliche
 Wissenschaft B, IZBG
Beitraege Zur Altbayerischen Kirchengeschichte RE
Beitraege Zur der Biblischen Hermeneutik IZBG
Beitraege Zur Evangelischen Theologie B, IZBG
Beitraege Zur Forderung Christlicher Theologie IZBG
Beitraege Zur Geschichte der Biblischen Exegese
 IZBG
Beitraege Zur Geschichte der Deutschen Sprache
 und Literatur RE
Beitraege Zur Namenforschung B
Beitraege Zur Wissenschaft Vom Alten und Neuen
 Testament IZBG
Bekehirncek IOB
Benedictina ETL, RE
Bericht des Historischin Vereins Bamberg RE
Berichte uber die Verhandlugn der Sachsischen
 Akademie der Wissenschaften zu Leipzig RE
Bern-Tubengen (Ehe.) IOB
Berytus ETL
Beth Mikra B
Bibbas (Manresa) NTA
Bibbia e Oriente ETL, IZBG, NTA
Bibel in der Welt B, IOB
Bibel und Kirche ETL, IZBG, NTA
Bibel und Leben ETL, NTA, RE
Bibel und Liturgie ETL, NTA
Bible et Terre Sainte IZBG
Bible et Vie Chretienne ETL, IZBG, NTA
Bible League Quarterly SISPL
Bible Lessons for Adults UMPI
Bible Lessons for Youth UMPI
Bible Science Newsletter SISPL
Bible Society Record IZBG, RPI

Bible Teacher for Adults UMPI
Bible Translator IZBG
Bible und Quran IBHR
Biblia Revuo IZBG
Biblica B, IRPL, NTA, RE
Biblica et Orientalias B
Biblical Archeologist B, CPI, CPLI, ETL, IBHR, IRPL, IZBG, NTA, RPI, SISPL
Biblical Research IZBG
Biblical Theology NTA
Biblical Theology Bulletin B, IZBG
Biblical Viewpoint SISPL
Bibliofilia RE
Bibliografia Nazionale Italiana RE
Bibliographie de Belgique RE
Bibliographie de la France RE
Bibliotheca Orientalis ETL, IZBG, NTA
Bibliotheca Sacra CPI, ETL, IRPL, IZBG, NTA, RE, RTA
Bibliothek und Wissenschaft RE
Bibliotheque D' Humanisme et Renaissance RE
Bibliotheque de l' Ecole des Chartes RE
Biblische Beitraege IZBG
Biblische Studien IZBG
Biblische Untersuchungen B
Biblische Zeitschrift ETL, IRPL, IZBG, NTA, RE
Biekorf RE
Bijdragen ETL, IZBG, NTA
Bijdragen en Mededelingen Betreffende de Geschiedenis der Nederlanden Re
Bijdragen en Mededelingen Uitger Door de Vereniging Gelre RE
Bijdragen. Tijdschrift voor Filosofie en Theologie RE
Bijdragen tot de Geschiedenis RE
Bijdragen tot de Taal-Land en Volkenkunde IBHR
Bild der Wissenschaft B
Bicla Bcoadranter SISPL
Biserica Ortodoxa Romana IOB
Biuletyn Historii Sztuki RE
Blatter fur Deutsche Landesgeschichte RE
Bodleian Library Record RE
Boek der Boeken IZBG
Boeken van het Oude Testament B
Bogoskovje IOB
Bogoslovni Vestnik B
Bogoslovska Smotra B
Boletin de Historia y Antiguedades RE

Boletin de la Real Academia de la Historia RE

Boletin de la Real Academia Espanola RE
Boletin del Instituto Caro y Cuervo IZBG

Boletin del Instituto de Estudios Helenicos B
Boletin del Seminario de Estudios de Arte y Arqueologia RE
Bollettino Bibliografiro Internazionale B
Bollettino D' Arte RE
Bollettino del Centro Camuno di Studi Preistorici IZBG
Bollettino dell' Amiciza Ebraico-Cristiana di Firanze B
Bollettino della Societa Geografica Italiano B
Bollettino della Societa Internazionale Scottista IZBG
Bollettino di Badia Greca di Grottaferrata RE
Bollettino Ligustico per la Storia e la Cultura Regionale RE
Bollettino Storico Bibliografico Subalpino RE
Bollettino Storico Piacentino RE
Bonner Biblische Beitrage B, ETL, IZBG
Bonner Geschichtsblatter RE
Bossche Bijdragen RE
Bracara Augusta RE
Bratskij Vestnik IOB
Brethren Life and Thought ETL, IRPL, RPI, RTA
British Journal of Sociology IBHR
Brotherhood Builder SBPI
Buenos Aires (Revista Biblica) IZBG
Buletin du Centre Protestant D' Etudes IOB
Buletin of the Catholic Research Institute China Academy B
Bulletin Archeologique IZBG
Bulletin D' Archeologie Algevienne B
Bulletin D' Etudes Orientalis de Institut Francais IBHR
Bulletin de Correspondance Hellenique B
Bulletin de l' Association Guillaume Bude B, ETL, RE
Bulletin de l' Institut de Recherche et D' Histoire des Textes RE
Bulletin de l' Institut Fondamentale D' Afrique Noire IBHR
Bulletin de l' Institut Francais D' Archeologie Orientale IZBG
Bulletin de l' Institut Historique Belge de Rome RE

Bulletin de l' Institut Royal du Patrimoine Artistique RE

Bulletin de la Classe des Lettres IZBG
Bulletin de la Commission Royale D' Histoire RE

Bulletin de la Commission Royale de Anciennes Lois et Ordonnances de Belgique RE
Bulletin de la Section D' Historie Moderne et Contemperaine RE
Bulletin de la Societe Archeologie et Historique de Nantes et de Loire Atlantique RE
Bulletin de la Societe Archeologique D' Eure et Loir RE
Bulletin de la Societe Archeologique et Historique du Limousin RE
Bulletin de la Societe D' Archeologie Copte IZBG, RE
Bulletin de la Societe D' Archeologie et de Statistique de la Drome RE
Bulletin de la Societe D' Art et D' Historie du Diocese de Liege RE
Bulletin de la Societe de Etudes Indochinoses IBHR
Bulletin de la Societe de l' Historie de l' Art Francais RE
Bulletin de la Societe de l' Historie du Protestantisme Francais ETL, RE
Bulletin de la Societe de Linguistique de Paris B
Bulletin de la Societe de'Archeologie Copte B
Bulletin de la Societe des Antiquaires de l' Ouest et des Musees de Poitiers RE
Bulletin de la Societe des Antiquaires de Normandie RE
Bulletin de la Societe des Etudes Litteraires, Scientifiques et
Bulletin de la Societe Francaise D' Egyptologie B
Bulletin de la Societe Francaise D' Etudes Marianles B
Bulletin de la Societe Historique et Archeologique du Perigord RE
Bulletin de la Societe Nationale des Antiquaires de France RE
Bulletin de la Societe Prehistorique Francaise IBHR
Bulletin de Litterature Ecclesiastique ETL, IZBG, NTA, RE
Bulletin de Theologie Ancienne et Medievale IZBG, RE
Bulletin de Theologie Biblique B

Bulletin del' Institut Francais D' Archeologie
Orientale B, IBHR

Bulletin des Etudes Portugaises, Publie Par
l' Institut Francais au Portugal RE
Bulletin des Musees Royaux D' Art et D' Histoire RE

Bulletin des Musees Royaux des Beaus Arts de
Belgique RE
Bulletin du Musee de Beyrouth B
Bulletin E. Renan IZBG
Bulletin et Memoirs de la Societe Archeologique
du Department D' Ille et Vilaine RE
Bulletin Hispanique RE
Bulletin Monumental RE
Bulletin of the American Academy of Religion IZBG
Bulletin of the American Schools of Oriental
Research B, ETL, IBHR, IZBG, NTA, SISPL
Bulletin of the Church History Association of
India IOB
Bulletin of the Department of Theology of the
World Presbyterian Alliance and the World Alliance
of Reformed Churches IOB
Bulletin of the Faculty of Arts, University
of Libya IBHR
Bulletin of the Institute of Archaeology B
Bulletin of the Institute of Historical Research RE
Bulletin of the John Rylands Library ETL, IZBG,
NTA, RE
Bulletin of the New York Public Library RE
Bulletin of the School of Oriental and African
Studies RE
Bulletin of the Society for African Church History
IOB
Bulletin of the United Biblical Societies IZBG
Bulletin Philologique et Historique du Comite
des Travaux Historiques et scientifiques RE
Bulletin Saint Jean-Baptist IBHR, IOB
Bulletin Secretariatus pro Non Christianis B, IOB
Bulletin Signaletique B
Bulletin Trimestriel de la Societe Academique
des Antiquaires de la Marinie RE
Bulletin Trimestriel de la Societe Archeologique
de Touraine RE
Bulletin Trimestriel de la Societe des Antiquaires
de Picardie RE
Bullettino dell' Istituto Storico Italiano per
Il Medio Evo e Archivio Muratoriano RE

Burgense. Collectanea Scientifica de la Real
Academia IZBG, NTA
Buried History SISPL
Burlington Magizine RE
Butraege Zur Wissenschaft von Alten und Neuen
Testament B
Byzantina RE
Byzantinische Forschungen RE
Byzantinische Zeitschrift RE
Byzantino Sloavica IBHR, RE
Byzantion ETL, RE
Cahiers Archeologiques, Fin de l' Antiquite
et Moyen Age RE
Cahiers Bruxellois RE
Cahiers D' Action Religieuse et Sociale IOB
Cahiers D' Etudes Cathares RE
Cahiers D' Histoire RE
Cahiers D' Historie Mondiale B, IBHR, RE
Cahiers de Civilisation Medievale B, RE
Cahiers de Josephologie NTA, RTA
Cahiers de la Revue Biblique IZBG
Cahiers des Religiones Africaines IBHR
Cahiers Internationaux de Sociologie IBHR
Cahiers Laennec ETL
Cahiers Leopold Delisle RE
Cahiers Renan IZBG
Cahiers Theologiques ETL
Cahiers Theologiques de l' Actualite Protestante
IZBG
California Publications in Classical Archaeology
and Semitic Philology, University of IZBG
Calvary Review SISPL
Calvin Theological Journal CPI, ETL, IRPL,
IZBG, RE, RPI
Calwer Hefte IZBG
Cambridge History of Iran IBHR
Canadian Historical Review RE
Canadian Journal of Theology ETL, IRPL, IZBG, RTA
Carinthia I. Geschichliche und Volkskunde.
Beitrage Zur Heimantkunde Karntens RE
Carkoven Vestnik IOB
Carmelus ETL, NTA, RE
Catechese IZBG
Catechistes IZBG
Cathedral Age RPI
Catholic Biblical Quarterly ETL, IRPL, IZBG,
NTA, RE, RPI
Catholic Business Education Review CPLI

Catholic Charities Review CPLI, RPI
Catholic Digest CPLI
Catholic Educator CPLI
Catholic Historical Review CPLI, ETL, GSSRPL, RE, RPI
Catholic Lawyer CPLI
Catholic Library World CPLI, RPI
Catholic School Journal CPLI, RPI
Catholic Theological Society of America Proceedings CPLI
Catholic Worker RPI
Catholic World, the CPLI, GSSRPL, RPI
Catholica (Copenhagen) ETL, NTA
Catholica (Munster) ETL, NTA
Catholica Unio IOB
Center Magazine GSSRPL
Central Asiatic Journal IBHR
Central Bible Quarterly SISPL
Central Christian Advocate UMPI
Central Conference of American Rabbis Journal B, IJP
Centre Protestant D' Etudes et de Documentation IOB
Ceres GSSRPL
Ceskoslovensky Casopis Historicky RE
Cesky Zapas IOB
Change GSSRPL
Chaplain RPI
Chicago Assyrian Dictionary B
Chicago Studies CPLI, ETL, NTA, RPI
Chicago Theological Seminary Register B, SISPL
Childrens Leadership SBPI
Choisir IOB
Christ to the World CPLI, IOB
Christelijk Oosten B, IOB, RE
Christian CPI
Christian Action UMPI
Christian Adventure UMPI
Christian Advocate GSSRPL, RPI
Christian Bookseller RPI
Christian Century GSSRPL, RPI
Christian Council Quarterly IOB
Christian Faith in Life-Supplement UMPI
Christian Graduate SISPL
Christian Herald GSSRPL, RPI
Christian Librarian CPI
Christian Life CPI, GSSRPL, RPI
Christian Ministry GSSRPL, RPI
Christian News from Israel IOB, IZBG

Christian Peace Conference IOB
Christian Reader GSSRPL
Christian Scholar IOB
Christian Scholar's Review NTA
Christian Standard GSSRPL
Christianisme au 20e Siecle IOB
Christianisme Social IOB
Christianity and Crisis GSSRPL, IRPL, RPI
Christianity Today CPI, GSSRPL, IRPL, IZBG, RPI
Christlich-Judisches Forum IOB
Christus B, ETL, IZBG, NTA, RTA
Chronique D' Egypte IZBG
Chrysostom IOB
Church Administration RPI, SBPI
Church and Society IRPL, RPI
Church Herald GSSRPL, RPI
Church History CPI, ETL, IRPL, RE, RPI
Church in Metropolis IOB
Church in the World IOB
Church Library Magazine RPI
Church Man IRPL, RPI
Church Messenger RPI
Church Quarterly ETL, IRPL, NTA, RPI
Church Recreation Magazine SBPI
Church School UMPI
Church Theological Review RPI
Church Times IOB
Church Training SBPI
Church Woman RPI
Ciencia Tomista ETL, IOB, IZBG, NTA, RE
Circuet Rider UMPI
Cistercienser Chronik RE
Citaux ETL, RE
Citeaux ETL, RE
Cithera CPLI
Citta di Vita ETL
Ciudad de Dios ETL, IZBG, NTA, RE
Civilta Cattolica ETL, IZBG, NTA, RE
Civitas ETL, IOB
Clairlieu. Tijdschrift Gewijd Aan de Geschiedenis der Kruisheren RE
Classica et Mediaevalia RE
Classical Folia RE
Classical Quarterly B, RE
Classical Review B, RE
Classical Weekly B
Classmate UMPI
Clergy Monthly NTA, RTA

Clergy Review CPLI, ETL, RE
Collage SBPI
Collationes RE
Collationes Brugenses et Gandavenses ETL, IOB, IZBG, NTA
Collationes Vlaoms Tijdschaft voor Theologie en Pastoral B
Collectanea Cisterciensia RE
Collectanea Franciscana B, ETL, IZBG, RE
Collectanea Mechliniensia ETL, IOB, IZBG, NTA
Collectanea Oridinis Cistericciensium Reformatorum ETL
Collectanea Theologica ETL, IZBG
Collection Lumiere et Vie IZBG
Colloquium (Auchland) NTA
Columbia CPLI, RPI
Commentaar op het Oude Testament B
Commentari RE
Commentary IZBG
Commenti Spirituali dell' Antico Testamento del Nuovo Testamento B
Commission SBPI
Commission Royale de Anciennes Lois et Ordonnances de Belgique, Bulletin de la RE
Commonlife Bulletin UMPI
Commonweal CPLI, GSSRPL, RPI
Communaute des Dissemines IOB
Communic ETL, NTA, RE
Communio Verbum Caro B
Communio Viatorum ETL, IRPL, IZBG, NTA, RE
Comparative Literature RE
Comparative Studies in Society and History RE
Compostellanum IZBG
Comptes Rendus B, IBHR
Comptes Rendus de l' Academie des Inscriptions et Belles Lettres IZBG
Comptes Rendus des Seances de l' Academie des Inscriptions et Belles Lettres RE
Comptes Rendus du Groupe Linguistique D' Etudes Chamito-Semitiques B
Computers in the Humanities B
Concept E. Papers from the Department on Studies in Evangelism IOB
Concept F. Documents du Department D' Etudes sur l' Evangelisation Iob
Concept G. Arbeiten aus dem Referat fur Fragen der Verkuendigung IOB
Concern RPI, UMPI

Concilium B, ETL, IOB, IZBG, NTA, RE
Concordia Historical Institute Quarterly ETL, RTA
Concordia Theological Monthly CPI, ETL, IRPL, IZBG, NTA, RPI, RTA
Confrontations. Revue Diocesaine de Tournai B, ETL
Congregationalist, the RPI
Congress Bi-Weekly IJP
Coniectanea Biblica Lund B
Coniectanea Biblica, New Testament Series Lund IZBG
Coniectanea Neotestamentica IZBG
Conservative Judaism IJP
Contacts IOB
Contempo SBPI
Contemporary Religions in Japan SISPL
Context SISPL
Continuum CPLI, ETL, IRPL, RPI
Copenhagen (Catholica) ETL, NTA
Cord RPI
Corpus Scriptorum Christianorum Orientalium B
Corsi di Cultura Sull' Arte Ravennate e Bizantina RE
Creation Research Society Quarterly SISPL
Credinta RPI
Criterio IOB
Criterion IRPI, RPI
Critic CPLI, GSSRPL, RPI
Cross and Crown CPLI, NTA
Cross Currents CPLI, GSSRPL, RPI
Crusader SBPI
Crusader Counselor SBPI
Crux SISPL
Cuadernos de Estudios Gallegos RE
Cuadernos de Historia de Espana RE
Cuadernos Teologicos IOB
Cultura Biblica ETL, IZBG, NTA
Cultura e Scuola B, IBHR
Cultura Neolatina RE
Current Anthropology IBHR
Current Developments in the Eastern European Churches IOB
Dansk Teologisk Tidsskrift ETL, IRPL, IZBG, NTA
De Homine Deo B
Deacon SBPI
Departement de la Marne Memoires de la Societe D' Agriculture, Commerce, Sciences et Arts, du RE
Deutsche Bibliographie RE
Deutsche Kunst und Denkmalpflete RE
Deutsche Literaturzeitung B, IBHR, IZBG, RE

Deutsche Vierteljahrsschrift fur
 Literaturwissenschaft und Geistegeschechte B, RE
Deutsche Zeitschrift fur Philosophie RE
Deutscher Evangelischer Kirchentag IOB
Deutsches Archiv fur der Erforschung des
 Mittelalters B, RE
Deutsches Pfarrerblatt B, IBHR
Diakonia CPLI, ETL, NTA, RPI
Dialog (Freiburg) IOB
Dialog (New York) ETL, IOB, IRPL, RPI
Dialogo IOB
Dialogue IOB
Dictionnaire D' Historie et de Geographie
 Ecclesiastiques B
Dictionnaire de Theologie Catholique B
Didaskalia B
Dienst am Wort B
Dietsche Warande en Belfort RE
Dimension SBPI
Dimensions in American Judaism RPI
Diocesaan Tijdschrift Hasselt ETL
Diogene RE
Diritto e Giurisprudenza ETL
Diritto Ecclesiastico RO
Discerner SISPL
Discoveries in the Judaean Desert B
Discovery SBPI
Dissertation Abstracts IZBG
Divinitas ETL, IZBG, NTA, RE
Divus Thomas ETL, IOB, IZBG, NTA, RE
Doctor Communis ETL, NTA, RE
Doctrine and Life ETL, NTA
Documenta IZBG
Documents from the Department for the Laity IOB
Dokumente. Zeitschrift fur Internationale
 Zusammenarbeit IOB
Dominicana CPLI
Downside Review ETL, IRPL, IZBG, RE , RTA
Drew Gateway IRPL, RPI
Dublin Review CPLI, ETL
Duchovna Kultura IOB
Duke Divinity School Review IRPL, RPI
Dumbarton Oaks Papers B
Dunwoodie Review IZBG
Durham University Journal IZBG
Dusseldorf (Kommentare und Beitrage zum Alten
 und Neuen Testament) B
Dusseldorfer Jahrbuch RE

East and West B
Ecanos-Jahrbuch ICB
Ecclesia (Val) IOB
Ecclesiastica Xaveriana B
Eccle Pratique des Hautes Etudes B, IBHR
Ecomcmia e Stcria RE
Economic History Review RE
Economisch Historisch Jaarboek RE
Ecumenical Notes IOB
Ecumenical Review GSSRPL, NTA, RE, RPI
Ecumenist CPLI, NTA
Education GSSRPL
Eglise et Mission ETL
Eglise et Theolcgie IZBG
Ehe. (Bern-Tubengen) IOB
Eigen Schoon en de Brabander RE
Ekklesia IOB
Elenchus Suppletorius ad Elerchum Bibliographe Biblicum B
Emuna IOB
Encounter GSSRPL, IBPL, IZBG, RPI
Encounter Today B
Encyclopedia Judaica B
Engage RPI
English Historical Review RE
English Studies RE
Environment GSSRPI
Envoy CPLI
Ephemerides Carmelitica ETL, IZBG, NTA, RE
Ephemerides Iuris Canonici ETL, RE
Ephemerides Liturgicae ETL, IZBG, NTA, RE
Ephemerides Mariolcgicae ETL, NTA, RE
Ephemerides Theologicae Lovanienses ETL, IZBG, NTA, RE
Epigraphica RE
Episcopal Overseas Mission Review IOB
Episcopal Recorder RPI
Episcopalian GSSRPL, RPI
Epworth Notes UMPI
Eranos RE
Eranos Jahrbuch IZBG
Erasmus. Speculum Scientiarum RE
Erbe und Auftrag ETL, IOB, IZBG, NTA
Eretz Israel IZBG
Erfurter Theologische Studien IZBG
Escritos del Vedat B
Esprit IOB
Esprit et Vie ETL, NTA

Estudio Augustiniano B
Estudios ETL
Estudios Biblicos ETL, IOB, NTA, RE
Estudios de Filosofia y Religion Orientales B
Estudios Eclesiasticos IZBG, RE
Estudios Franciscanos RE
Estudios Josefiros B
Estudios Lulianos RE
Estudios Marianos B
Estudios Trinitarios B
Eternity IZBG
Eternity Magazine CPI, GSSRPL, RPI
Ethiopia Observer IOB
Ethnographisch-Archaeologische Zeitschrift IBHT
Ethnomusicology IBHR
Ethologcia IBHR
Etudes CPLI, ETL, IZBG, NTA, RE
Etudes Carmelitaines IZBG
Etudes Celtiques RE
Etudes Classiques ETL, IZBG, RE
Etudes de Papyrologie B
Etudes et Travaux B
Etudes Franciscaines ETL, NTA, RE
Etudes Gregoriennes RE
Etudes Moriales B
Etudes Philosophiques ETL, RE
Etudes Teilhardiennes ETL
Etudes Theologiques et Religieuses ETL, IRPL, IZBG, NTA, RE
Eucharist RPI
Euntes Docete ETL, NTA, RE
Euphorion. Zeitschrift fur Literaturgeschichte RE
European Judaism IJP
Evangelical Quarterly CPI, IRPL, IZBG, RPI
Evangelijus Flet IOB
Evangelisch Katholischer Kommentar B
Evangelische Erziekar IBHR
Evangelische Kommentare B, IBHR, IZBG
Evangelische Theologie ETL, IZBG, NTA, RE, RTA
Evangelische Welt ICB
Evangelisches Pfarrerblatt IOB
Evangeliser ETL
Evangelishas Missionamagazin IOB
Evangile IZBG
Event RPI
Expedition B, IZBG
Explore UMPI
Explore Resource Kit UMPI

Explore Teacher's Guide UMPI
Expository Times ETL, IRPL, IZBG, RTA
Extension Magazine CPLI, RPI
Fabula. Zeitschrift fur Erzahlforschung RE
Facalta di Letare e Filosafia dell' Universita degli Studi di Trieste, Annoli della IBHR
Face to Face UMPI
Faith and Forum RPI
Faith and Order Trends IOB
Faith and Thought SISPL
Faith at Work RPI
Fede e Civilta IOB
Federation der Societes D' Histoire et D' Archeologie de l' Aisne, Memoires de la RE
Fellowship RPI
Fides et Historici SISPL
Findsh Teologisk Tidsskrift IOB
Five/Six UMPI
Fivista Italiana di Numismatica e Scienze Affini RE
Foi et Le Temps RE
Foi et Vie ETL, IRPI
Foi Vivante (Suisse) ETL
Foliu Orientalia IBHR
Folk Religion and the Worldview in the South Western Pacific IBHR
Folklore IZBG, RE
Fomenta Social IOB
For Biblisk Tro IOB
Forschungen und Berichte IBHR
Forschungen und Fortschritte ETL
Forschungen Zur Osteuropaischen Geschichte RE
Forschungen Zur Religion und Literatur des Alten und Neuen Testaments B
Forschungen Zur Religion und Literatur des Alten und Neuen Testaments Izbg
Forum IOB
Foundation Studies in Christian Faith Study-Selected Reading UMPI
Foundations IRPL, RPI
Franciscan Herald RPI
Franciscan Message RPI
Franciscan Studies CPLI, ETL, IZBG, NTA, RE, RPI
Franciscana ETL, RE
Franciscanum B
Franciskaans Leven ETL
Frankfurter Hefte IOB
Franziskanische Studien ETL, IOB, IZBG, NTA, RE
Free University Quarterly RTA

Freiburg (Dialog) IOB
Freiburger Diozesan Archiv RE
Freiburger Rundbrief IOB, IZBG
Freiburger Zeitschrift fur Philosophie und Theologie ETL, NTA, RE
Freide uber Israel IOB
French Review RE
French Studies RE
Friar RPI
Friends Journal RPI
Frontier CPI, IRPL
Fruhmittelalrerliche Studien RE
Furrow CPLI, NTA
Gateway SBPI
Gazette des Beaus Arts RE
Geist und Leben ETL, IZBG, NTA, RE
Gemeenschap der Kerken IOB
Geneva RE
Geneve-Afrique IOB
Gentse Bijdrager tot de Kunstgeschiedenis en de Oudheidkunde RE
Geographical Journal B
Geographical Review B
Geographische Zeitschrift B
Gereformeerd Theologisch Tijdschrift ETL, IZBG, NTA, RE, RTA
Germanisch Romanische Monatsschrift RE
Geschichte und Kunst des Trierer Landes und Seiner Nachbargebiete, Trierer Zeitschrift fur RE
Geschichtliche Landeskunde RE
Geschiedenis en Oudheidkundige Kring voor Leuven en Omgeving, Mededlingen van de ETL, RE
Gesta RE
Getuigenis B, IOB
Gidoggyosasang IOB
Giornale Critico della Filosofia Italiana ETL, RE
Giornale Storico della Letteratura Italiana RE
Giornali Italiano di Filologia B
Giurisprudenza Italiana ETL
Glasgow University Oriental Society Transactions B
Gnomon ETL, NTA, RE
Good Work CPLI
Gottingische Gelehrte Anzeigen B, RE
Goya. Revista de Arte RE
Grande Lessico del Neue Testamente B
Greek Orthodox Theological Review IRPL, RPI
Greek, Roman, and Byzantine Studies RE
Gregorianae, Pontificiae Universitatis B

Gregorianium ETL, IZBG, NTA, RE, RTA

Gregorios o Palamas IOB
Grosse Entschluss, der IOB
Guardian IOB
Guide SBPI
Gulden Passer RE
Gymnasium B
Hadassah Magazine IJP
Handbuch der Orientalistik B
Handeling van het Genootschap voor Geschiedenis
Gesticht Onder de Benaming Societe D' Emulation
de Bruges RE
Handelingen der Maatschappij voor Geschiedenis
en Oudheidkunde Te Gent Re
Handes Amsorya B
Hansische Geschichtsblatter RE
Hartford Quarterly IRPL, RTA
Harvard Semitic Series B
Harvard Studies in Classical Philology B, IBHP
Harvard Theological Review B, ETL, IRPL, IZBG,
NTA, RE, RPI, RTA
Harvard Theological Studies IZBG
Hearthstone SISPL
Hebrew Union College Annual ETL, NTA
Hechos y Dichos IOB
Heerbaan IOB
Heidelberger Jahrbucher RE
Heilig Land B, IZBG
Heilige Land in Vergangenheit und Gegenwart IZBG
Heiliger Dienst IOB
Helmantica RE
Hemecht. Zeitschrift fur Luxemburger Geschichte RE
Herald of Holiness GSSBPL
Herder Correspondence CPLI, ETL, RPI
Herder Korrespondenz IZBG
Hermes. Zeitschrift fur Klassische Philologie RE
Hervormde Teolcgiese Studies B, IZBG
Hesperis Tamuda RE
Hevrew Unicn Xollege Annual IZBG
Heythrop Journal CPLI, ETL, IZBG, RE
Hi Times UMPI
Hibbert Journal ETL, RTA
His CPI, GSSBPL
Hispania. Revista Espanola de Historia RE
Hispania Sacra ETL, RE
Hispanic Review RE
Histerisenes Jahrbuch der Gorresgeuschaft B

Histoire du Droit et des Institutions des Anciens Pays Bourguignons, Comtois et Romands Memoires de la Societe Pour l' RE

Historia B, RE
Historia. Zeitschrift fur Alte Geschichte RE
Historica RE
Historical Journal RE
Historical Magazine of the Protestant Episcopal Church RPI
Historique du Comite des Travaux Historiques et scientifiques, Bulletin Philologique et RE
Historische Zeitschrift B, IOB, RE
Historisches Jahrbuch der Gorresgesellschaft B, RE
Historisk Tidsskrift (Oslo) RE
History RE
History and Theory RE
History of Religions ETL, GSSRPL, IBHR, IRPL, IZBG, RE, RPI
History Today RE
Hochland IOB, RE
Holland (Ministerium) B
Home Life SBPI
Home Missions SBPI
Homelitica en Biblica ETL, IZBG
Homiletic and Pastoral Review CPLI, NTA
Hospital Progress CPLI
Hsientai Hsuehyuan B
Humanist RPI
Iglesia Viva B
Igreja e Missac IOB
Illustrated London News B
Imago Mundi RE
In Lichte der Reformation IOB
Index Quaderri Camerti di Studi Romanistici B
Indian Ecclesiastical Studies B, NTA
Indian Journal of Theology IZBG, NTA, RTA
Indice Historico Espanol RE
Indogermanische Forschungen B
Indo-Iranian Journal B, IBHR
Information Evangelisation IOB
Information Historique RE
Information Service (New York) IOB
Information Service, Secretariat for Promoting Christian Unity IOB
Informations Catholiques Internationales ETL, IOB
Innsbrucker Beitraege Zur Kulturwissenschaft IBHR
Insight CPLI

International Journal for the Philosophy of Religion B

International Journal of Religious Education SISPL
International Reformed Bulletin IOB
International Review of Missions B, CPI, ETL, IBHR, IRPL, RPI, RTA
International Review of Social History RE
Internationale Kirchliche Zeitschrift ETL, IZBG, NTA, RE
Internationales Jahrbuch fur Religions-Sociologie IOB
Internationales Katholiche Informatie IOB
Interpretation ETL, IRPL, IZBG, NTA, RE, RPI, RTA
Ipse hic Elerchus Bibliographicus Biblicus B
Iranica Antiqua B
Iranistische Mittelungen IBHR
Iraq IZBG
Irenikon ETL, IRPL, IZBG, NTA, RE
Irish Ecclesiastical Record CPLI, ETL, IOB, RE
Irish Historical Studies RE
Irish Theological Quarterly CPLI, ETL, IZBG, RE
Isis RE
Islam RE
Islamic Quarterly B
Israel Digest IJP
Israel Exploration Journal ETL, IZBG, NTA
Israel Forum IZBG
Israel Magazine IJP
Israelitisches Wochenblatt IZBG
Istina IRPL, NTA, RE
Istituto Storico Italiano per Il Medio Evo e Archivio Muratoriano, Bullettino dell' RE
Italaia Medioevale e Umanistica RE
Italiana (Revista Biblica) IZBG
Ius Canonicum RE
Ius Commune RE
Iustitia ETL
Jaarbericht van het Vooraziatisch Egyptisch Genootschap ex Oriente Lux IBHR
Jaarbericht van het Vooraziatisch Egyptisch Genotschap ex Oriente Lux IZBG
Jaarbock voor de Eredienst IOB
Jaarboek Werkgenootschap van Katholieke Theologen in Nederland B
Jahrbuch der Berliner Museen RE
Jahrbuch der Gesellschaft fur Niedersachsische Kirchengeschichte RE

Jahrbuch der Hessischen Kirchengeschichtlichen Vereinigung IOB
Jahrbuch der Kunsthistorischen Sammlungen Wien RE
Jahrbuch der Osterreichischen Byzantinistichen Gesellschaft IOB
Jahrbuch der Osterreichischin Byzantinistik RE
Jahrbuch der Stallichen Kunstsammulugen in Baden-Wurttemberg IBHR
Jahrbuch des Deutschen Archaelogischen Instituts B
Jahrbuch des Instituts fur Christliche Sozialwissenschaften IOB
Jahrbuch des Kolnischen Geschichtsvereins RE
Jahrbuch des Kunsthistorischen Instiutes der Universitat Graz RE
Jahrbuch des Martin Luther-Bundes IOB
Jahrbuch des Museums fur Volkenbunder zu Leipzig IBHR
Jahrbuch Evangelischer Mission IOB
Jahrbuch fur Antike und Christentum IZBG, RE
Jahrbuch fur die Geschichte Mittelingen und Ostdeutschlands RE
Jahrbuch fur Frankische Landesforschung RE
Jahrbuch fur Geschichte Osteuropas IOB
Jahrbuch fur Landeskunde voor Niederosterreich RE
Jahrbuch fur Liturgik und Hymnologie B, IOB, RE
Jahrbuch fur Mystiche Theologie ETL
Jahrbuch fur Numismatik und Geldgeschichte B, RE
Jahrbuch fur Wirtschaftsgeschichte RE
Jahrbucher fur Geschichte Osteuropas RE
Japan Missionary Bulletin IOB
Japanese Religions IOB
Jarrbericht van het Vooraziatisch Egyptisch Genootschap ex Oriente Lux B
Jewish Digest IJP
Jewish Educator IJP, RTA
Jewish Frontier GSSRPL, IJP
Jewish Heritage IJP
Jewish Journal of Sociology B, IBHR
Jewish Life IJP, RPI
Jewish Observer and Middle East Review IJP
Jewish Quarterly Review ETL, IJP, IRPL, IZBG, RE, RPI
Jewish Social Studies IZBG
Jewish Spectator GSSRPL, IJP, RPI
Johannesburg (African Studies) IBHR, IOB
Jordan Lectures in Comparative Religions ETL
Journal Asiatique IZBG, RE
Journal de la Societe des Americanistes IBHR

Journal des Moskauer Patriarchats IZBG
Journal des Savants B, RE
Journal for the Scientific Study of Religion IRPL, RE, RPI
Journal for the Study of Judaism IZBG
Journal for the Study of Judaism in the Persian Helenistic and Roman Periods B
Journal for Theology and the Church IRPL, RPI
Journal of African History IBHR, RE
Journal of American Oriental Society IZBG
Journal of American Research Center in Egypt B
Journal of Ancient Near Eastern Society of Columbia B, SISPL
Journal of Applied Behavorial Science SISPL
Journal of Biblical Literature ETL, GSSRPL, IJP, IRPL, IZBG, NTA, RE, RPI, RTA
Journal of Christian Education B, SISPL
Journal of Church and State IRPL, RPI
Journal of Church Music RPI
Journal of Classical Studies B
Journal of Contemporary History RE
Journal of Cuneiform Studies IZBG
Journal of Ecclesiastical History ETL, GSSRPL, IRPL, IZBG, RE, RPI
Journal of Ecomonic History RE
Journal of Economic and Social History of the Orient B
Journal of Ecumenical Studies CPLI, ETL, IRPL, IZBG, RE, RPI
Journal of English and Germanic Philology RE
Journal of Ethiopian Studies B
Journal of Glass Studies B, N
Journal of Hebraic Studies, the B
Journal of Historical Studies ETL, IBHR, IZBG, NTA
Journal of Jewish Communal Service IJP
Journal of Jewish Lore and Philosophy B
Journal of Jewish Studies ETL, IZBG, NTA
Journal of Juristic Papyrology B
Journal of Linguistics SISPL
Journal of Marriage and the Family GSSRPL, IOB
Journal of Modern African Studies GSSRPL
Journal of Modern History RE
Journal of Near Eastern Studies ETL, IZBG, NTA, RPI
Journal of Pastoral Care IRPL, RPI
Journal of Presbyterian History IRPL, RPI
Journal of Religion GSSRPL, IRPL, IZBG, RE, RPI
Journal of Religion and Health IRPL, RPI
Journal of Religion in Africa RE, SISPL

Journal of Religious History ETL, IRPL, IZBG, RE
Journal of Religious Thought IRPL, RPI
Journal of Roman Studies B, RE
Journal of Semitic Studies ETL, IRPL, IZBG, NTA
Journal of Social Psychology IBHR
Journal of the American Academy of Religion
ETL, GSSRPL, IRPL, IZBG, NTA, RE, RPI
Journal of the British Archaeological Association
RE
Journal of the Economic and Social History of
the Orient RE
Journal of the Evangelical Theological Society B
Journal of the Historical Society of the Church
in Wales RE
Journal of the History of Ideas B, RE
Journal of the History of Philosophy RE
Journal of the Northwest Semitic Languages B
Journal of the Polynesian Society IBHR
Journal of the Royal Asiatic Society of Great
Britain and Ireland RE
Journal of the Royal Society of Antiquaries
of Ireland RE
Journal of the University of Bombay IBHR
Journal of the Warburg and Courtauld Institutes RE
Journal of Theological Studies ETL, IRPL, IZBG,
RE, RTA
Judaica IZBG
Judaism ETL, IBHR, IJP, IOB, IRPL, IZBG, RPI
Junge Kirche IOB
Junior Hi Times UMPI
Jurist RE
Jus ETL
Justice dans de Monde ETL
Kairos ETL, IZBG, NTA, RE
Kant Studien ETL, RE
Katallagete B, IRPL, RPI
Katechetische Blatter IZBG
Katholiek Archief ETL
Katholische Erzieher B
Katholischen Missionen IOB
Katholisches Missionejahrbuch der Schweiz IOB
Keeping Posted IJP
Kerk en Missie ETL
Kerk en Theologie B, IOB
Kerkelijk Leven IOB
Kerygma und Dogma ETL, IRPL, IZBG, RE, RTA
Kindergarten UMPI
Kirche Im Osten RE

Kirchenblatt fur die Reformierte Schweiz B
Kirchlichen Dienst IOB
Kirchliches Jahrbuch fur die Evangelische Kirche in Deutschland IOB
Kirjath Sepher IZBG
Kirke og Luther IOB
Kirkehistorike Samlinger RE
Kliene Pauly B
Klio. Beitrage Zur Alten Geschichte Berlin et Wiesbaden RE
Kommentare und Beitrage zum Alten und Neuen Testament (Dusseldorf) B
Kommunist IOB
Kosmos en Oecumene IOB
Kostnicke Jiskry IOB
Kratkie Soobscenija Institute Narodov Azii IZBG
Krestanska Revue IOB, IZBG
Kristel Forum IOB
Kristen Gemenskap IOB
Kulturarbeit IOB
Kultuurleven IOB
Kunst und Kirche IOB
Kwartalnik Historyczny RE
Kyrios. Vierteljahresschrift fur Kirchen und Geistesgeschichte Osteruopas RE
Kyrkohistorisk Arsskrift RE
L' Osservatore CPII
Language. Journal of the Linguistic Society of America IBHR, IOB, IZBG
Lateinamerika Jahrbuch RE
Latomus ETL, RE
Laurentianum RE
Laval Theologique et Philosophique ETL, NTA
Learning for Living RTA
Lebendige Seelsorge IOB
Lebendiges Zeugnis IOB
Lecciones Cristianas UMPI
Lelkopasztor IOB
Leodium RE
Leshonenu IZBG
Letopis IZBG
Lettres Romanis RE
Leuvense Bijdragen RE
Levant. Journal of the British School of Archaeology in Jerusalem Sispl
Lexikon der Christichen Ikonographie B
Lexington Theological Quarterly ETL, IRPL, NTA, RPI
Libri e Riviste D' Italia B

Liguorian CPLI, RPI
Limburg RE
Linguistica Biblica IZBG
Linguistische Berichte IZBG
Lingusitica Biblica B
Link GSSRPL, RPI
Literaturwissenschaftliches Jahrbuch RE
Liturgical Arts CPLI, RPI
Liturgie und Monchtum ETL, IZBG
Liturgisches Jahrbuch B, RE
Living Light CPLI
Living Word CPLI
Logos RPI
London (Africa) IOB
London (Sobornost) IOB, NTA
London (Tablet) CPLI
Louvain Studies CPLI, NTA
Lown Institute for Judaiistic Studies IZBG
Lumen ETL, IOB
Lumen (Madrid) IOB
Lumen Vitae CPLI, ETL, IZBG
Lumiere et Vie CPLI, ETL, IZBG, RE
Lunds Universitets Arsskrift IZBG
Lusitania Sacra RE
Luther Jahrbuch RE
Lutheran GSSRPL, RPI
Lutheran Forum RPI
Lutheran Quarterly ETL, IRPL, IZBG, RPI
Lutheran Standard GSSRPL, RPI
Lutheran Theological Seminary Review SISPL
Lutheran Witness GSSRPL, RPI
Lutheran World IRPI, IRPL
Lutherische Monatshefte ETL, IZBG, NTA
Lutherische Rundschau ETL, NTA
Maasfouw RE
Madrid (Augustinus) B, IOB
Madrid (Lumen) IOB
Mainzer Zeitschrift RE
Maison Dieu ETL, NTA, RE
Man, the Journal of the Royal Anthropologist Institute IBHR
Manresa (Bibbas) NTA
Manuscripta CPLI, RE
Marburger Theologische Studien IZBG
Marian Studies B, CPLI
Marianum ETL, NTA, RE
Mariologische Studien B
Marriage CPLI, RPI

Masses Ouvrieres IOB
Materialdienst des Konfessionskundlichen Instituts
E, IOB
Mature Years UMPI
McCormick Quarterly IBPL, RPI
Mededlingen en Verhandelingen van het
Vooraziatisch-Egytisch Genootschap "ex Oriente
Lux" ETL
Mededlingen van de Geschiedenis en Oudheidkundige
Kring voor Leuven en Omgeving ETL, RE
Mededlingen van het Nederlands Historie Instituut
Te Rome RE
Mediaeval and Renaissance RE
Mediaeval Scandinavia RE
Mediaeval Studies RE
Medieval Archaeology RE
Medieval Studies E, IBHR
Medievalia et Humanistica RE
Medium Aevum RE
Melanges D' Archeologie et D' Histoire RE
Melanges D' Archeologie et D' Historier de l'
Ecole Francaise de Rome IBHR
Melanges de l' Institut Dominicain D' Etudes
Crientales E, IZBG
Melanges de l' Instiut Domincain D' Etudes
Orientales de Caire RE
Melanges de l' Universite St. Joseph E, IBHR,
IZBG, RE
Melanges de la Casa de Velazquez RE
Melanges de Science Religieuse ETL, IZBG, NTA, RE
Melita Theclogica ETL, IZBG, NTA
Memoires de la Federation der Societes D' Histcire
et D' Archeolcgie de l' Aisne RE
Memoires de la Federation des Societes Historie
et Archeclogie de Paris et de l' Ile de France RE
Memoires de la Societe Archeolcgie et Historique
de la Charente RE
Memoires de la Societe D' Agriculture, Commerce,
Sciences et Arts, du Departement de la Marne RE
Memoires de la Societe Pour l' Histoire du Droit
et des Institutions des Anciens Pays Bourguignons,
Comtois et Romands RE
Memoirs de la Societe Archeologique du Department
D' Ille et Vilaine, Bulletin et RE
Memorie de Deputazione di Storia Patria per
Le Province di Romagna, Atti e RE
Memorie Storiche Forogiuliesi RE
Mennonite GSSRPL, ICB, RPI

Mennonite Quarterly Review IRPL, RPI

Messager de l' Exauchat de Patriarche Russe en Europe Occidentale IOB
Messager Orthodoxe IOB

Messenger GSSRPL, RPI
Methodist History IRPL, RPI
Methodist Story UMPI
Methodist Student UMPI
Methodist Teacher UMPI
Methodist Woman UMPI
Metonoia GSSRPL, RPI
Metropolitan Museum of Art Bulletin RE
Mid America CPLI, RE
Middle East Journal GSSRPL
Middle East Studies Association Bulletin IBHR
Migration Today IOB
Migrations IOB
Milarbeit IOB
Ministerium (Holland) B
Ministry IOB
Miscelanea Comillas FTL, IZBG, NTA, RE
Miscelanea de Estudics Arabes y Hebreos B
Miscellanea Franciscana RE
Mision Avierta al Servicio de al Fe B
Misiones Extranjeras IOB
Missie Integraal IOB
Missiewerk IOB
Missionalia Hispanica RE
Missionary Research Library IOB, RE
Missioni Catholiche IOB
Mitropolia Ardealului IOB
Mitropolia Banatului IOB
Mitropolia Moldavei si Sucevei IOB, RE
Mitropolia Olterici IOB, RE
Mitteilungen der Deutschen Orient-Gesellschaft IZBG
Mitteilungen des Instituts fur Orientforschung E, IBHR, IZBG
Mitteilungen des Instituts fur Osterreichesche Geschichtsforschung RE
Mitteilungen des Oesterreichischen Staatsarchivs RE
Mitteilungen und Forschungsbeitrage der Cusanus Gesellschaft RE
Mitteilungen Zur Geschichte des Benediktiner Ordens und Seiner Zweige, Studien und RE
Mitteilunger der Deutschen Orient Gesellschaft E, IBHR

Mitteilunger des Deutschen Archaeologischen Instituts B, IBHR
Mittellanteinisches Jahrbuch RE
Mnemosyne RE
Modern Churchman B, ETL, IRPL, NTA
Modern Language Notes IZBG, RE
Modern Language Quarterly RE
Modern Language Review RE
Modern Philology RE
Modern Schoolman CPLI, RE
Modern Society CPLI
Molad IZBG
Momentum CPLI
Monastic Studies CPLI
Monde Juie, la Revue du Centre de Documentation Juife Contemporaine IZBG
Monitor Ecclesiasticus ETL
Month CPLI, ETL, NTA, RE
Monthly Letter About Evangelism IOB
Monuments Historuques de la France RE
Moody Monthly CPI, GSSRPL
Moreana. Bulletin Thomas More RE
Motive GSSPRL, RPI
Moyen Age RE
Munchener Studien Zur Sprachwissenschaft B, IBHR
Munchener Theologische Zeitschrift ETL, IZBG, NTA, RE
Munster (Catholica) ETL, NTA
Munster, Zeitschrift fur Christliche Kunst und Kunstwissenschaft ICB, RE
Musart CPLI
Musees de Geneve IBHR
Museon ETL, IZBG, NTA, RE
Museum Helveticum B
Museum of Far Eastern Antiquities, the IBHR
Music Ministry SISPL, UMPI
Musica Disciplina. a Yearbook of the History of Music RE
Musik und Altar ICB
Musik und Kirche IOB
Muslim World IRPL, RPI
Mysterium ETL, IZBG, NTA
Nabozenska Revue IOB
Nachrichten der Akademie der Wissenschaften in Gottingen RE
Nachrichter der Akademie der Wissenschaften zu Gottingen B
Namurcum RE

Nasza Przeszlosc RE

National Catholic Education Association Bulletin CPLI

National Catholic Guidance Conference Journal CPLI, RPI

National Catholic Reporter CPLI

National Christian Council Review IOB

National Geographic B

National Guild of Catholic Psychiatrists Bulletin CPLI

National Jewish Monthly IJP

Natural Law Forum CPLI

Naturaleza y Gracia B

Near East Council of Churches IOB

Near East Reporter IJP

Nederduitse Gereformeerde Teologiese Tydskrif B, IBHR, IZBG

Nederlands Archief voor Kerkgeschiedenis IOB, RE

Nederlands Archievenblad RE

Nederlands Katholische Stemmen ETL

Nederlands Kunsthistorisch Jaarboek RE

Nederlands Theclogisch Tijdschrift ETL, IRPL, IZBG, NTA, RE

Neophilologus RE

Neue Ordnung ETL, IOB

Neue Rundschau IOB

Neue Zeitschrift fur Missionswissenschaft IZBG, RE

Neue Zeitschrift fur Systematische Theologie und Religionsphilosophie ETL, IRPL

Neue Zeitschrift fur Systematische Theologie und Religionsphilosophie Re

Neue Zeitschrift fur Systematische Theologie und Religionsphilosophie RTA

Neues Forum IOB

Neukirchener Studienbucher ETL

Neuphilologische Mitteilungen RE

Neutestamentliche Abhandlungen IBHR, IZBG

New Blackfriars CPLI, ETL

New Book Review RPI

New Christian IOB

New City CPLI

New Creation UMPI

New Creation Leaders Guide UMPI

New Creation Resource Packet UMPI

New Scholasticism CPLI, ETL, RE

New Testament Abstracts IZBG

New Testament Studies CPI, ETL, IRPL, IZBG, NTA, RE, RPI

New World Outlook RPI
New York (Dialog) ETL, IOB, IRPL, RPI

New York (Information Service) IOB
Newman-Studien IOB
Newsletter, National Council of Churches Committee on the Church and Jewish People IOB, SBPI
Niederdeutsche Beitrage Zur Kunstgeschichte RE
Niedersachsisches Jahrbuch fur Landesgeschichte RE
Nieuwe Mens IOB
Nordisk Tidsskrift for Bok och Biblioteksvasen RE
Norsk Teclogisk Tidsckrift ETL
Norsk Teologisk Tidsskrift ETL, IRPL, IZBG, NTA
Norsk Tidsskrift for Misjon IOB
North American Liturgical Week CPLI
Notes Africaines IBHR
Notes on Translation SISPL
Noticias Cristianas de Israel IZBG
Notre Catechese IZBG
Notre Dame Journal of Education CPLI
Nottingham Mediaeval Studies RE
Nouva Rivista Storica RE
Nouvelle Revue Theologique CPLI, ETL, IZBG, NTA, RE
Nouvelles Chretiennes D' Israel B
Nova et Vetera ETL, IZBG, NTA
Nova et Vetera (Suisse) B, ETL
Novare RE
Novum Testamentum ETL, IRPL, IZBG, NTA, RE, RTA
Numen IZBG, RE
Numen, International Review for the History of Religions ETL, IRPL, NTA
Numismatic Chronicle RE
Numismatic Chronicle and Journal B
Nunc et Senyser IOB
Nuntius Sodalicii Neotestamentici Upsaliensis IZBG
Nursery Days UMPI
Ny Kyrklig Tidsskrift ETL, IZBG
Oberbayerisches Archiv RE
Occasional Bulletin SISPL
Odrodzenie i Reformacja W Polsce RE
Oecumene IOB
Oecumenica B
Oekumenische Diskussion IOB
Oekumenische Rundschau B, IOB
Oesterreichische Bibliographie RE

Oesterreichische Zeitschrift fur Kunst und Denkmalpflege RE

Oesterreichisches Archiv fur Kirchenrecht ETL, IOB, RE
Oesterreichisches Klerusblatt ETL

Official News Digest RPI
Offizieller Bericht der Vollversammlung des Lutherischen Weltbundes Iob
Oikoumenikon IOB
One Church RPI
One Geestelijk Leven B
One/Two UMPI
Ons Geestelijk IOB
Opuscula Atheniensia IBHR
Oratorium RE
Orbis Catholicus IZBG
Ordens Korrespondenz B
Oriens IZBG, RE
Oriens Antiquus IZBG
Oriens Christianus IZBG, RE
Orient Syrien ETL, IZBG, NTA
Oriental Institute Communications B
Orientalia ETL, IZBG, NTA, RE
Orientalia Christiana Periodica ETL, NTA, RE, RTA
Orientalia et Biblica Iovaniensia B, IZBG
Orientalia Lovaniensia Periodica B
Orientalia Suecana B, IBHR
Orientalistische Literaturzeitung ETL, IZBG, NTA, RE
Oriente Christiano IOB
Oriente Moderno IBHR
Orientierung ETL, NTA
Orpheus. Rivista di Umanita Classica e Cristiana RE
Orthodox Church RPI
Orthodox Life RPI
Orthodox Word RPI
Orthodoxia IOB
Oslo (Historisk Tidsskrift) RE
Osterreichische Zeitschrift fur Volkskunde IBHR
Osteuropa IOB
Ostkirchliche Studien ETL, NTA, RE
Other Side SISPL
Oud Holland RE
Oude Land van Loon RE
Oud-Katholiek IOB
Oudtestamentische Studien B, IZBG

Ou-Testamentiese Werkgemeenskap van Suid-Afrika
IZBG
Outlook SBPI
Outreach SBPI
Oxoniensia RE
Paedagogica Historica RE
Pages Documentaires IOB
Palabra de Clero ETL, NTA
Palabra Inspirada ETL
Palestine Exploration Quarterly ETL, IRPL,
IZBG, NTA
Palestinskii Sbaornik IZBG
Palestra del Clero IZBG
Palladia. Rivista di Storia dell' Architettura RE
Pantheon. Internationale Zeitschrift fur Kunst RE
Par l' Institut Francais au Portugal Bulletin
des Etudes Portugaises, Publie RE
Paroisse et Liturgie IZBG
Parola del Passato B, IBHR
Parola per l' Assemblea Festiva, la B
Parole de l' Orient B, IZBG, RE
Parole di Vita B
Parole et Mission B, IBHR
Parole et Pain ETL
Past and Present RE
Pastor Bonus ETL
Pastoral Blatter ETL, NTA
Pastoral Counselor SISPL
Pastoral Life RPI
Pastoral Psychology CPI, GSSRPL, IRPL, RPI, RTA
Pastoraltheologie, Wissenschaft und Pranxis IOB
Patrologia Latina B
Patterns of Prejudice IJP
Paul and Qumran IBHR
Pays Lorrain RE
Pazmaveb IZBG
Pedagogic Reporter IJP
Pensamiento RE
Pensamiento Cristiano SISPL
Pensee Catholique, la B
Pentecostal Evangel GSSRPL
Perfice Munus ETL
Periodica de Re Morali, Canonica, Liturgica RE
Perkins School of Theology Journal NTA
Perspectiva Teologica B
Perspective IRPL, RPI
Perspectives de Catholicite IOB
Perspektive der Zukunft B

Philippiana Sacra B

Philippine Studies B, IBHR
Philological Quarterly RE
Philologus. Zeitschrift fur das Klassische Altertum RE
Philosophia Reformata IOB, RE
Philosophical Review RE
Philosophical Studies CPLI
Philosophische Rundschau IBHR
Philosophischer Literaturanzeiger B, RE
Philosophisches Jahrbuch B, RE
Philosophy Today CPLI
Phoenix ETL
Phoibos ETL
Phylon GSSRPL
Plain Truth SISPL
Planbook for Adults UMPI
Polish Ecumenical Review IOB
Pope Speaks CPLI, RPI
Porefthendes IOB
Positions Lutheriennes B, IOB, IZBG
Practical Anthropology CPI, IRPL
Pravoslavna Misao IBHR, IOB
Prawo Kanoniczne RE
Preaching CPLI
Predicador Evangelicio IOB
Presbyterian Alliance and the World Alliance of Reformed Churches, Bulletin of the Department of Theology of the World IOB
Presbyterian Journal SISPL
Presbyterian Life GSSRPL, RPI
Presbyterian Outlook RPI
Presbyterian Survey RPI
Preschool Leadership SBPI
Presence Orthodoxe B
Pretoria Oriental Studies ETL
Priest CPLI
Princeton Seminary Bulletin ETL, IRPL, IZBG, RPI
Prism IOB
Probe SBPI
Proceedings of the American Academy for Jewish Research B
Proceedings of the American Philosophical Society B
Proceedings of the British Academy RE
Proceedings of the College Theology Society CPLI
Proceedings of the Israel Academy of Sciences and Humanities B

Proceedings of the World Congress of Jewish
Studies B
Proche Orient Chretien RE
Proclaim SBPI
Program Quarterly UMPI
Project IOB
Protestantesimo IZBG
Protestantischen Kirchen der Tschechoslowakei IZBG
Province du Maine RE
Prozdor IZBG
Przeglad Historyczny RE
Przeglad Orientalistyczny B, IZBG
Psychology for Living UMPI
Psychology Today GSSRPL
Publications de la Section Historique de l'
Institut Ducal de Luxembourg RE
Publications de la Societe Historique et
Archologique dans Le Limbourg a Maestricht RE
Publications of the Modern Language Association RE
Quadermi di Semiliatica B
Quaderni Storici RE
Quadrivium RE
Quaerendo RE
Quaestiones Disputatae ETL, IZBG
Quaker History IRPL, RPI
Quaker Life RPI
Quartalschrift fur Christliche Alterumskunde
und Kirchengeschichte, Romanische RE
Quarterly Review RPI
Quarterly Review of Historical Studies, the IBHR
Quatember IOB
Quellen und Forschungen aus Italienischen Archiven
und Bibliotheken RE
Questions de Vida Cristia B
Questions Liturgiques RE
Rassegna di Ascetica e Mistica B
Rassegna di Letteratura Tomistica RE
Rassegna di Studi Etiopici B
Rassegna Mensile di Israel B, IBHR, IZBG
Rassegna Storica del Risorgimento RE
Rassegna Storica Toscana RE
Razon y Fe ETL, NTA, RE
Real UMPI
Real Class Guide UMPI
Real Resource Packet UMPI
Reallexikon fur Antike und Christentum B
Recherches Augustiniennes B, RE
Recherches Bibliques B

Recherches de Science Religieuse ETL, IRPL, IZBG, NTA, RE
Recherches de Theologie Ancienne et Medievale ETL, IZBG, NTA, RE
Recherches et Debats du Centre Catholiques des Intellectuals Francais IOB
Rechtsforshung Zeitschrift fur Vergleichinde Rechtsgeschichte,
Rechtsforshung Zeitschrift fur Vergleichinde Rechtsgeschichte, Einschliesslich der Ethnologischen B
Reconciliation IOB
Reconstructionist IJP
Recontre Assyriologique Internationale B
Recontre Oecumenique IOB
Records of the American Catholic Historical Society of Philadelphia RE
Recueil Dalloz ETL
Recusant History RE
Reformatasok Lajsja IOB
Reformation Review IOB
Reformatus Egykaz IOB
Reforme IOB
Reformed and Presbyterian World IRPL, RPI
Reformed Review IRPL, IZBG, RPI
Reformed Theological Review ETL, IRPL, IZBG, NTA
Reformierte Kirchenzeitung IOB
Regelrecht IOB
Regnum Dei ETL, RE
Religion and Society IOB
Religion in Geschichte und Gegenwart ETL
Religion Teacher's Journal CPLI
Religion, Wissenschaft, Kultur IZBG
Religion y Cultura B, IOB
Religious and Theological Abstracts IZBG
Religious Book Guide UMPI
Religious Education GSSRPL, IJP, RPI
Religious Humanism GSSRPL
Religious Studies IRPL, RPI
Renaiscence CPLI
Renaissance and Modern Studies RE
Renaissance Quarterly RE
Rendiconti de Scienze Morali IZBG
Rendiconti dell' Istituto Lombardo di Scienze e Lettere RE
Rendiconti dell' Istituto Nazionale D' Archeolgia e Storia dell' Arte Re
Rendiconti della Academia Nazionale dei Lincei IBHR

Rendiconti della Pontifica Accademia Romana de Archaeologia IBHR
Rendus des Seances de l' Academie des Inscriptions et Belles Lettres, Comptes RE
Renewal IRPL, RPI
Reniconti della Portifica Accademia Romana di Archeologia RE
Renovation ETL
Report from the Capital SBPI
Reporter for Conscience's Sake RPI
Resonance CPLI
Response RTA, SBPI, UMPI
Response in Worship Music the Acts IOB
Review and Expositor ETL, IRPL, IZBG, NTA
Review for Religious CPLI, ETL, NTA, RPI
Review of English Studies RE
Review of Politics CPLI, RE
Review of Religion SISPL
Review of Religious Research IRPL, RE, RPI
Review of Social Economy CPLI
Revista Agustiniana de Espiritualidad B, ETL, NTA
Revista Biblica (Argentina) B
Revista Biblica (Buenos Aires) IZBG
Revista Biblica (Italiana) IZBG
Revista de Archivos, Bibliotecas y Museos RE
Revista de Cultura Biblica ETL, IZBG, NTA
Revista de Cultura Teologica ETL, NTA
Revista de Espiritualidad RE
Revista de Filologia Espanola RE
Revista de Indias RE
Revista degli Studi Orientali IZBG
Revista di Cultura Tehologica IZBG
Revista di Pastorale Liturgica B
Revista di Teologia Morale B
Revista Eclesiastica Brasileria ETL, IZBG, NTA, RE
Revista Ecumenica "Ut Unum Sint" ETL
Revista Espanola de Derecho Canonico RE
Revista Espanola de Teologia ETL, IZBG, NTA, RE
Revue Archeologique RE
Revue Belge D' Archeolcgie et D' Historie de l' Art RE
Revue Belge D' Historie Contemporaine RE
Revue Belge de Musicolcgie RE
Revue Belge de Numismatique et de Sigillcgraphie RE
Revue Belge de Philologie et D' Histoire RE
Revue Benedictine ETL, NTA, RE
Revue Biblique ETL, IRPL, IZBG, NTA, RE
Revue D' Archeclogique B

Revue D' Ascetique et de Mystique ETL, IZBG, NTA, RE
Revue D' Auvergne RE
Revue D' Egyptclcgie B, IBHR
Revue D' Histoire de l' Amerique Francaise RE
Revue D' Histoire de l' Eglise de France RE
Revue D' Histoire de Philosophie et de Theologie ETL
Revue D' Histcire des Religions RE
Revue D' Histcire des Sciences et de Leurs Applications RE
Revue D' Histcire des Textes B
Revue D' Histcire Diplomatique RE
Revue D' Histcire Ecclesiastique ETL, IRPL, IZBG, NTA, RE
Revue D' Histoire Economique Sociale RE
Revue D' Histoire et de Philosophie Religieuses ETL, IRPL, IZBG, NTA, RE
Revue D' Histcire Litteraire de la France RE
Revue D' Histcire Mitteilungen RE
Revue D' Histcire Moderne et Contemporaine RE
Revue de Droit Canonique RE
Revue de Etudes Augustiniennes ETL, NTA
Revue de l' Anranchin et du Pays de Granville RE
Revue de l' Art RE
Revue de l' Histoire de la Medicine Hebraique IBHR, IZBG
Revue de l' Histoire des Religions ETL, IRPL, IZBG, NTA
Revue de l' Institut des Belles Letters Arabes B, IBHR
Revue de l' Occident Musulman et de la Mediterranee IBHR
Revue de l' Universite D' Ottawa CPLI, ETL, IZBG, RE
Revue de la Haute Auvergne RE
Revue de Litteratur Comparee RE
Revue de Metaphysiqye et de Morale RE
Revue de Philclogie, de Litterature et D' Histoire Anciennes RE
Revue de Qumran ETL, IRPL, IZBG, RE, RTA
Revue de Synthese RE
Revue de Theolcgie et de Philosophie ETL, IZBG, NTA, RE
Revue del' Evangelisation IOB
Revue des Communautes Religieuses ETL
Revue des Etudes Anciennes B, IBHR
Revue des Etudes Armeniennes B, IBHR, RE

Revue des Etudes Augustiniennes RE

Revue des Etudes Byzantines B, IBHR, RE
Revue des Etudes Grecques RE
Revue des Etudes Islamiques B, IBHR
Revue des Etudes Italiennes RE
Revue des Etudes Juives B, IBHR, IZBG, RE
Revue des Etudes Latines RE
Revue des Etudes Slaves RE
Revue des Etudes Sud-Est Europeenes IBHR, RE
Revue des Sciences Humaines RE
Revue des Sciences Philosophiques et Theologiques B, ETL, IBHR, IZBG, NTA, RE
Revue des Sciences Religieuses ETL, IRPL, IZBG, NTA
Revue des Sciences Religieuses de l' Universite de Strasbourg RE
Revue Diocesaine de Namur ETL
Revue Diocesaine de Tournai ETL
Revue du Droit Canonique ETL, IOB
Revue du Louvre et des Museede Frcme B, IBHR
Revue du Louvre et des Musees de France RE
Revue du Moyen Age Latina RE
Revue du Nord RE
Revue du Vivarais RE
Revue Generale RE
Revue Historique B, IZBG, RE
Revue Historique du Droit Francais et Etranger RE
Revue Hittite et Asianique B, IBHR
Revue Internationale de Philosophie RE
Revue Internationale des Droits de l' Antiquite IZBG, RE
Revue Mabillon RE
Revue Numismatique B, RE
Revue Philosophique de la France et de l' Etranger RE
Revue Philosophique de Louvain CPLI, ETL, RE
Revue Roumaine D' Histoire IZBG, RE
Revue Theologique de Louvain RE
Revue Thomiste ETL, IZBG, NTA, RE
Rheinische Vierteljahrsblatter RE
Rheinisches Museum fur Philologie IZBG
Ribista Rosminiana di Filosofia e di Cultura RE
Ricerche Bibliche e Religiose ETL
Rinascimento RE
Risk IOB
Risorgimento RE
Rivista Biblica ETL, NTA, RE
Rivista degli Studi Orientali B, ETL, IBHR, RE

Rivista del Diritto Matrimoniale e Dello Stato Delle Persone ETL
Rivista di Archeologia Cristiana RE
Rivista di Ascetica e Mistica ETL, NTA
Rivista di Cultura Classica e Medioevale RE
Rivista di Diritto Civile ETL
Rivista di Filologia ETL
Rivista di Filologia e di Istruzione Classica RE
Rivista di Filosofia Neoscolastica RE
Rivista di Liturgia B
Rivista di Pedagogia e Scienze Religiose B
Rivista di Storia del Diritto Italiano RE
Rivista di Storia della Chiesa in Italia RE
Rivista di Storia e Letteratura Religiosa RE
Rivista di Studi Classici ETL
Rivista di Studi Fenici B
Rivista Internazionale de Filosofia de Diritto ETL
Rivista Storica Italiana RE
Roczniki Historyczne RE
Roczniki Humanistyczne RE
Roczniki Orientalistyczny IZBG
Roczniki Reologiczro Kanoniczne ETL, NTA
Roczniki Teologiczne Chrzescijanskiej Akademii Teologicznej IZBG
Roczniki Teologiczno Kanoniczne IZBG, RE
Romance Philology RE
Romania RE
Romanic Review RE
Romanische Forschungen RE
Romanische Quartalschrift fur Christliche Alterumskunde und Kirchengeschichte RE
Romanistisches Jahrbuch RE
Romische Historische Mitteilungen RE
Romische Quartalschrift ETL, IOB, NTA
Romisches Jahrbuch fur Kunstgeschichte RE
Roundtable UMPI
Royal Service SBPI
Ruch Biblijny i Liturgiczny ETL, IZBG, NTA
Sacerdos ETL
Sacra Doctrina ETL, NTA, RE
Sacred Music CPLI, RPI
Sacris Erudiri ETL, IZBG, NTA, RE
Saeculum IZBG, RE
Salesianum IZBG, RE
Salmanticensis ETL, IZBG, NTA, RE
Santissima Eucharistia IOB
Sapienza ETL, NTA, RE
Scandinavian Economic History Review RE

Schema XIII CPLI
Schriften des Deutschen Instituts fur Wissenschaftlishe Padogogik ETL
Schweizer Buchhandel RE
Schweizer Rundschau IOB
Schweizerische Theologische Umschau IOB
Schweizerische Zeitschrift fur Geschichte RE
Schweizerisches Archiv fur Volkskunde IBHR, RE
Science et Esprit ETL, IZBG, NTA, RE
Sciences Ecclesiastiques ETL, RTA
Scottish Historical Review RE
Scottish Journal of Theology ETL, IRPL, IZBG, RTA
Scripta Mercaturae RE
Scripta Theologica B
Scriptorium RE
Scriptorium Victoriense RE
Scripture CPLI, ETL
Scripture Bulletin CPLI, ETL, IZBG, NTA
Scuola Cattolica ETL, IZBG, NTA, RE
Scuola Pasitiva Serie Iv IBHR
Seanchas Ard Mhacha RE
Search ICB, SEPI
Secretariado Trinitario ETL
Sefarad ETL, IZBG, NTA, RE
Sein und Sendung B
Selecciones de Libros B
Self-Realization Magazine RPI
Semana Biblica Espanola B
Semana Espanola de Teologia B
Semeur IOB
Seminario Conciliar IZBG
Seminarios ETL
Seminarium ETL
Semitica IZBG
Series (United Methodist Student) UMPI
Series (United Methodist Teacher) UMPI
Serran RPI
Shenhsueh Yu Cjiaohui B
Sicilia Archeologica IBHR
Siculorum Gymnasium B, RE
Sighted Pathways GSSRPL
Sign CPLI, RPI
Signes du Temps ICB
Signos de los Tiempos B
Sinhagbondan IOB
Sinhagyeiogu IOB
Sister Formation Bulletin CPLI
Sisters Today CPLI, RPI

Sitzungsberichte der Bayerischen Akademie der Wissenschaften RE
Sitzungsberichte der Deutschen Akademie der Wissenschaften IZBG, RE
Sitzungsberichte der Heidelberger Akademie der Wissenschaften IZBG, RE
Sitzungsberichte der Oesterreicheschen Akademie der Wissenschaften Izbq
Sitzungsberichte der Oesterreichischen Akademie der Wissenschaften RE
Sitzungsberichte der Sachsischen Adademie der Wissenschaften zu Leipzig RE
Sjalocm IOB
Skrifter Utgitt Av Det Norske Videnskaps Akademie i Oslo IZBG
Slavia RE
Slavia Antiqua RE
Slavia Occidentalis RE
Sluzba Slova IZBG
Sobornost (London) IOB, NTA
Social Action IRPI, RPI
Social Compass ETL, RE, RTA
Social Justice Review CPLI, RPI
Social Questions Bulletin RPI
Societe Archeclogie et Historique de Nantes et de Loire Atlantique, Bulletin de la RE
Societe Historique et Archologique dans Le Limbourg a Maestricht, Publications de la RE
Societes Historie et Archeologie de Paris et de l' Ile de France, Memoires de la Federation des RE
Sociologia Religiosa IBHR
Sociological Analysis IBHR
Sociologisch Bulletin IOB
Solia RPI
Sophia. Rassegna Critica di Filosofia e Storia della Filosofia RE
Soundings IRPI, RPI
South East Asia Journal of Theology IRPL, NTA
South Indian Churchman IOB
Southern Baptist Educator SBPI
Southwestern Journal of Theology CPI, ETL, IRPL, IZBG, NTA, RPI, RTA, SBPI
Southwestern News SBPI
Soviet Studies in History RE
Span SBPI
Spectrum RPI
Speculum B, RE, SISPL

Spicilegium Historicum Congregationis Ssmi Redemptoris RE
Spiegel Historiael RE
Spire SBPI
Spirit CPLI
Spiritual Life CPLI, RPI
Spiritus IOB
Sprachforschung auf dem Gebiet der Indogermanischen Sprachen, Zeitschrift fur Vergleichende B
Sprawozdania Z Czynnosci Wydawniczej i Posiedzen Naukoeych Oraz Kronika RE
Springfielder IRPI, RPI
St. Anthony Messenger CPLI, RPI
St. Nomata NTA
St. Vladimir's Theological Quarterly ETL, IRPI, IZBG, NTA, RPI
Stained Glass RPI
Starinar RE
Start SBPI
Stimme der Generde IOB
Stimme der Orthodoxie B, IOB
Stimmen der Zeit CPLI, ETL, IZBG, NTA, RE
Storia Contemporanea RE
Streeven B, IOB, IZBG, RE
Strenna Storica Bolognese RE
Stromata IOB, IZBG, RE
Student SBPI
Studi Biblici IZBG
Studi Classici e Orientali B, IBHR
Studi Danteschi RE
Studi di Saciolcgia IBHR
Studi e Materiali di Storia della Religioni B, ETL, IBHR, IZBG, RE
Studi Francescani B, RE
Studi Mahrebini IBHR
Studi Medievali RE
Studi Mediolatini e Volgari RE
Studi Micenci Ed Egeo-Anatolici IBHR
Studi Romani B, RE
Studi Semitici IZBG
Studi Senesi RE
Studi Storici RE
Studi Storici dell' Ordine dei Servi di Maria RE
Studi Urbinati di Storia, Filosofia e Letteratura RE
Studia et Documenta Historiae et Iuris B, RE
Studia Evangelica IBHR

Studia Hibernica RE
Studia Historica Slovaca RE
Studia Islamica B, IBHR
Studia Liturgica IRPL, IZBG, NTA, RE
Studia Missionalia RE
Studia Monastica RE
Studia Montis Reglii ETL
Studia Moralia B
Studia Neophilologica RE
Studia Orientalia B, IBHR, IZBG
Studia Orientalia Christiana B, RE
Studia Papyrologica B, IBHR
Studia Patavina ETL, NTA, RE
Studia Patristica B
Studia Picena RE
Studia Theologica ETL, IRPL, IZBG, NTA, RE
Studia Theologica Varsaviensia RE
Studia Warminkie B
Studia Zrodloznawcze RE
Studien und Mitteilungen Zur Geschichte des Benediktiner Ordens und Seiner Zweige RE
Studien zum Alten und Neuen Testament IZBG
Studien Zur Umwelt des Neuen Testaments IZBG
Studies CPLI
Studies in Biblical Theology IZBG
Studies in Bibliography and Booklore IJP
Studies in Christian Living UMPI
Studies in Comparative Religion B, IBHR
Studies in English Literature RE
Studies in Islam IBHR
Studies in Medieval and Renaissance History RE
Studies in Philology RE
Studies in Religion IZBG
Studies in the Geography of Israel IZBG
Studies in the History of Religions B
Studies in the Renaissance RE
Studies Journal of the British Institute of Archaeology at Anakara, Anatolian B, IBHR
Studies on the Texts of the Desert of Judah ETL
Studies on Voltaire and the XVIIIth Century RE
Studii Biblici Franciscani Liber Annuus ETL, IZBG, NTA
Studii Teologice B, RE
Studium ETL, NTA
Studium Generale IOB
Studium Legionense B
Study Encounter IRPL, RPI
Stuttgarter Bibelstudien B, IZBG

Stuttgarter Biblische Monographien IZBG
Suchness RPI
Sudost-Forschungen IBHR
Suisse (Foi Vivante) ETL
Suisse (Nova et Vetera) B, ETL
Sumer B, ETL, IZBG
Summit RPI
Sunday Night UMPI
Supplement RE
Svensk Exegetisk Arsbok ETL, IZBG, NTA, RE
Svensk Teologisk Kvartalskrift ETL, IRPL, IZBG,
NTA, RE
Symbolae Osloenses B, IBHR, IZBG
Synagogue School Quarterly IJP
Synthronon Art et Archeologie de la Fin de l'
Antiquite IBHR
Syria IZBG
Tablet (London) CPLI
Tarbiz ETL, IZBG, RTA
Taxandria RE
Te Elfder Ure IOB
Teilhard Review CPLI
Temenos. Studies in Comparative Religion RE
Tempo RPI
Teologia del Presente B
Teologia Espiritual B, IOB
Teologinen Aikakauskirja B, IZBG
Terra Santa B
Terre Sainte IZBG
Testimonianze NTA
Texte und Untersuchungen B, IZBG
Textus B, IZBG
Themelios SISPL
Theokratia B
Theologia IOB
Theologia Evangelica IZBG
Theologia Practica B, IOB
Theologia Viatorum IZBG
Theologiai Azemla ICB
Theologica B
Theological Dictionary of the New Testament B
Theological Education IRPL, RPI
Theological Educator GSSRPL, SBPI
Theological Studies CPLI, ETL, IRPL, IZBG,
NTA, RE, RPI, RTA
Theologicka Priloha Krestanske Revue IZBG
Theologie en Zielzorg IOB
Theologie in Praktijk IOB

Theologie Pastorale au Rwanda et Burundi B
Theologie. Pastorale et Spiritualite ETL
Theologie und Glaube ETL, IZBG, NTA, RE
Theologie und Philosophie ETL, IZBG, NTA, RE
Theologisch Praktische Quartalschrift IZBG, RE
Theologische Literaturzeitung IZBG
Theologische Akademie IBHR
Theologische Bericht B
Theologische Bucherei IZBG
Theologische Existenz Heute B, IZBG
Theologische Forschung IZBG
Theologische Literaturzeitung ETL, IRPL, NTA, RE
Theologische Quartalschrift ETL, IBHR, NTA, RE
Theologische Revue ETL, IZBG, NTA, RE
Theologische Rundschau ETL, IRPL, IZBG, RE, RTA
Theologische Studien ETL, IZBG
Theologische Zeitschrift ETL, IRPL, IZBG, NTA, RE, RTA
Theologisches Handworter zum Alten Testament B
Theologisches Jahrbuch IZBG
Theologisches Worterbuch zum Alten Testament B
Theologisches Worterbuch zum Neue Testament B
Theologisch-Praktische Quartelschrift B
Theology ETL, IRPL, IZBG, NTA
Theology and Life RTA
Theology Digest CPLI, ETL, IZBG, RPI
Theology Today ETL, IRPL, IZBG, NTA, RPI, RTA
These Times GSSRPL
Thesis Theological Cassettes UMPI
Thomist CPLI, ETL, RE
Thought CPLI, RE, RPI
Three/Four UMPI
Tidsskrift for Teologi og Kirche ETL, IZBG
Tijdschrift voor Geschiedenis RE
Tijdschrift voor Liturgie IZBG
Tijdschrift voor Nederlandse Tall en Letterkunde RE
Tijdschrift voor Philosophie RE
Tijdschrift voor Rechtsgeschiedenis B, RE
Tijdschrift voor Theologie ETL, IZBG, NTA, RE
Times Literary Supplement B
Today CPLI
Today's Education GSSRPL
Today's Family Digest CPLI
Together RPI
Toledo Archdiocesan Messenger RPI
Tomorrow's World SISPL
Traditio CPLI, ETL, NTA, RE, RPI
Tradition IJP, NTA

Tradition und Erneuerung IBHR, IOB

Transactions and Proceedings of the American Philological Association Re
Transactions of the Royal Historical Society RE

Travaux et Jours IOB
Travaux et Memoires du Centre de Recherche D' Histoire et Civilisation Byzantines RE

Trierer Theologische Studien IZBG
Trierer Theologische Zeitschrift ETL, IZBG, NTA, RE
Trierer Zeitschrift fur Geschichte und Kunst des Trierer Landes und Seiner Nachbargebiete RE
Trimestriel de la Societe Academique des Antiquaires de la Marinie, Bulletin RE
Triumph CPLI, RPI
Tro och Liv IOB
True Light RPI
Tubinger Theologische Quartalschrift ETL, IZBG
Turkish Review of Archaeology IBHR
Tuuk Arkeclogi Dergisi IBHR
Twelve/Fifteen UMPI
Tyndale Bulletin IZBG
Ugarit Forschungen B
Ukrainian Orthodox Work RPI
Umeni RE
Umschau in Wissenschaft und Technik B
Una Sancta ETL, IRPL, IZBG, NTA, RPI
Unam Sanctam IZBG
Union Seminary Quarterly Review ETL, IRPL, RPI, RTA
Unitarian Universalist World RPI
Unitas ETL, NTA
United Bible Societies Bulletin B
United Church Review IOB
United Evangelical Action CPI, GSSRPL, RPI
United Methodist Student (Series) UMPI
United Methodist Teacher (Series) UMPI
United Synagogue Review CPLI, RPI
University of Birmingham Historical Journal RE
University of California Publications in Classical Archaelogy and Semitic Philology IZBG
Ut Unum Sint IOB
Val (Ecclesia) IOB
Var Losen IOB
Verbum Caro ETL, IRPL, IZBG
Verbum Domini ETL, IZBG, NTA
Verdad y Vida RE

Vereeniging tot Uitgaff der Bronnen van het Oud Vaderlandsche Recht, Verslagen en Mededeelingen der RE
Verhandelingen der Amsterdam Akademie van Wetenschappen B
Verhandlugn der Sachsischen Akademie der Wissenschaften zu Leipzig, Berichte uber die RE
Verhandlungen der Akademie van Wetenschappen B
Verhandlungen der Naturforschenden Gesleischaft in Basel IBHR
Verkundigung und Forschung ETL, IOB, IZBG, NTA
Vers l' Unite Chretienne ETL, IOB
Verslagen en Mededeelingen der Vereeniging tot Uitgaff der Bronnen van het Oud Vaderlandsche Recht RE
Verslagen en Mededelingen van de Leiegouw RE
Vetera Christianorum RE
Vetus Testamentum ETL, IRPL, IZBG, NTA, RTA
Vie Consacree ETL
Vie Spirituelle IZBG
Vierteljahresschrift fur Kirchen und Geistesgeschichte Osteruopas, Kyrios. RE
Vierteljahrhefte fur Zeitgeschichte RE
Vierteljahrsschrift fur Literaturwissenschaft und Geistegeschechte, Deutsche B, RE
Vierteljahrsschrift fur Social und Wirtschaftsgeschishte RE
Vigilae Christianae ETL, IRPL, IZBG, NTA, RE
Vigilia IOB
Vision SBPI
Vita Religiosa ETL
Vital Christianity GSSRPL, RPI
Vivante Afrique IOB
Vivarium RE
Voprosy Filosofu IOB
Vorgare IOB
Vox Evangelica ETL, IZBG, NTA
Vox Reformata NTA
Vozes IOB
Vrije Fries RE
Wallraf Richartz Jahrbuch RE
War Cry GSSRPL
Way CPLI, NTA, RPI
Wege zum Menschen ETL, IOB
Welt der Slaven IOB
Welt des Islams IOB
Welt des Orients IZBG
Wencling IOB

Wereldwijd ICB
Werkgenootschap voor Katholieke Theologen in Nederland ETL, ICB
Werkshefte ICB
Wesley Quarterly UMPI
Wesleyan Studies in Religion IZBG, STSPL
Weslyan Theological Journal STSPL
West African Archaeological Newsletter IBHR
Westfalen. Hefte fur Geschichte, Kunst und Volkskunde RE
Westfalische Forschungen RE
Westfalische Zeitschrift RE
Westminister Theological Journal CPI, ETL, IRPI, IZBG, NTA, RPI, RTA
Wichmann Jahrbuch fur Kirchengeschichte Im Bistum Berlin RE
Wiener Zeitschrift fur Kunde des Morgenlandes B, ETL, IZBG
Wiener Zeitschrift fur Philosophie ETL
Wissenschafliche Untersuchungen zum Neue Testament B
Wissenschaft UN Prozis in Kirche und Gesellschaft B
Wissenschaft und Weisheit ETL, IZBG, NTA
Wissenschaft und Weltbild IZBG
Wissenschaftliche Monographien zum Alten und Neuen Testament ETL, IZBG
Wissenschaftliche Untersuchungen zum Neuen Testament IZBG
Wissenschaftliche Zeitschrift der Friedrich Schiller Universitat Jena Re
Wissenschaftliche Zeitschrift der Humbolt Universitat zu Berlin RE
Wissenschaftliche Zeitschrift der Karl Marx Universitat Re IZBG
Wissenschaftliche Zeitschrift der Martin Luther Universitat Halle Wittenberg IBHR, IZBG
Wissenschaftliche Zeitschrift der Martin Luther Universitat Halte Wittenberg RERE
Wissenschaftliche Zeitschrift der Universitat Greifswald IZBG
Wissenschaftliche Zeitschrift der Universitat Jena IZBG
Wissenschaftliche Zeitschrift der Universitat Rostock RE
Witness RPI
Word RPI
Workers with Youth UMPI

World Archaeolcgy SISPL

World Call IOE
World Justice CPLI, ICB
World Mission CPLI, ICB
World Order RPI
World Outlock IOB
World View GSSRPL, RPI
World Vision SISPI
Worship CPLI, IRPL, IZBG, RPI
Wort und Dienst IZBG
Wort und Wahrheit IOB, IZBG
Wurzburger Diozesangeschichtsblatter RE
Yearbcok cf Liturgical Studies B
Years Ahead SBPI
Yediot IZBG
Young Judaean IJP
Your Church RPI
Youth Leader UMPI
Youth Leadership SBPI
Youth Teacher and Counselor UMPI
Zapiski Historyczne RE
Zeichen der Zeit B, ICB
Zeitschrift der Deutschen Morgenlandischen Gesellschaft ETL, IZBG, NTA, RE
Zeitschrift der Gavigny Stiftung fur Rechtsgeschichte Romanische Abteilung RE
Zeitschrift der Gesellschaft fur Schleswig Holsteinische Geschichte RE
Zeitschrift der Martin Luther Universitat Halle Wittenberg, Wissenschaftliche IBHR, IZBG
Zeitschrift der Martin Luther Universitat Halte Wittenberg, Wissenschaftliche RERE
Zeitschrift des Aachener Geschichtsvereins RE
Zeitschrift des Bergischen Geschichtsvereins RE
Zeitschrift des Deutschen Palastina Vereins ETL, NTA, RE
Zeitschrift des Deutschen Vereins fur Kunstwisswenschaft RE
Zeitschrift Deutschen Palastinavereins IZBG
Zeitschrift fur Agypitsche Sprache und Alterumskunde IZBG
Zeitschrift fur Agyptische Sprache und Alterumskunde B
Zeitschrift fur Assyriologie und Vorderasiatische Archaeolcgie ETL, IZBG
Zeitschrift fur Bayerische Kircheneschichte RE
Zeitschrift fur Bayerische Landergerchichte RE

Zeitschrift fur Bibliothekswissen und
Bibliographie RE
Zeitschrift fur Celtische Philologie RE
Zeitschrift fur Deutsche Philologie RE
Zeitschrift fur Deutsches Altertum und Deutsche
Literatur RE
Zeitschrift fur die Alttestamentliche Wissenschaft
ETL, IRPL, IZBG, RTA
Zeitschrift fur die Geschichte des Oberrheins RE
Zeitschrift fur die Geschichte und Altertumskunde
Ermlands RE
Zeitschrift fur die Neutestamentliche Wissenschaft
ETL, IRPL, IZBG, NTA, RE, RTA
Zeitschrift fur Ethnologie B, IBHR
Zeitschrift fur Evangelische Ethik ETL, IRPL, RTA
Zeitschrift fur Franzosische Sprache und Literatur
RE
Zeitschrift fur Geschichte des Judentums B
Zeitschrift fur Geschichtswissenschaft RE
Zeitschrift fur Jagdwissenshaft IBHR
Zeitschrift fur Katholische Theologie ETL,
IZBG, NTA
Zeitschrift fur Kirchengeschichte RE
Zeitschrift fur Missionwissenschaft und
Religionswissenschaft ETL, IRPL, RE
Zeitschrift fur Ostforschung RE
Zeitschrift fur Papyrologie und Epigraphik B
Zeitschrift fur Philosophische Forschung ETL, RE
Zeitschrift fur Religions und Geistesgeschichte
ETL, IRPL, IZBG, NTA, RE, RTA
Zeitschrift fur Schweizerische Archaologie und
Kunstgeschichte RE
Zeitschrift fur Schweizerische Kirchengeschichte
ICB, RE
Zeitschrift fur Slavische Philologie RE
Zeitschrift fur Systemantische Theologie IZBG
Zeitschrift fur Theologie und Kirche ETL, IRPL,
IZBG, RE, RTA
Zeitschrift fur Vergleichende Sprachforschung
auf dem Gebiet der Indogermanischen Sprachen B
Zeitschrift fur Vergleichinde Rechtsgeschichte,
Einschliesslich der Ethnologischen Rechtsforshung
B, IBHR
Zeszyty Naukowe Katolickiego Uniwersytetu
Lubelskiego B, RE
Zintralblatt fur Bubliothekswesen RE
Zion IZBG
Zurnal Moskovskoj Patriarchii B, IBHR

Zwingliana IZEG
Zwischen Den Zeiten IOB
Zygon GSSRPL, IRPL, RPI

INVERTED TITLE LIST

INVERTED TITLE LISTING

Aachener Kunstblatter RE
Aan de Geschiedenis der Kruisheren, Clairlieu. Tijdschrift Gewijd RE
Abhandlungen, Neutestamentliche IBHR, IZBG
Abhandlungen und Berichte des Staatlichen Museum fur Volkunde in Dresden IBHR
Abhandlungen Zur Theologie des Alten und Neuen Testaments B, IZBG
About Evangelism, Monthly Letter IOB
Abr-Nahrain ETL, IZBG
Abstracts, Dissertation IZBG
Abstracts, New Testament IZBG
Abstracts, Religious and Theological IZBG
Academia, Burgense. Collectanea Scientifica de la Real IZBG, NTA
Academia de la Historia, Boletin de la Real RE
Academia Espanola, Boletin de la Real RE
Academia Internazionale dei Lincei ETL
Academia Nazionale dei Lincei, Rendiconti della IBHR
Academiae Scientiarum Fennicae, Annales IZBG
Academiae Scientiarum Hungaricae, Acta Antiqua IBHR
Academiae Scientiarum Hungaricae, Acta Ethnographica IBHR
Academie des Inscriptions et Belles Lettres, Comptes Rendus de l' Izbg
Academie des Inscriptions et Belles Lettres, Comptes Rendus des Seances de l' RE
Academie Revue de Belgique. Bulletin de la Classe des Beaux Arts RE
Academie Revue de Belgique. Bulletin de la Classe des Lettres et des Sciences Morales et Politiques RE
Academie Royale de Belgique B
Academie Theologie, Annuaire de l' B
Academique des Antiquaires de la Marinie, Bulletin Trimestriel de la Societe RE
Academy, Buletin of the Catholic Research Institute China B
Academy, Proceedings of the British RE

Academy for Jewish Research, Proceedings of the American B
Academy of Religion, Bulletin of the American IZBG
Academy of Religion, Journal of the American ETL, GSSRPL, IRPL, IZBG, NTA, RE, RPI
Academy of Sciences and Humanities, Proceedings of the Israel B
Accademia Romana de Archaeologia, Rendiconti della Pontifica IBHR
Accademia Romana di Archeologia, Atti della Pontificia B
Accademia Romana di Archeologia, Peniconti della Pontifica RE
Accademie e Biblioteche D' Italia B
Accent SBPI, UMPI
Accent on Youth UMPI
Accion Metodista UMPI
Accrediting Association of Bible Colleges Newsletter SISPL
Acta Antiqua IZBG
Acta Antiqua Academiae Scientiarum Hungaricae IBHR
Acta Apostalicae Sedis CPLI, ETL
Acta Archaeologica Ljubliana IZBG
Acta Ethnographica Academiae Scientiarum Hungaricae IBHR
Acta Historiae Neerlandica RE
Acta Historica RE
Acta Iranica IBHR
Acta Orientalia Budapest IZBG
Acta Poloniae Historica RE
Acta Seminarii Neotestamentici Upsaliensis ETL, IZBG
Acta Universitatis Gotoburgensis IZBG
Acta Universitatis Upsaliensis IZBG
Actes du Congres International de Numismatique B
Actes du Congres International de Papyrologie B
Actes du Congres International des Etudes Byzantines B
Actes du Congres International des Orientalistes B
Action, Christian UMPI
Action, Social IRPL, RPI
Action, United Evangelical CPI, GSSRPL, RPI
Action Religieuse et Sociale, Cahiers D' IOB
Acts, Response in Worship Music the IOB
Actualidad Biblica ETL
Actualite Protestante, Cahiers Theologiques de l' IZBG
A.D. RPI

Adademie der Wissenschaften zu Leipzig, Sitzungsberichte der Sachsischen RE
Administration, Church RPI, SBPI
Adult Bible Course UMPI
Adult Bible Studies UMPI
Adult Leader UMPI
Adult Leadership SBPI
Adult Student SBPI
Adult Teacher UMPI
Adults, Bible Lessons for UMPI
Adults, Bible Teacher for UMPI
Adults, Planbook for UMPI
Advance RPI
Advent Christian Witness RPI
Adventure, Christian UMPI
Advocate, Central Christian UMPI
Advocate, Christian GSSRPL, RPI
Aegyptus IZBG
Aevi. Bulletin du Cange, Archivum Latinitatis Medii RE
Aevum, Medium RE
Aevum. Rassegna di Scienze Storiche, Linguistiche e Filclogiche B, IZBG, RE
Aevum. Rassegna di Scienze Storiche, Linguistiche e Filclogiche B, IZBG, RE
Affini, Rivista Italiana di Numismatica e Scienze RE
Africa, Journal of Religion in RE, SISPL
Africa (London) IOB
Africa Theological Journal SISPL
Africaines, Antiquites B, IBHR
Africaines, Cahiers des Religiones IBHR
Africaines, Notes IBHR
African Church History, Bulletin of the Society for IOB
African History, Journal of IBHR, RE
African Studies IBHR
African Studies, Bulletin of the School of Oriental and RE
African Studies (Johannesburg) IBHR, IOB
African Studies, Journal of Modern GSSRPL
Afrika und Ubersee IBHR
Afrique Noire, Bulletin de l' Institut Fondamentale D' IBHR
Age, Archives D' Historie Doctrinale et Litteraire du Moyen B
Age, Cathedral RPI
Age, Moyen RE

Age Cahiers Archeologiques, Fin de l' Antiquite et Moyen RE

Age Latina, Revue du Moyen RE
Agriculture, Commerce, Sciences et Arts, du Departement de la Marne Memoires de la Societe D' RE
Agustiniana de Espiritualidad, Revista B, ETL, NTA
Agustiniano, Archivo Teologico ETL
Aikakauskirja, Teologinen B, IZBG
Aires, Buenos (Revista Biblica) IZBG
Aisne, Memoires de la Federation der Societes D' Histoire et D' Archeologie de l' RE
Akademi i Oslc, Avhandlinger Utgitt Av Det Norsk Videnskaps IZBG
Akademie, Theologische IBHR
Akademie der Wissenschaften, Anzeiger der Oestereichischen RE
Akademie der Wissenschaften, Sitzungsberichte der Bayerischen RE
Akademie der Wissenschaften, Sitzungsberichte der Deutschen IZBG, RE
Akademie der Wissenschaften, Sitzungsberichte der Heidelberger IZBG, RE
Akademie der Wissenschaften, Sitzungsberichte der Oesterreicheschen IZBG
Akademie der Wissenschaften, Sitzungsberichte der Oesterreichischen Re
Akademie der Wissenschaften in Gottingen, Nachrichten der RE
Akademie der Wissenschaften zu Gottingen, Nachrichter der B
Akademie der Wissenschaften zu Leipzig, Berichte uber die Verhandlugn der Sachsischen RE
Akademie i Oslc, Skrifter Utgitt Av Det Norske Videnskaps IZBG
Akademii Teolcgicznej, Roczniki Teologiczne Chrzescijanskiej IZBG
Akkadusches Handworterbuch B
Akten des Internationale Kongresses B
Al Andalus. Revista de las Escuelas de Estudios Arabes RE
Algemeen Nederlands Tijdschrift voor Wijsbegeerte en Psychologie ETL
Algevienne, Bulletin D' Archeologie B
Alliance and the World Alliance of Reformed Churches, Bulletin of the Department of Theology of the World Presbyterian IOB

Alliance of Reformed Churches, Bulletin of the Department of Theology of the World Presbyterian Alliance and the World IOB

Al-Machriq B
Alsace, Archives de l' Eglise D' RE

Altar, Musik und IOB
Altbayerischen Kirchengeschichte, Beitraege Zur RE
Alte Geschichte, Historia. Zeitschrift fur RE
Alten Geschichte Berlin et Wiesbaden, Klio. Beitrage Zur RE
Alten Testament, Theologisches Handworter zum B
Alten Testament, Theologisches Worterbuch zum B
Alten und Neuen Testament, Butraege Zur Wissenschaft von B
Alten und Neuen Testament, Beitraege Zur Wissenschaft Vom IZBG
Alten und Neuen Testament, Kommentare und Beitrage zum (Dusseldorf) B
Alten und Neuen Testament, Studien zum IZBG
Alten und Neuen Testaments, Abhandlungen Zur Theologie des B, IZBG
Alten und Neuen Testaments, Forschungen Zur Religion und Literatur des B, IZBG
Alter Orient und Altes Testament B, IZBG
Altertum ETL, IZBG
Altertum, Philologus. Zeitschrift fur das Klassische RE
Altertumskunde, Basler Zeitschrift fur Geschichte und RE
Altertumswissenschaft, Anzeiger fur die B, IBHR
Alterumskunde und Kirchengeschichte, Romanische Quartalschrift fur Christliche RE
Altes Testament, Alter Orient und B, IZBG
Altestamentliche Wissenschaft, Beihefte Zur Zeitschrift fur die B, IZBG
Am Tische des Wortes B
America CPLI, RPI
America, Language. Journal of the Linguistic Society of IBHR, ICB, IZBG
America, Mid CPLI, RE
America Indigena IBHR
America Proceedings, Cathclic Theological Society of CPLI
American Academy for Jewish Research, Proceedings of the B
American Academy of Religion, Bulletin of the IZBG

American Academy of Religion, Journal of the
ETL, GSSRPL, IRPL, IZBG, NTA, RE, RPI

American Anthropologist IBHR
American Benedictine Review NTA, RPI

American Catholic Historical Records CPLI
American Catholic Historical Society of
Philadelphia, Records of the Re
American Catholic Philosophical Association
Proceedings CPLI
American Church Quarterly NTA
American Ecclesiastical Review RE
American Historical Review RE
American Jewish Archives IJP
American Jewish Historical Quarterly IJP
American Journal of Archaeology B, ETL, IBHR,
IZBG, SISPL
American Journal of Jurisprudence CPLI
American Journal of Legal History RE
American Journal of Philology B, IBHR
American Journal of Sociology GSSRPL
American Judaism, Dimensions in RPI
American Liturgical Week, North CPLI
American Opinion GSSRPL
American Oriental Society, Journal of IZBG
American Philological Association, Transactions
and Proceedings of the RE
American Philological Association Transaction
Proceeding B
American Philosophical Society, Proceedings
of the B
American Quarterly IRPL
American Rabbis Journal, Central Conference
of B, IJP
American Research Center in Egypt, Journal of B
American Scholar GSSRPL
American School of Oriental Research, Annual
of the IZBG
American Schools of Oriental Research, Bulletin
of the B, ETL, IBHR, IZBG, NTA, SISPL
American Sociological Review GSSRPL
American Studies in Papyrology B
American Zionist IJP
Americanistes, Journal de la Societe des IBHR
Americano, Archivo Ibero RE
Amerique Francaise, Revue D' Histoire de l' RE
Ami du Clerge IZBG

Amiciza Ebraicc-Cristiana di Firanze, Bcllettino dell' B

Amico del Clero ETL
Amministrativa, Annali della Fondazione Italiana per la Storia RE
Amsorya, Handes B
Amtsblatt der Evangelischen Kirche in Deutschland IOB
Amtsblatt der Evangelisch-Iutherischen Kirche in Thuringen IOB
Amtsblatt des Evangelischen Konsistoriums in Grerfswald ICB
Anadolu Sanatu Arastermalan IBHR
Anakara, Anatclian Studies Journal of the British Institute cf Archaeolcgy at B, IBHR
Analecta Augustiniana RE
Analecta Biblica IZBG
Analecta Bcllandiana RE
Analecta Cisterciensia RE
Analecta Cracovina B
Analecta Gregoriana ETL
Analecta Lovaniensia Biblica et Orientalia B, IZBG
Analecta Ordinis Fratrum Minorum ETL
Analecta Orientalia IZBG
Analecta Praemcnstratensia ETL, RE
Analecta Sacra Tarraconensia RE
Analecta Sacri Ordinis Cistercionis ETL
Analecta Sacri Ordinis Fratrum Praedicatorum ETL
Analysis, Sociological IBHR
Anatclian Studies Journal of the British Institute cf Archaeolcgy at Anakara B, IBHR
Ancienne et Medievale, Bulletin de Theologie IZBG, RE
Ancienne et Medievale, Recherches de Theologie ETL, IZBG, NTA, RE
Anciennes, Revue des Etudes B, IBHR
Anciennes Lois et Ordonnances de Belgique, Bulletin de la Commission Royale de RE
Anciennes Revue de Philologie, de Litterature et D' Histoire RE
Anciens Pays Bourguignons, Comtois et Romands Memoires de la Societe Pour l' Histoire du Droit et des Institutions des RE
Anciens Pays et Assemblees D' Etats RE
Ancient Near Eastern Society of Columbia, Journal cf B, SISPL
Ancient Society B

Andalus. Revista de las Escuelas de Estudios Arabes, al RE
Andover Newton Quarterly B, ETL, IBHR, IRPL, IZBG, NTA, RTA, SISPL
Andrews University Seminary Studies B, ETL, IBHR, IRPL, IZBG, NTA, SISPL
Angelicum IZBG, NTA, RE
Anglia. Zeitschrift fur Englische Philologie RE
Anglican Theological Review B, ETL, IBHR, IRPL, IZBG, NTA, SISPL
Anima IOB
Anima, Vierteljahrsschrift fur Praktische Seelsorge IZBG
Annalen der Historischen Vereins fur der Niererrhein RE
Annalen van het Thijmgenootschap B, ICB, RE
Annales Academiae Scientiarum Fennicae IZBG
Annales Archeologiques Arabe Syriennes B, IBHR
Annales de Bourgogne RE
Annales de Bretagne RE
Annales de Demographie Historique RE
Annales de Ethiopie B
Annales de l' Est RE
Annales de l' Institut Archeologique du Luxembourg RE
Annales de l' Ordre Souverain Militaire de Malte RE
Annales de l' Universite de Paris RE
Annales de la Societe Archeologique de Namur RE
Annales de Sociologie IBHR
Annales du Centre D' Etude des Religiones B
Annales du Midi RE
Annales du Service des Antiquites de l' Egypte B
Annales. Economies, Societes, Civilisations B, RE
Annales. Economies, Societes, Civilisations B, RE
Annales Historiques de la Revolution Francaise RE
Annales Islamologiques IBHR
Annali del Facolta di Filosofia e Letter di UN-Versita Statale de Milano RE
Annali del' Istituto Orientale di Napoli B, ETL, IBHR, IZBG
Annali della Fondazione Italiana per la Storia Amministrativa RE
Annali della Scuola Normale Superiore di Pisa B, RE
Annali di Sociologia IBHR
Annali di Storia del Diritto RE
Annali di Storia Economica e Sociale RE
Annals GSSRPL
Annee Canonique ETL, RE

Annee Philologique B

Annoli della Facalta di Letare e Filosafia dell' Universita degli Studi di Trieste IBHR
Annua, Antholcgica RE

Annuaire D' Histoire Liegeoise RE
Annuaire de l' Academie Theolcgie B
Annuaire de l' Institut de Philologie et D' Historie Orientales et Slaves B, IBHR
Annuaire de la Societe D' Histoire et D' Archeolcgie de la Lorraine RE
Annual, Hebrew Union College ETL, NTA
Annual, Hevrew Unicn Xollege IZBG
Annual Egyptolcgical Bibliography B
Annual of the American School of Oriental Research IZBG
Annual of the Department of Antiquities of Jordan B
Annual cf the Swedish Theclogical Institute B IBHR, IZBG, NTA
Annuale Mediaevale RE
Annuario di Studi Ebraici B
Annuarium Histcriae Conciliorum ETL, RE
Annuus, Studii Biblici Franciscani Liber ETL, IZBG, NTA
Anranchiñ et du Pays de Granville, Revue de l' RE
Antemurale RE
Anthologica Annua RE
Anthony Messenger, St. CPLI, RPI
Anthropolcgical Quarterly CPLI, IBHR
Anthropolcgist, American IBHR
Anthropolcgist Institute Man, the Journal of the Royal IBHR
Anthropclcgy, Arctic IBHR
Anthropolcgy, Current IBHR
Anthropclcgy, Practical CPI, IRPL
Anthropos ETL, IOB, IZBG
Antica e Mcderna, Arte RE
Antiche Provincie Modenesi, Atti e Memorie de Deputazione di Stcria Patria per Le RE
Antico Testamento del Nuovo Testamentc, Commenti Spirituali dell' B
Anti-Defamaticn League Bulletin IJP
Antiguedades, Boletin de Histcria y RE
Antik Tanulmanyck IBHR
Antike und Christentum, Jahrbuch fur IZBG, RE
Antike und Christentum, Reallexikon fur B
Antike Welt B

Antiken Judentums und des Urchristentums,
Arbeiten Zur Geschichte des B

Antiqua, Acta IZBG
Antiqua, Iranica B

Antiqua, Slavia RE
Antiqua Academiae Scientiarum Hungaricae, Acta IBHR
Antiquaires de France, Bulletin de la Societe Nationale des RE
Antiquaires de l' Ouest et des Musees de Poitiers, Bulletin de la Societe des RE
Antiquaires de la Marinie, Bulletin Trimestriel de la Societe Academique des RE
Antiquaires de Normandie, Bulletin de la Societe des RE
Antiquaires de Picardie, Bulletin Trimestriel de la Societe des RE
Antiquaries Journal B, RE
Antiquaries of Ireland, Journal of the Royal Society of RE
Antiquite, Revue Internationale des Droits de l' IZBG, RE
Antiquite, Synthronon Art et Archeologie de la Fin de l' IBHR
Antiquite Classique B, ETL, IBHR, RE
Antiquite et Moyen Age Cahiers Archeologiques, Fin de l' RE
Antiquites Africaines B, IBHR
Antiquites de l' Egypte, Annales du Service des B
Antiquities, the Museum of Far Eastern IBHR
Antiquities of Jordan, Annual of the Department of B
Antiquity B, SISPL
Antiquus, Oriens IZBG
Antonianum ETL, IZBG, NTA, RE
Antropologica IBHR
Anuario de Estudios Medievales RE
Anuario de Historia del Derecho Espanol RE
Anzeigen, Gottingische Gelehrte B, RE
Anzeiger, Archaeologischer B, IZBG
Anzeiger der Oestereichischen Akademie der Wissenschaften RE
Anzeiger fur die Altertumswissenschaft B, IBHR
Apollinaris ETL, RE
Apostalicae Sedis, Acta CPLI, ETL
Apostolado Sacerdotal IZBG

Applications, Revue D' Histoire des Sciences et de Leurs RE
Applied Behavorial Science, Journal of SISPL
Aquinas RE
Aquinas Ephemerides Thomisticae ETL
Arabe Syriennes, Annales Archeologiques B, IBHR
Arabes, al Andalus. Revista de las Escuelas de Estudios RE
Arabes, Revue de l' Institut des Belles Letters B, IBHR
Arabes y Hebreos, Miscelanea de Estudios B
Arastermalan, Anadolu Sanatu IBHR
Arbeiten aus dem Referat fur Fragen der Verkuendigung, Concept G. Iob
Arbeiten Zur Geschichte des Antiken Judentums und des Urchristentums B
Arbeiten Zur Neutestamentlichen Textforschung IZBG
Arbeiten Zur Theclogie IZBG
Arbor RE
Archaelogischen Instituts, Jahrbuch des Deutschen B
Archaelogy and Semitic Philology, University of California Publications in Classical IZBG
Archaeclogia, Rendiconti della Pontifica Accademia Romana de IBHR
Archaeologia Cantiana RE
Archaeologica Ljubliana, Acta IZBG
Archaeological Association, Journal of the British RE
Archaeological Jcurnal RE
Archaeologische Bibliographie B
Archaeclogische Mitteilungen aus Iran B
Archaeologischen Instituts, Mitteilunger des Deutschen B, IBHR
Archaeologischer Anzeiger B, IZBG
Archaeolcgy B, IZBG
Archaeolcgy, American Journal of B, ETL, IBHR, IZBG, SISPL
Archaeolcgy, Australian Journal of Biblical IZBG
Archaeolcgy, Bulletin of the Institute of B
Archaeolcgy, Medieval RE
Archaeology, Turkish Review of IBHR
Archaeclcgy at Anakara, Anatolian Studies Journal cf the British Institute of B, IBHR
Archaeology in Jerusalem, Levant. Journal cf the British School of Sispl
Archdiocesan Messenger, Tcledo RPI
Archeologia RE

Archeologia, Atti della Pontificia Accademia Romana di B

Archeologia, Reniconti della Pontifica Accademia Romana di RE
Archeologia Classica B
Archeologia Cristiana, Rivista di RE
Archeologia e Storia dell' Arte, Rendiconti dell' Istituto Nazionale D' RE
Archeologia e Storia Patria, Atti e Memorie de Societa Istriana di RE
Archeologica, Sicilia IBHR
Archeologie Algevienne, Bulletin D' B
Archeologie Copte, Bulletin de la Societe D' IZBG, RE
Archeologie de la Fin de l' Antiquite, Synthronon Art et IBHR
Archeologie de la Lorraine, Annuai de la Societe D' Histoi et D' RE
Archeologie de Paris et de l' Ile de France, Memoires de la Federation des Societes Historie et RE
Archeologie et de Statistique de la Drome, Bulletin de la Societe D' Re
Archeologie et D' Histoire, Melanges D' RE
Archeologie et D' Historie de l' Art, Revue Belge D' RF
Archeologie et D' Historier de l' Ecole Francaise de Rome, Melanges D' Ibhr
Archeologie et Historique de la Charente, Memoires de la Societe RE
Archeologie et Historique de Nantes et de Loire Atlantique, Bulletin de la Societe RE
Archeologie Orientale, Bulletin de l' Institut Francais D' IZBG
Archeologie Orientale, Bulletin del' Institut Francais D' E, IBHR
Archeologie Vivante B
Archeologique, Bulletin IZBG
Archeologique, Revue RE
Archeologique, Revue D' B
Archeologique D' Eure et Loir, Bulletin de la Societe RE
Archeologique de Namur, Annales de la Societe RE
Archeologique de Touraine, Bulletin Trimestriel de la Societe RE
Archeologique du Department D' Ille et Vilaine, Bulletin et Memoirs de la Societe RE

Archeologique du Luxembourg, Annales de l' Institut RE
Archeologique du Perigord, Bulletin de la Societe Historique et RE
Archeologique et Historique du Limousin, Bulletin de la Societe RE
Archeologiques, Fin de l' Antiquite et Moyen Age Cahiers RE
Archeologiques Arabe Syriennes, Annales B, IBHR
Archeologist, Biblical B, CPI, CPLI, ETL, IBHR, IBPL, IZBG, NTA, RPI, SISPL
Archief, Kathcliek ETL
Archief voor de Geschiedenis van de Katholieke Kerk in Nederland ETL, ICB, RE
Archief voor Kerkgeschiedenis, Nederlands IOB, RE
Archievenblad, Nederlands RE
Architettura, Palladia. Rivista di Storia dell' RE
Archiv, Freiburger Diczesan RE
Archiv, Oberbayerisches RE
Archiv fur Begriffsgeschichte B
Archiv fur das Studium der Neueren Sprachen und Literaturen RE
Archiv fur der Erforschung des Mittelalters, Deutsches B, RE
Archiv fur Diplomatik Schriftgeschichte, Siegel und Wappenkunde RE
Archiv fur Diplomatik Schriftgeschichte, Siegel und Wappenkunde RE
Archiv fur Geschichte der Philosophie B, RE
Archiv fur Katholisches Kirchenrecht ETL, IBHR, RE
Archiv fur Kirchenrecht, Oesterreichisches ETL, ICB, RE
Archiv fur Kulturgeschichte B, IOB, RE
Archiv fur Liturgiewissenschaft B, ETL, IBHR, IZBG, RE
Archiv fur Mittelrheinische Kirchengeschichte IOB, RE
Archiv fur Orientforschung B, ETL, IZBG
Archiv fur Osterreichische Geschichte RE
Archiv fur Papyrusforschung B
Archiv fur Rechts und Sozialphilosophie ETL
Archiv fur Reformationsgeschichte ETL, IRPL, RE, RTA
Archiv fur Schlesische Kirchengeschichte RE
Archiv fur Volkskunde, Schweizerisches IBHR, RE
Archiv Orientalni B, ETL, IBHR, IZBG, RE
Archiva Ecclesiae ETL, RE
Archivalische Zeitschrift RE

Archivar RE
Archiven und Bibliotheken, Quellen und Forschungen aus Italienischen Re
Archives, American Jewish IJP
Archives, Archivum. Revue Internationale des RE
Archives D' Histoire Doctrinale et Litteraire du Paris RE
Archives D' Historie Doctrinale et Litteraire du Moyen Age B
Archives de l' Eglise D' Alsace RE
Archives de l' Historie des Sciences B
Archives de Philosophie ETL, RE
Archives de Philosophie du Droit RE
Archives de Sociologie de Religions B, ETL, IBHR, RE
Archives et Bibliotheques de Belgique RE
Archives Internationales D' Histoire des Sciences RE
Archivio di Societa Romana di Storia Patria RE
Archivio Giuridico "Filippo Serafini" ETL, RE
Archivio Glottologico Italiano B
Archivio Italiano per la Storia della Pieta RE
Archivio Muratoriano, Bullettino dell' Istituto Storico Italiano per Il Medio Evo e RE
Archivio Storico Italiano RE
Archivio Storico Lombardo RE
Archivio Storico per la Sicilia Orientale RE
Archivio Storico per Le Province Napoletane RE
Archivio Storico per Le Province Parmensi RE
Archivio Veneto RE
Archivium Hibernicum RE
Archivo Espanol de Arqueologia B
Archivo Espanol de Arte RE
Archivo Hispalense IZBG
Archivo Ibero Americano RE
Archivo Teologico Agustiniano ETL
Archivo Teologico Granadino IZBG, RE
Archivos, Bibliotecas y Museos Revista de RE
Archivos Leoneses RE
Archivum Franciscanum Historicum ETL, RE
Archivum Fratrum Praedicatorum ETL, RE
Archivum Historicum Societatis Iesu ETL, RE
Archivum Latinitatis Medii Aevi. Bulletin du Cange RE
Archivum Linguisticum IZBG
Archivum. Revue Internationale des Archives RE
Archiwa, Biblioteki Muzea Koscielne RE
Archiwa, Biblioteki Muzea Koscielne RE

Archolcgique dans Le Limbourg a Maestricht, Publications de la Societe Historique et RE

Arctic Anthropology IBHR
Ard Mhacha, Seanchas RE

Ardealului, Mitropclia IOB
Argentina (Revista Biblica) B
Arhivic Venetc RE
Ariel IJP
Arkeologi Dergisi, Tuuk IBHR
Armenian Church IBHR
Armeniennes, Revue des Etudes B, IBHR, RE
Arqueclogia, Archivc Espanol de B
Arqueologia, Boletin del Seminaric de Estudios de Arte y RE
Ars Orientalis IBHR
Arsbok, Svensk Exegetisk ETL, IZBG, NTA, RE
Arsbck for Kristen Humanism IOB
Arsskrift, Kyrkohistorisk RE
Arsskrift, Lunds Universitets IZBG
Art, Revue Belge D' Archeologie et D' Historie de l' RE
Art, Revue de l' RE
Art Bulletin RE
Art Bulletin, Metropolitan Museum of RE
Art et Archeologic dc la Fin de l' Antiquite, Synthronon IBHR
Art et D' Histcire, Bulletin des Musees Royaux D' RE
Art et D' Historie du Diocese de Liege, Bulletin de la Societe D' RE
Art Journal RE
Arte, Archivc Espancl de RE
Arte, Bcllettino D' RE
Arte, Goya. Revista de RE
Arte Antica e Moderna RE
Arte Atti dell' Istituto Veneto di Scienze, Lettere di RF
Arte Lombarda RE
Arte Ravennate e Bizantina, Corsi di Cultura Sull' RE
Arte y Arqueolcgia, Boletin del Seminaric de Estudios de RE
Artistique, Bulletin de l' Institut Royal du Patrimcine RE
Artistiques du Lot Bulletin de la Societe des Etudes Litteraires, Scientifiques et RE

Arts, Academie Revue de Belgique. Bulletin de la Classe des Beaux RE

Arts, Gazette des Beaus RE
Arts, Liturgical CPLI, RPI

Arts, University of Libya Bulletin of the Faculty of IBHR
Arts Asiatiques IBHR
Arts de Belgique, Bulletin des Musees Royaux des Beaus RE
Arts, du Departement de la Marne Memoires de la Societe D' Agriculture, Commerce, Sciences et RE
Arts et Traditions Populaires RE
Artz und Christ IOB
Ascetica e Mistica, Rassegna di B
Ascetica e Mistica, Rivista di ETL, NTA
Ascetique et de Mystique, Revue D' ETL, IZBG, NTA, RE
Asia Journal of Theology, South East IRPL, NTA
Asian Folklore Studies IBHR
Asianique, Revue Hittite et B, IBHR
Asiatic Journal, Central IBHR
Asiatic Society of Great Britain and Ireland, Journal of the Royal RE
Asiatique, Journal IZBG, RE
Asiatiques, Arts IBHR
Asiatische Studien ETL, IZBG
Asprenas ETL, IZBG, RE
Assemblea Festiva, la Parola per l' B
Assemblees D' Etats, Anciens Pays et RE
Assemblees die Seigneur B
Association, Journal of the British Archaeological RE
Association, Publications of the Modern Language RE
Association, Transactions and Proceedings of the American Philological RE
Association Bulletin, Middle East Studies IBHR
Association Bulletin, National Catholic Education CPLI
Association Guillaume Bude, Bulletin de l' B, ETL, RE
Association of Bible Colleges Newsletter, Accrediting SISPL
Association of India, Bulletin of the Church History IOB

Association Proceedings, American Catholic Philosophical CPLI
Association Transaction Proceeding, American Philological P
Associazione Biblica Italiana, Esegesi Biblica ETL
Associazione Biblica Italiana, Esegesi Biblica ETL
Assyrian Dictionary, Chicago B
Assyriologique Internationale, Recontre B
Atheniensia, Opuscula IBHR
Atlantique, Bulletin de la Societe Archeologie et Historique de Nantes et de Loire RE
Attempto ETL
Atti dell' Istituto Veneto di Scienze, Lettere di Arte RE
Atti dell' Istituto Veneto di Scienze, Lettere di Arte RE
Atti della Pontificia Accademia Romana di Archeologia P
Atti della Settimana Biblica B
Atti di Societa Ligure di Storia Patria RE
Atti e Memorie de Deputazione di Storia Patria per Le Antiche Provincie Modenesi RE
Atti e Memorie de Deputazione di Storia Patria per Le Province di Romagna RE
Atti e Memorie de Societa Istriana di Archeologia e Storia Patria RE
Auchland (Colloquium) NTA
Auftrag, Erbe und ETL, IOB, IZBG, NTA
Augusta, Bracara RE
Augustinian Studies RE
Augustiniana IBHR, RE
Augustiniana, Analecta RE
Augustiniano, Estudio B
Augustinianum B, ETL, IBHR, IZBG, NTA
Augustiniennes, Recherches B, RE
Augustiniennes, Revue de Etudes ETL, NTA
Augustiniennes, Revue des Etudes RE
Augustinus (Madrid) B, IOB
Australasian Catholic Record ETL, NTA, RTA
Australian Biblical Review ETL, IZBG, NTA
Australian Journal of Biblical Archaeology IZBG
Auvergne, Revue D' RE
Auvergne, Revue de la Haute RE
Av Det Norsk Videnskaps Akademi i Oslo, Avhandlinger Utgitt IZBG
Av Det Norske Videnskaps Akademie i Oslo, Skrifter Utgitt IZBG
Ave Maria CPLI, RPI

Avhandlinger Utgitt Av Det Norsk Videnskaps Akademi i Oslo IZBG
Avierta al Servicio de al Fe, Mision B
Aware SBPI
Azemla, Theologiai IOB
Azii, Kratkie Soobscenija Institute Narodov IZBG
Background Information IOB
Baden-Wurttemberg, Jahrbuch der Stallichen Kunstsammulugen in IBHR
Badia Greca di Grottaferrata, Bollettino di RE
Baghader Mitteilungen B, IBHR
Bamberg, Bericht des Historischin Vereins RE
Banatului, Mitropolia IOB
Banner GSSRPI, RPI
Baptist Bulletin GSSRPL, RPI
Baptist Educator, Southern SBPI
Baptist Herald RPI
Baptist History and Heritage SBPI
Baptist Leader RPI
Baptist Men's Journal SBPI
Baptist Quarterly IRPL, IZBG, RTA
Baptist World IOB, SBPL
Basler Zeitschrift fur Geschichte und Altertumskunde RE
Bausteine NTA
Bayerischen Akademie der Wissenschaften, Sitzungsberichte der RE
Bazmaveb B
Bcoadranter, Biola SISPL
Beaus Arts, Gazette des RE
Beaus Arts de Belgique, Bulletin des Musees Royaux des RE
Beaux Arts, Academie Revue de Belgique. Bulletin de la Classe des RE
Begriffsgeschichte, Archiv fur B
Behavorial Science, Journal of Applied SISPL
Beihefte Zur Zeitschrift fur die Altestamentliche Wissenschaft B, IZBG
Beitraege, Biblische IZBG
Beitraege Zur Altbayerischen Kirchengeschichte RE
Beitraege Zur der Biblischen Hermeneutik IZBG
Beitraege Zur Evangelischen Theologie B, IZBG
Beitraege Zur Forderung Christlicher Theologie IZBG
Beitraege Zur Geschichte der Biblischen Exegese IZBG
Beitraege Zur Geschichte der Deutschen Sprache und Literatur RE
Beitraege Zur Kulturwissenschaft, Innsbrucker IBHR

Beitraege Zur Namenforschung B

Beitraege Zur Wissenschaft Vom Alten und Neuen Testament IZBG
Beitrage, Bonner Biblische B, ETL, IZBG

Beitrage zum Alten und Neuen Testament, Kommentare und (Dusseldorf) B
Beitrage Zur Alten Geschichte Berlin et Wiesbaden, Klio. RE
Beitrage Zur Heimartkunde, Carinthia I. Geschichliche und Volkskunde. KARNTENS RE
Beitrage Zur Kunstgeschichte, Niederdeutsche RE
Bekehirncek ICB
Belfort, Dietsche Warande en RE
Belge D' Archeclogie et D' Historie de l' Art, Revue RE
Belge D' Historie Contemporaine, Revue RE
Belge de Musicclogie, Revue RE
Belge de Numismatique et de Sigillographie, Revue RE
Belge de Philologie et D' Histoire, Revue RE
Belge de Rome, Bulletin de l' Institut Historique RE
Belgique, Academie Royale de B
Belgique, Archives et Bibliotheques de RE
Belgique, Bibliographie de RE
Belgique, Bulletin de la Commission Royale de Anciennes Lois et Ordonnances de RE
Belgique, Bulletin des Musees Royaux des Beaus Arts de RE
Belgique. Bulletin de la Classe des Beaux Arts, Academie Revue de RE
Belgique. Bulletin de la Classe des Lettres et des Sciences Morales et Politiques, Academie Revue de RE
Belles Letters Arabes, Revue de l' Institut des B, IBHR
Belles Lettres, Comptes Rendus de l' Academie des Inscriptions et Izbg
Belles Lettres, Comptes Rendus des Seances de l' Academie des Inscriptions et RE
Benaming Societe D' Emulation de Bruges, Handeling van het Genootschap vocr Geschiedenis Gesticht Onder de RE
Benedictina ETL, RE
Benedictine, Revue ETL, NTA, RE
Benedictine Review, American NTA, RPI

Benediktiner Ordens und Seiner Zweige, Studien
und Mitteilungen Zur Geschichte des RE
Bericht, Theologische B
Bericht der Vollversammlung des Lutherischen
Weltbundes, Offizieller Iob
Bericht des Historischin Vereins Bamberg RE
Berichte, Forschungen und IBHR
Berichte, Linguistische IZBG
Berichte des Staatlichen Museum fur Volkunde
in Dresden, Abhandlungen und IBHR
Berichte uber die Verhandlugn der Sachsischen
Akademie der Wissenschaften zu Leipzig RE
Berlin et Wiesbaden, Klio. Beitrage Zur Alten
Geschichte RE
Berliner Museen, Jahrbuch der RE
Bern-Tubengen (Ehe.) IOB
Berytus ETL
Beth Mikra B
Betreffende de Geschiedenis der Nederlanden,
Bijdragen en Mededelingen RE
Beyrouth, Bulletin du Musee de B
Bibbas (Manresa) NTA
Bibbia e Oriente ETL, IZBG, NTA
Bibel in der Welt B, IOB
Bibel und Kirche ETL, IZBG, NTA
Bibel und Leben ETL, NTA, RE
Bibel und Liturgie ETL, NTA
Bibelstudien, Stuttgarter B, IZBG
Bible Colleges Newsletter, Accrediting
Association of SISPL
Bible Course, Adult UMPI
Bible et Terre Sainte IZBG
Bible et Vie Chretienne ETL, IZBG, NTA
Bible League Quarterly SISPL
Bible Lessons for Adults UMPI
Bible Lessons for Youth UMPI
Bible Quarterly, Central SISPL
Bible Science Newsletter SISPL
Bible Societies Bulletin, United B
Bible Society Record IZBG, RPI
Bible Studies, Adult UMPI
Bible Teacher for Adults UMPI
Bible Translator IZBG
Bible und Quran IBHR
Biblia Revuo IZBG
Biblica B, IBPL, NTA, RE
Biblica, Actualidad ETL
Biblica, Analecta IZBG

Biblica, Atti della Settimana B

Biblica, Cultura ETL, IZBG, NTA
Biblica, Homelitica en ETL, IZBG
Biblica, Linguistica IZBG
Biblica, Lingusitica B
Biblica, New Testament Series Lund Coniectanea IZBG
Biblica, Revista (Argentina) B
Biblica, Revista (Buenos Aires) IZBG
Biblica, Revista (Italiana) IZBG
Biblica, Revista de Cultura ETL, IZBG, NTA
Biblica, Rivista ETL, NTA, RE
Biblica Associazione Biblica Italiana, Esegesi ETL
Biblica Espancla, Semana B
Biblica et Orientalia, Analecta Lovaniensia B, IZBG
Biblica et Orientalias B
Biblica Italiana, Esegesi Biblica Associazione ETL
Biblica Lovaniensia, Orientalia et B, IZBG
Biblica Lund, Coniectanea B
Biblical Archaeology, Australian Journal of IZBG
Biblical Archeologist B, CPI, CPLI, ETL, IBHR, IRPL, IZBG, NTA, RPI, SISPL
Biblical Literature, Journal of ETL, GSSRPL, IJP, IRPL, IZBG, NTA, RE, RPI, RTA
Biblical Quarterly, Catholic ETL, IRPL, IZBG, NTA, RE, RPI
Biblical Research IZBG
Biblical Review, Australian ETL, IZBG, NTA
Biblical Societies, Bulletin of the United IZBG
Biblical Theology NTA
Biblical Theology, Studies in IZBG
Biblical Theolcgy Bulletin B, IZBG
Biblical Viewpcint SISPL
Bibliche e Religiose, Ricerche ETL
Biblici, Studi IZBG
Biblici Franciscani Liber Annuus, Studii ETL, IZBG, NTA
Biblicos, Estudios ETL, IOB, NTA, RE
Biblicum, Elenchus Suppletorius ad Elenchum Bibliographe B
Biblicus, Ipse hic Elenchus Bibliographicus B
Biblijny i Liturgiczny, Ruch ETL, IZBG, NTA
Bibliofilia RE
Bibliografia Nazionale Italiana RE
Bibliografico Subalpinc, Bollettino Storico RE
Bibliografiro Internazionale, Bollettino B

Bibliographe Biblicum, Elenchus Suppletorius ad Elenchum B

Bibliographicus Biblicus, Ipse hic Elenchus B
Bibliographie, Archaeologische B

Bibliographie, Deutsche RE
Bibliographie, Oesterreichische RE
Bibliographie de Belgique RE
Bibliographie de la France RE
Bibliography, Annual Egyptological B
Bibliography and Booklore, Studies in IJP
Biblioteche D' Italia, Accademie e B
Biblioteksvasen, Nordisk Tidsskrift for Bok och RE
Bibliotheca Orientalis ETL, IZBG, NTA
Bibliotheca Sacra CPI, ETL, IRPL, IZBG, NTA, RE, RTA
Bibliothek und Wissenschaft RE
Bibliotheken, Quellen und Forschungen aus Italienischen Archiven und Re
Bibliotheque D' Humanisme et Renaissance RE
Bibliotheque de l' Ecole des Chartes RE
Bibliotheques de Belgique, Archives et RE
Biblique, Bulletin de Theologie B
Biblique, Cahiers de la Revue IZBG
Biblique, Revue ETL, IRPL, IZBG, NTA, RE
Bibliques, Recherches B
Biblische Beitraege IZBG
Biblische Beitrage, Bonner B, ETL, IZBG
Biblische Monographien, Stuttgarter IZBG
Biblische Studien IZBG
Biblische Untersuchungen B
Biblische Zeitschrift ETL, IRPL, IZBG, NTA, RE
Biblischen Exegese, Beitraege Zur Geschichte der IZBG
Biblischen Hermeneutik, Beitraege Zur der IZBG
Biblisk Tro, for IOB
Biekorf RE
Bijdragen ETL, IZBG, NTA
Bijdragen, Bossche RE
Bijdragen, Leuvense RE
Bijdragen en Mededelingen Betreffende de Geschiedenis der Nederlanden Re
Bijdragen en Mededelingen Uitger Door de Vereniging Gelre RE
Bijdragen. Tijdschrift voor Filosofie en Theologie RE
Bijdragen tot de Geschiedenis RE

Bijdragen tot de Kunstgeschiedenis en de Oudheidkunde, Gentse RE
Bijdragen tot de Taal-Land en Volkenkunde IBHR
Bild der Wissenschaft B
Bicla Bcoadranter SISPL
Birmingham Historical Journal, University of RE
Biserica Ortodoxa Romana IOB
Biuletyn Historii Sztuki RE
Bi-Weekly, Congress IJP
Bizantina, Corsi di Cultura Sull' Arte Ravennate e RE
Blackfriars, New CPLI, ETL
Blatter, Katechetische IZBG
Blatter, Pastoral ETL, NTA
Blatter fur Deutsche Landesgeschichte RE
Bodleian Library Record RE
Boek der Boeken IZBG
Boeken, Boek der IZBG
Boeken van het Oude Testament B
Bogoskovje ICB
Bogoslovni Vestnik B
Bogoslovska Smotra B
Bok och Biblioteksvasen, Nordisk Tidsskrift for RE
Boletin de Historia y Antiguedades RE
Boletin de la Real Academia de la Historia RE
Boletin de la Real Academia Espanola RE
Boletin del Instituto Caro y Cuervo IZBG
Boletin del Instituto de Estudios Helenicos B
Boletin del Seminario de Estudios de Arte y Arqueologia RE
Bollandiana, Analecta RE
Bollettino Bibliografiro Internazionale B
Bollettino D' Arte RE
Bollettino del Centro Camuno di Studi Preistorici IZBG
Bollettino dell' Amiciza Ebraico-Cristiana di Firanze B
Bollettino della Societa Geografica Italiano B
Bollettino della Societa Internazionale Scottista IZBG
Bollettino di Badia Greca di Grottaferrata RE
Bollettino Ligustico per la Storia e la Cultura Regionale RE
Bollettino Storico Bibliografico Subalpino RE
Bollettino Storico Piacentino RE
Bolognese, Strenna Storica RE
Bombay, Journal of the University of IBHR
Bonner Biblische Beitrage B, ETL, IZBG

Bonner Geschichtsblatter RE
Bonus, Pastor ETL
Book Guide, Religious UMPI
Book Review, New RPI
Booklore, Studies in Bibliography and IJP
Bookseller, Christian RPI
Bossche Bijdragen RE
Bourgogne, Annales de RE
Bourguignons, Comtois et Romands Memoires de la Societe Pour l' Histoire du Droit et des Institutions des Anciens Pays RE
Brabander, Eigen Schoon en de RE
Bracara Augusta RE
Brasileria, Revista Eclesiastica ETL, IZBG, NTA, RE
Bratskij Vestnik IOB
Bretagne, Annales de RE
Brethern Life and Thought ETL, IRPL, RPI, RTA
Britain and Ireland, Journal of the Royal Asiatic Society of Great RE
British Academy, Proceedings of the RE
British Archaeological Association, Journal of the RE
British Institute of Archaeology at Anakara, Anatolian Studies Journal of the B, IBHR
British Journal of Sociology IBHR
British School of Archaeology in Jerusalem, Levant. Journal of the SISPL
Brotherhood Builder SBPI
Brugenses et Gandavenses, Collationes ETL, IOB, IZBG, NTA
Bruges, Handeling van het Genootschap voor Geschiedenis Gesticht Onder de Benaming Societe D' Emulation de RE
Bruxellois, Cahiers RE
Bucherei, Theologische IZBG
Buchhandel, Schweizer RE
Budapest, Acta Orientalia IZBG
Bude, Bulletin de l' Association Guillaume B, ETL, RE
Buenos Aires (Revista Biblica) IZBG
Builder, Brotherhood SBPI
Buletin du Centre Protestant D' Etudes IOB
Buletin of the Catholic Research Institute China Academy B
Bulletin, Anti-Defamation League IJP
Bulletin, Art RE
Bulletin, Baptist GSSRPL, RPI

Bulletin, Biblical Theology B, IZBG

Bulletin, Commonlife UMPI
Bulletin, International Reformed IOB
Bulletin, Japan Missionary IOB
Bulletin, Metropolitan Museum of Art RE
Bulletin, Middle East Studies Association IBHR
Bulletin, National Catholic Education Association CPLI
Bulletin, National Guild of Catholic Psychiatrists CPLI
Bulletin, Occasional SISPL
Bulletin, Princeton Seminary ETL, IRPL, IZBG, RPI
Bulletin, Scripture CPLI, ETL, IZBG, NTA
Bulletin, Sister Formation CPLI
Bulletin, Social Questions RPI
Bulletin, Sociologisch IOB
Bulletin, Tyndale IZBG
Bulletin, United Bible Societies B
Bulletin Archeclogique IZBG
Bulletin D' Archeologie Algevienne B
Bulletin D' Etudes Orientalis de Institut Francais IBHR
Bulletin de Correspondance Hellenique B
Bulletin de l' Association Guillaume Bude B, ETL, RE
Bulletin de l' Institut de Recherche et D' Histoire des Textes RE
Bulletin de l' Institut Fondamentale D' Afrique Noire IBHR
Bulletin de l' Institut Francais D' Archeologie Orientale IZBG
Bulletin de l' Institut Historique Belge de Rome RE
Bulletin de l' Institut Royal du Patrimoine Artistique RE
Bulletin de la Classe des Beaux Arts, Academie Revue de Belgique. RE
Bulletin de la Classe des Lettres IZBG
Bulletin de la Classe des Lettres et des Sciences Morales et Politiques, Academie Revue de Belgique. RE
Bulletin de la Commission Royale D' Histoire RE
Bulletin de la Commission Royale de Anciennes Lois et Ordonnances de Belgique RE
Bulletin de la Section D' Historie Moderne et Contemperaine RE
Bulletin de la Societe Archeolcgie et Historique de Nantes et de Loire Atlantique RE

Bulletin de la Societe Archeologique D' Eure et Loir RE

Bulletin de la Societe Archeologique et Historique du Limousin RE
Bulletin de la Societe D' Archeologie Copte IZBG, RE
Bulletin de la Societe D' Archeologie et de Statistique de la Drome RE
Bulletin de la Societe D' Art et D' Historie du Diocese de Liege RE
Bulletin de la Societe de Etudes Indochinoses IBHR
Bulletin de la Societe de l' Historie de l' Art Francais RE
Bulletin de la Societe de l' Historie du Protestantisme Francais ETL, RE
Bulletin de la Societe de Linguietique de Paris B
Bulletin de la Societe de'Archeologie Copte B
Bulletin de la Societe des Antiquaires de l' Ouest et des Musees de Poitiers RE
Bulletin de la Societe des Antiquaires de Normandie RE
Bulletin de la Societe des Etudes Litteraires, Scientifiques et Artistiques du Lot RE
Bulletin de la Societe des Etudes Litteraires, Scientifiques et
Bulletin de la Societe Francaise D' Egyptologie B
Bulletin de la Societe Francaise D' Etudes Marianles B
Bulletin de la Societe Historique et Archeologique du Perigord RE
Bulletin de la Societe Nationale des Antiquaires de France RE
Bulletin de la Societe Prehistorique Francaise IBHR
Bulletin de Litterature Ecclesiastique ETL, IZBG, NTA, RE
Bulletin de Theologie Ancienne et Medievale IZBG, RE
Bulletin de Theologie Biblique B
Bulletin del' Institut Francais D' Archeologie Orientale B, IBHR
Bulletin des Etudes Portugaises, Publie Par l' Institut Francais au Portugal RE
Bulletin des Etudes Portugaises, Publie Par l' Institut Francais au Portugal RE
Bulletin des Musees Royaux D' Art et D' Histoire RE
Bulletin des Musees Royaux des Beaus Arts de Belgique RE

Bulletin du Cange, Archivum Latinitatis Medii Aevi. RE
Bulletin du Musee de Beyrouth B
Bulletin E. Renan IZBG
Bulletin et Memoirs de la Societe Archeologique du Department D' Ille et Vilaine RE
Bulletin Hispanique RE
Bulletin Monumental RE
Bulletin of the American Academy of Religion IZBG
Bulletin of the American Schools of Oriental Research B, ETL, IBHR, IZBG, NTA, SISPL
Bulletin of the Church History Association of India ICB
Bulletin of the Department of Theology of the World Presbyterian Alliance and the World Alliance of Reformed Churches IOB
Bulletin of the Faculty of Arts, University of Libya IBHR
Bulletin of the Faculty of Arts, University of Libya IBHR
Bulletin of the Institute of Archaeology B
Bulletin of the Institute of Historical Research RE
Bulletin of the John Rylands Library ETL, IZBG, NTA, RE
Bulletin of the New York Public Library RE
Bulletin of the School of Oriental and African Studies RE
Bulletin of the Society for African Church History IOB
Bulletin of the United Biblical Societies IZBG
Bulletin Philologique et Historique du Comite des Travaux Historiques et scientifiques RE
Bulletin Saint Jean-Baptist IBHR, IOB
Bulletin Secretariatus pro Non Christianis B, IOB
Bulletin Signaletique B
Bulletin Theomas More, Moreana. RE
Bulletin Trimestriel de la Societe Academique des Antiquaires de la Marinie RE
Bulletin Trimestriel de la Societe Archeologique de Touraine RE
Bulletin Trimestriel de la Societe des Antiquaires de Picardie RE
Bullettino dell' Istituto Storico Italiano per Il Medio Evo e Archivio Muratoriano RE
Burgense. Collectanea Scientifica de la Real Academia IZBG, NTA
Buried History SISPL
Burlington Magizine RE

Burundi. Theologie Pastorale au Rwanda et B Business Education Review, Catholic CPLI Butraege Zur Wissenschaft von Alten und Neuen Testament Byzantina RE Byzantine Studies Greek, Roman, and RE Byzantines. Actes du Congres International des Etudes Byzantines. Revue des Etudes B. IBHR. RE Byzantines, Travaux et Memoires du Centre de Recherche D' Histoire et Civilisation RE Byzantinische Forschungen RE Byzantinische Zeitschrift RE Byzantinistichen Gesellschaft, Jahrbuch der Osterreichischen TCB Byzantinistik, Jahrbuch der Osterreichischin RE Byzantino Sloavica IRHR, RE Byzantion ETL, RE Cahiers Archeologiques. Fin de l' Antiquite et Moven Age RE Cahiers Archeologiques, Fin de l' Antiquite et Moven Age RE Cahiers Bruxellois RF Cahiers D' Action Religieuse et Sociale IOB Cahiers D' Etudes Cathares RE Cahiers D' Histoire RE Cahiers D' Historie Mondiale B, IBHR, RE Cahiers de Civilisation Medievale B, RE Cahiers de Josephologie NTA, RTA Cahiers de la Revue Biblique IZBG Cahiers des Religiones Africaines IBHR Cahiers Internationaux de Sociologie IBHR Cahiers Laennec ETL Cahiers Leopold Delisle RE Cahiers Renan IZEG Cahiers Theologiques ETL Cahiers Theologiques de l' Actualite Protestante IZBG Caire, Melanges de l'Instiut Domincain D' Etudes Orientales de RE California Publications in Classical Archaelogy and Semitic Philology, University of IZBG Calvary Review SISPL Calvin Theological Journal CPI, ETL, IRPL, IZBG, RE, RPI Calwer Hefte IZBG Cambridge History of Iran IBHR

Camerti di Studi Romanistici, Index Quaderri B

Camuno di Studi Preistorici, Bollettino del Centro IZBG
Canadian Historical Review RE
Canadian Journal of Theology ETL, IRPL, IZBG, RTA
Cange, Archivum Latinitatis Medii Aevi. Bulletin du RE
Canonici, Ephemerides Iuris ETL, RE
Canonico, Revista Espanola de Derecho RE
Canonicum, Ius RE
Canonique, Annee ETL, RE
Canonique, Revue de Droit RE
Canonique, Revue du Droit ETL, IOB
Cantiana, Archaeologia RE
Capital, Report from the SBPI
Care, Journal of Pastoral IRPL, RPI
Carinthia I. Geschichliche und Volkskunde. Beitrage Zur Heimantkunde Karntens RE
Carkoven Vestnik IOB
Carmelitaines, Etudes IZBG
Carmelitica, Ephemerides ETL, IZBG, NTA, RE
Carmelus ETL, NTA, RE
Caro, Communio Verbum B
Caro y Cuervo, Boletin del Instituto IZBG
Casa de Velazquez, Melanges de la RE
Casopis Historicky, Ceskoslovensky RE
Cassettes, Thesis Theological UMPI
Catechese IZBG
Catechese, Notre IZBG
Catechistes IZBG
Cathares, Cahiers D' Etudes RE
Cathedral Age RPI
Catholic Biblical Quarterly ETL, IRPL, IZBG, NTA, RE, RPI
Catholic Business Education Review CPLI
Catholic Charities Review CPLI, RPI
Catholic Digest CPLI
Catholic Education Association Bulletin, National CPLI
Catholic Educator CPLI
Catholic Guidance Conference Journal, National CPLI, RPI
Catholic Historical Records, American CPLI
Catholic Historical Review CPLI, ETL, GSSRPL, RE, RPI
Catholic Historical Society of Philadelphia, Records of the American Re
Catholic Lawyer CPLI
Catholic Library World CPLI, RPI

Catholic Philosophical Association Proceedings, American CPLI
Catholic Psychiatrists Bulletin, National Guild of CPLI
Catholic Record, Australasian ETL, NTA, RTA
Catholic Reporter, National CPLI
Catholic Research Institute China Academy, Buletin of the B
Catholic School Journal CPLI, RPI
Catholic Theological Society of America Proceedings CPLI
Catholic Worker RPI
Catholic World, the CPLI, GSSRPL, RPI
Catholic World, the CPLI, GSSRPL, RPI
Catholica (Copenhagen) ETL, NTA
Catholica (Munster) ETL, NTA
Catholica Unio IOB
Catholiche, Missioni IOB
Catholicite, Perspectives de IOB
Catholicus, Orbis IZBG
Catholique, Dictionnaire de Theologie B
Catholique, la Pensee B
Catholiques des Intellectuals Francais, Recherches et Debats du Centre IOB
Catholiques Internationales, Informations ETL, IOB
Cattolica, Civilta ETL, IZBG, NTA, RE
Cattolica, Scuola ETL, IZBG, NTA, RE
Celtiques, Etudes RE
Center in Egypt, Journal of American Research B
Center Magazine GSSRPL
Central Asiatic Journal IBHR
Central Bible Quarterly SISPL
Central Christian Advocate UMPI
Central Conference of American Rabbis Journal B, IJP
Centre Catholiques des Intellectuals Francais, Recherches et Debats du IOB
Centre D' Etude des Religiones, Annales du B
Centre de Documentation Juife Contemporaine, Monde Juie. la Revue du IZBG
Centre de Recherche D' Histoire et Civilisation Byzantines, Travaux et Memoires du RE
Centre Protestant D' Etudes, Buletin du IOB
Centre Protestant D' Etudes et de Documentation IOB
Centro Camuno di Studi Preistorici, Bollettino del IZBG
Century, Christian GSSRPL, RPI
Century, Studies on Voltaire and the XVIIIth RE

Ceres GSSRPL
Ceskoslovensky Casopis Historicky RE
Cesky Zapas ICB
Chamito-Semitiques, Comptes Rendus du Groupe Linguistique D' Etudes B
Change GSSRPL
Chaplain RPI
Charente, Memoires de la Societe Archeologie et Historique de la RE
Charities Review, Catholic CPLI, RPI
Chartes, Bibliotheque de l' Ecole des RE
Chicago Assyrian Dictionary B
Chicago Studies CPLI, ETL, NTA, RPI
Chicago Theological Seminary Register B, SISPL
Chiesa in Italia, Rivista di Storia della RE
Childrens Leadership SBPI
China Academy, Buletin of the Catholic Research Institute B
Choisir IOB
Chretien, Proche Orient RE
Chretienne, Bible et Vie ETL, IZBG, NTA
Chretiennes D' Israel, Nouvelles B
Christ, Artz und IOB
Christ to the World CPLI, IOB
Christelijk Oosten B, IOB, RE
Christentum, Jahrbuch fur Antike und IZBG, RE
Christentum, Reallexikon fur Antike und B
Christian CPI
Christian, New ICB
Christian Action UMPI
Christian Adventure UMPI
Christian Advocate GSSRPL, RPI
Christian Advocate, Central UMPI
Christian Bookseller RPI
Christian Century GSSRPL, RPI
Christian Council Quarterly IOB
Christian Council Review, National IOB
Christian Education, Journal of B, SISPL
Christian Faith in Life-Supplement UMPI
Christian Faith Study-Selected Reading, Foundation Studies in UMPI
Christian Graduate SISPL
Christian Herald GSSRPL, RPI
Christian Librarian CPI
Christian Life CPI, GSSRPL, RPI
Christian Living, Studies in UMPI
Christian Ministry GSSRPL, RPI
Christian News from Israel IOB, IZBG

Christian Peace Conference IOB
Christian Reader GSSRPL
Christian Scholar IOB
Christian Scholar's Review NTA
Christian Standard GSSRPL
Christian Unity Information Service, Secretariat for Promoting IOB
Christian Witness, Advent RPI
Christiana, Studia Orientalia B, RE
Christiana Periodica, Orientalia ETL, NTA, RE, RTA
Christianis, Bulletin Secretariatus pro Non B, IOB
Christianisme au 20e Siecle IOB
Christianisme Social IOB
Christianity and Crisis GSSRPL, IRPL, RPI
Christianity Today CPI, GSSRPL, IRPL, IZBG, RPI
Christiano, Oriente IOB
Christianorum Orientalium, Corpus Scriptorum B
Christianus, Oriens IZBG, RE
Christichen Ikonographie, Lexikon der B
Christliche Alterumskunde und Kirchengeschichte, Romanische Quartalschrift fur RE
Christliche Kunst und Kunstwissenschaft Munster, Zeitschrift fur IOB, RE
Christliche Sozialwissenschaften, Jahrbuch des Instituts fur IOB
Christlicher Theologie, Beitraege Zur Forderung IZBG
Christlich-Judisches Forum IOB
Christus B, ETL, IZBG, NTA, RTA
Chronicle, Numismatic RE
Chronicle and Journal, Numismatic B
Chronik, Cistercienser RE
Chronique D' Egypte IZBG
Chrysostom IOB
Chrzescijanskiej Akademii Teologicznej, Roczniki Teologiczne IZBG
Church, Armenian IBHR
Church, Historical Magazine of the Protestant Episcopal RPI
Church, Journal for Theology and the IRPL, RPI
Church, One RPI
Church, Orthodox RPI
Church Administration RPI, SBPI
Church and Jewish People Newsletter, National Council of Churches Committee on the IOB, SBPI
Church and Society IRPL, RPI
Church and State, Journal of IRPL, RPI
Church Herald GSSRPL, RPI

Church History CPI, ETL, IRPL, RE, RPI

Church History, Bulletin of the Society for African IOB
Church History Association of India, Bulletin of the IOB
Church in Metropolis IOB
Church in the World IOB
Church in Wales, Journal of the Historical Society of the RE
Church Library Magazine RPI
Church Man IRPL, RPI
Church Messenger RPI
Church Music, Journal of RPI
Church Quarterly ETL, IRPL, NTA, RPI
Church Quarterly, American NTA
Church Recreation Magazine SBPI
Church Review, United IOB
Church School UMPI
Church Theological Review RPI
Church Times IOB
Church Training SBPI
Church Woman RPI
Churches, Bulletin of the Department of Theology of the World Presbyterian Alliance and the World Alliance of Reformed IOB
Churches, Current Developments in the Eastern European IOB
Churches, Near East Council of IOB
Churches Committee on the Church and Jewish People Newsletter, National Council of IOB, SBPI
Churchman, Modern B, ETL, IRPL, NTA
Churchman, South Indian IOB
Ciencia Tomista ETL, IOB, IZBG, NTA, RE
Circuet Rider UMPI
Cistercienis, Analecta Sacri Ordinis ETL
Cistercienser Chronik RE
Cisterciensia, Analecta RE
Cisterciensia, Collectanea RE
Cistericciensium Reformatorum, Collectanea Oridinis ETL
Citaux ETL, RE
Citeaux ETL, RE
Cithera CPLI
Citta di Vita ETL
City, New CPLI
Ciudad de Dios ETL, IZBG, NTA, RE
Civile, Rivista di Diritto ETL

Civilisation Byzantines, Travaux et Memoires du Centre de Recherche D' Histoire et RE

Civilisation Medievale, Cahiers de B, RE
Civilisations Annales. Economies, Societes, B, RE

Civilta, Fede e IOB
Civilta Cattolica ETL, IZBG, NTA, RE
Civitas ETL, IOB
Cjiaohui, Shenhsueh Yu B
Clairlieu. Tijdschrift Gewijd Aan de Geschiedenis der Kruisheren RE
Class Guide, Real UMPI
Classe des Beaux Arts, Academie Revue de Belgique. Bulletin de la RE
Classe des Lettres, Bulletin de la IZBG
Classe des Lettres et des Sciences Morales et Politiques, Academie Revue de Belgique. Bulletin de la RE
Classica, Archeologia B
Classica, Rivista di Filologia e di Istruzione RE
Classica e Cristiana, Orpheus. Rivista di Umanita RE
Classica e Medioevale, Rivista di Cultura RE
Classica et Mediaevalia RE
Classical Archaelogy and Semitic Philology, University of California Publications in IZBG
Classical Folia RE
Classical Philology, Harvard Studies in B, IBHR
Classical Quarterly B, RE
Classical Review B, RE
Classical Studies, Journal of B
Classical Weekly B
Classici, Rivista di Studi ETL
Classici e Orientali, Studi B, IBHR
Classique, Antiquite B, ETL, IBHR, RE
Classiques, Etudes ETL, IZBG, RE
Classmate UMPI
Clerge, Ami du IZBG
Clergy Monthly NTA, RTA
Clergy Review CPLI, ETL, RE
Clero, Amico del ETL
Clero, Palabra de ETL, NTA
Clero, Palestra del IZBG
Collage SBPI
Collationes RE
Collationes Brugenses et Gandavenses ETL, IOB, IZBG, NTA

Collationes Vlaoms Tijdschaft voor Theologie en Pastoral B
Collectanea Cisterciensia RE
Collectanea Franciscana B, ETL, IZBG, RE
Collectanea Mechliniensia ETL, IOB, IZBG, NTA
Collectanea Oridinis Cistericciensium Reformatorum ETL
Collectanea Scientifica de la Real Academia, Burgense. IZBG, NTA
Collectanea Theologica ETL, IZBG
Collection Lumiere et Vie IZBG
College Annual, Hebrew Union ETL, NTA
College Theology Society, Proceedings of the CPLI
Colleges Newsletter, Accrediting Association of Bible SISPL
Colloquium (Auchland) NTA
Columbia CPLI, RPI
Columbia, Journal of Ancient Near Eastern Society of B, SISPL
Comillas, Miscelanea ETL, IZBG, NTA, RE
Comite des Travaux Historiques et scientifiques, Bulletin Philclogique et Historique du RE
Commentaar op het Oude Testament B
Commentari RE
Commentary IZBG
Commenti Spirituali dell' Antico Testamento del Nuovo Testamento B
Commission SBPI
Commission Royale D' Histoire, Bulletin de la RE
Commission Royale de Anciennes Lois et Ordonnances de Belgique, Bulletin de la RE
Committee on the Church and Jewish People Newsletter, National Council of Churches IOB, SBPI
Commonlife Bulletin UMPI
Commonweal CPLI, GSSRPL, RPI
Communal Service, Journal of Jewish IJP
Communaute des Dissemines IOB
Communautes Religieuses, Revue des ETL
Commune, Ius RE
Communications, Oriental Institute B
Communio ETL, NTA, RE
Communio Verbum Caro B
Communio Viatorum ETL, IRPL, IZBG, NTA, RE
Communis, Doctor ETL, NTA, RE
Comparative Literature RE
Comparative Religion, Studies in B, IBHR
Comparative Religion, Temenos. Studies in RE

Comparative Religions, Jordan Lectures in ETL
Comparative Studies in Society and History RE
Comparee, Revue de Litteratur RE
Compass, Social ETL, RE, RTA
Compostellanum IZBG
Comptes Rendus B, IBHR
Comptes Rendus de l' Academie des Inscriptions et Belles Lettres IZBG
Comptes Rendus des Seances de l' Academie des Inscriptions et Belles Lettres RE
Comptes Rendus du Groupe Linguistique D' Etudes Chamito-Semitiques B
Computers in the Humanities B
Concept E. Papers from the Department on Studies in Evangelism IOB
Concept F. Documents du Department D' Etudes sur l' Evangelisation Iob
Concept G. Arbeiten aus dem Referat fur Fragen der Verkuendigung IOB
Concern RPI, UMPI
Conciliar, Seminario IZBG
Conciliorum, Annuarium Historiae ETL, RE
Concilium B, ETL, IOB, IZBG, NTA, RE
Concordia Historical Institute Quarterly ETL, RTA
Concordia Theological Monthly CPI, ETL, IRPL, IZBG, NTA, RPI, RTA
Conference, Christian Peace IOB
Conference Journal, National Catholic Guidance CPLI, RPI
Conference of American Rabbis Journal, Central B, IJP
Confrontations. Revue Diocesaine de Tournai B, ETL
Congregationalist, the RPI
Congregationalist, the RPI
Congregationis Ssmi Redemptoris, Spicilegium Historicum RE
Congres International de Numismatique, Actes du B
Congres International de Papyrologie, Actes du B
Congres International des Etudes Byzantines, Actes du B
Congres International des Orientalistes, Actes du B
Congress Bi-Weekly IJP
Congress of Jewish Studies, Proceedings of the World B
Coniectanea Biblica, New Testament Series Lund IZBG
Coniectanea Biblica Lund B

Coniectanea Biblica, New Testament Series Lund IZBG
Coniectanea Neotestamentica IZBG
Conscience's Sake, Reporter for RPI
Conservative Judaism IJP
Contacts IOB
Contemperaine, Bulletin de la Section D' Historie Moderne et RE
Contempo SBPI
Contemporaine, Monde Juie. la Revue du Centre de Documentation Juife IZBG
Contemporaine, Revue Belge D' Historie RE
Contemporaine, Revue D' Histoire Moderne et RE
Contemporanea, Storia RE
Contemporary History, Journal of RE
Contemporary Religions in Japan SISPL
Context SISPL
Continuum CPLI, ETI, IRPL, RPI
Copenhagen (Catholica) ETL, NTA
Copte, Bulletin de la Societe D' Archeologie IZBG, RE
Copte, Bulletin de la Societe de'Archeolcgie B
Cord RPI
Corpus Scriptorum Christianorum Orientalium B
Correspondance Hellenique, Bulletin de B
Correspondence, Herder CPLI, ETL, RPI
Corsi di Cultura Sull' Arte Ravennate e Bizantina RE
Council of Churches, Near East IOB
Council of Churches Committee on the Church and Jewish People Newsletter, National IOB, SBPI
Council Quarterly, Christian IOB
Council Review, National Christian IOB
Counselor, Crusader SBPI
Counselor, Pastoral SISPL
Course, Adult Bible UMPI
Courtauld Institutes, Journal of the Warburg and RE
Cracovina, Analecta B
Creation, New UMPI
Creation Leaders Guide, New UMPI
Creation Research Society Quarterly SISPL
Creation Resource Packet, New UMPI
Credinta RPI
Crisis, Christianity and GSSRPL, IRPL, RPI
Cristia, Questions de Vida B
Cristiana, Orpheus. Rivista di Umanita Classica e RE
Cristiana, Rivista di Archeologia RE

Cristianas, Lecciones UMPI
Cristianas de Israel, Noticias IZBG
Cristiano, Pensamiento SISPL
Criterio IOB
Criterion IRPL, RPI
Critic CPLI, GSSRPL, RPI
Critica di Filosofia e Storia della Filosofia, Sophia. Rassegna RE
Critico della Filosofia Italiana, Giornale ETL, RE
Cross and Crown CPLI, NTA
Cross Currents CPLI, GSSRPL, RPI
Crown, Cross and CPLI, NTA
Crusader SBPI
Crusader Counselor SBPI
Crux SISPL
Cuadernos de Estudios Gallegos RE
Cuadernos de Historia de Espana RE
Cuadernos Teologicos IOB
Cuervo, Boletin del Instituto Caro y IZBG
Cultura, Religion y B, IOB
Cultura, Ribista Rosminiana di Filosofia e di RE
Cultura Biblica ETL, IZBG, NTA
Cultura Biblica, Revista de ETL, IZBG, NTA
Cultura Classica e Medioevale, Rivista di RE
Cultura e Scuola B, IBHR
Cultura Neolatina RE
Cultura Regionale, Bollettino Ligustico per la Storia e la RE
Cultura Sull' Arte Ravennate e Bizantina, Corsi di RE
Cultura Teholcgica, Revista di IZBG
Cultura Teologica, Revista de ETL, NTA
Cuneiform Studies, Journal of IZBG
Current Anthropology IBHR
Current Develcpments in the Eastern European Churches IOB
Currents, Cross CPLI, GSSRPL, RPI
Cusanus Gesellschaft, Mitteilungen und Forschungsbeitrage der RE
Czynnosci Wydawniczej i Posiedzen Naukoeych Oraz Kronika, Sprawozdania Z RE
Dalloz, Recueil ETL
Dame Journal of Education, Notre CPLI
Dansk Teologisk Tidsskrift ETL, IRPL, IZBG, NTA
Danteschi, Studi RE
D' Archeologie de l' Aisne, Memoires de la Federation der Societes D' Histoire et RE
Days, Nursery UMPI

De Hcmine Deo B

Deacon SBPI
De'Archeologie Copte, Bulletin de la Societe B
Debats du Centre Catholiques des Intellectuals Francais, Recherches et IOB
Del' Evangelisation, Revue IOB
Del' Institut Francais D' Archeologie Orientale, Bulletin B, IBHR
Del' Istituto Orientale di Napoli, Annali B, ETL, IBHR, IZBG
Delisle, Cahiers Leopold RE
Dell' Arte, Rendiconti dell' Istituto Nazionale D' Archeologia e Storia RE
Delle Persone, Rivista del Diritto Matrimoniale e Dello Statc ETL
Dello Stato Delle Persone, Rivista del Diritto Matrimoniale e ETL
Demographie Historique, Annales de RE
Denkmalpflege, Oesterreichische Zeitschrift fur Kunst und RE
Denkmalpflete, Deutsche Kunst und RE
Deo, de Hcmine B
Departement de la Marne Memoires de la Societe D' Agriculture, Commerce, Sciences et Arts, du RE
Department D' Etudes sur l' Evangelisation, Concept F. Documents du Iob
Department D' Ille et Vilaine, Bulletin et Memoirs de la Societe Archeologique du RE
Department for the Laity, Documents from the IOB
Department of Antiquities of Jordan, Annual of the B
Department of Theology of the World Presbyterian Alliance and the World Alliance of Reformed Churches, Bulletin of the IOB
Department on Studies in Evangelism, Concept E. Papers from the IOB
Deputazione di Storia Patria per Le Antiche Provincie Modenesi, Atti e Memorie de RE
Deputazione di Storia Patria per Le Province di Romagna, Atti e Memorie de RE
Derecho Canonico, Revista Espanola de RE
Derecho Espanol, Anuario de Historia del RE
Dergisi, Tuuk Arkeologi IBHR
Desert, Discoveries in the Judaean B
Desert of Judah, Studies on the Texts of the ETL
Det Norsk Videnskaps Akademi i Oslo, Avhandlinger Utgitt Av IZBG

Det Norske Videnskaps Akademie i Oslo, Skrifter Utgitt Av IZBG
Deutsche Bibliographie RE
Deutsche Kunst und Denkmalpflete RE
Deutsche Landesgeschichte, Blatter fur RE
Deutsche Literaturzeitung B, IBHR, IZBG, RE
Deutsche Vierteljahrsschrift fur Literaturwissenschaft und Geistegeschechte B, RE
Deutsche Zeitschrift fur Philosophie RE
Deutschen Akademie der Wissenschaften, Sitzungsberichte der IZBG, RE
Deutschen Archaelogischen Instituts, Jahrbuch des B
Deutschen Archaeologischen Instituts, Mitteilunger des B, IBHR
Deutschen Instituts fur Wissenschaftlishe Padogogik, Schriften des Etl
Deutschen Orient Gesellschaft, Mitteilunger der B, IBHR
Deutschen Orient-Gesellschaft, Mitteilungen der IZBG
Deutschen Sprache und Literatur, Beitraege Zur Geschichte der RE
Deutscher Evangelischer Kirchentag IOB
Deutsches Archiv fur der Erforschung des Mittelalters B, RE
Deutsches Pfarrerblatt B, IBHR
Deutschland, Amtsblatt der Evangelischen Kirche in IOB
Deutschland, Kirchliches Jahrbuch fur die Evangelische Kirche in IOB
Developments in the Eastern European Churches, Current IOB
D' Histoire, Bulletin des Musees Royaux D' Art et RE
D' Histoire, Melanges D' Archeologie et RE
D' Historie de l' Art, Revue Belge D' Archeologie et RE
D' Historie du Diocese de Liege, Bulletin de la Societe D' Art et RE
D' Historier de l' Ecole Francaise de Rome, Melanges D' Archeologie et IBHR
Diakonia CPLI, ETI, NTA, RPI
Dialog (Freiburg) IOB
Dialog (New York) ETI, IOB, IRPL, RPI
Dialogo IOB
Dialogue IOB
Dichos, Hechos y IOB

Dictionary, Chicago Assyrian B
Dictionary of the New Testament, Theological B
Dictionnaire D' Historie et de Geographie Ecclesiastiques B
Dictionnaire de Theologie Catholique B
Didaskalia B
Dienst, Heiliger IOB
Dienst, Kirchlichen IOB
Dienst am Wort B
Dietsche Warande en Belfort RE
Dieu, Maison ETL, NTA, RE
Digest, Catholic CPLI
Digest, Israel IJP
Digest, Jewish IJP
Digest, Official News RPI
Digest, Theology CPLI, ETL, IZBG, RPI
Digest, Today's Family CPLI
Dimension SBPI
Dimensions in American Judaism RPI
Diocesaan Tijdschrift Hasselt ETL
Diocesaine de Namur, Revue ETL
Diocesaine de Tournai, Confrontations. Revue B, ETL
Diocesaine de Tournai, Revue ETL
Diocese de Liege, Bulletin de la Societe D' Art et D' Historie du RE
Diogene RE
Dios, Ciudad de ETL, IZBG, NTA, RE
Diczesan Archiv, Freiburger RE
Diplomatik Schriftgeschichte, Siegel und Wappenkunde Archiv fur RE
Diplomatique, Revue D' Histoire RE
Diritto, Annali di Storia del RE
Diritto, Rivista Internazionale de Filosofia de ETL
Diritto Civile, Rivista di ETL
Diritto e Giurisprudenza ETL
Diritto Ecclesiastico RQ
Diritto Italiano, Rivista di Storia del RE
Diritto Matrimoniale e Dello Stato Delle Persone, Rivista del ETL
Discerner SISPL
Disciplina. a Yearbook of the History of Music, Musica RE
Discoveries in the Judaean Desert B
Discovery SBPI
Diskussion, Oekumenische IOB
Disputatae, Quaestiones ETL, IZBG

Dissemines, Communaute des IOB

Dissertation Abstracts IZBG
Divinitas ETL, IZBG, NTA, RE

Divinity School Review, Duke IRPL, RPI
Divus Thomas ETL, IOB, IZBG, NTA, RE
Docete, Euntes ETL, NTA, RE
Doctor Communis ETL, NTA, RE
Doctrina, Sacra ETL, NTA, RE
Doctrinale et Iitteraire du Moyen Age, Archives D' Historie E
Doctrinale et Litteraire du Paris, Archives D' Histoire RE
Doctrine and Life ETL, NTA
Documenta IZBG
Documenta Historiae et Iuris, Studia et B, RE
Documentaires, Pages IOB
Documentation, Centre Protestant D' Etudes et de IOB
Documentation Juife Contemporaine, Monde Juie. la Revue du Centre de IZBG
Documents du Department D' Etudes sur l' Evangelisation, Concept F. Iob
Documents from the Department for the Laity IOB
Dogma, Kerygma und ETL, IRPL, IZBG, RE, RTA
Dokumente. Zeitschrift fur Internationale Zusammenarbeit IOB
Domincain D' Etudes Orientales de Caire, Melanges de l' Instiut RE
Dominicain D' Etudes Orientales, Melanges de l' Institut B, IZBG
Dominicana CPLI
Door de Vereniging Gelre, Bijdragen en Mededelingen Uitger RE
Downside Review ETL, IRPL, IZBG, RE , RTA
Dresden, Abhandlungen und Berichte des Staatlichen Museum fur Volkunde in IBHR
Drew Gateway IRPL, RPI
Droit, Archives de Philosophie du RE
Droit Canonique, Revue de RE
Droit Canonique, Revue du ETL, IOB
Droit et des Institutions des Anciens Pays Bourguignons, Comtois et Romands Memoires de la Societe Pour l' Histoire du RE
Droit Francais et Etranger, Revue Historique du RE
Droits de l' Antiquite, Revue Internationale des IZBG, RE

Drome, Bulletin de la Societe D' Archeologie et de Statistique de la Re
Dublin Review CPLI, ETL
Ducal de Luxembourg, Publications de la Section Historique de l' Institut RE
Duchovna Kultura IOB
Duke Divinity School Review IRPL, RPI
Dumbarton Oaks Papers B
Dunwoodie Review IZBG
Durham University Journal IZBG
Dusseldorf (Kommentare und Beitrage zum Alten und Neuen Testament) B
Dusseldorfer Jahrbuch RE
East and West B
East Asia Journal of Theology, South IRPL, NTA
East Council of Churches, Near IOB
East Journal, Middle GSSRPL
East Reporter, Near IJP
East Review, Jewish Observer and Middle IJP
East Studies Association Bulletin, Middle IBHR
Eastern Antiquities, the Museum of Far IBHR
Eastern European Churches, Current Developments in the IOB
Eastern Society of Columbia, Journal of Ancient Near B, SISPL
Eastern Studies, Journal of Near ETL, IZBG, NTA, RPI
Ebraici, Annuario di Studi B
Ebraico-Cristiana di Firanze, Bollettino dell' Amiciza B
Ecanos-Jahrbuch IOB
Ecclesia (Val) IOB
Ecclesiae, Archiva ETL, RE
Ecclesiastica Xaveriana B
Ecclesiastical History, Journal of ETL, GSSRPL, IRPL, IZBG, RE, RPI
Ecclesiastical Record, Irish CPLI, ETL, IOB, RE
Ecclesiastical Review, American RE
Ecclesiastical Studies, Indian B, NTA
Ecclesiastico, Diritto RQ
Ecclesiasticus, Monitor ETL
Ecclesiastique, Bulletin de Litterature ETL, IZBG, NTA, RE
Ecclesiastique, Revue D' Histoire ETL, IRPL, IZBG, NTA, RE
Ecclesiastiques, Dictionnaire D' Historie et de Geographie B
Ecclesiastiques, Sciences ETL, RTA

Eclesiastica Brasileria, Revista ETL, IZBG, NTA, RE
Eclesiasticos, Estudios IZBG, RE
Ecole des Chartes, Bibliotheque de l' RE
Ecole Francaise de Rome, Melanges D' Archeologie et D' Historier de l' IBHR
Ecole Pratique des Hautes Etudes B, IBHR
Economia e Storia RE
Economic History, Journal of RE
Economic and Social History of the Orient, Journal of B
Economic and Social History of the Orient, Journal of the RE
Economic History Review RE
Economic History Review, Scandinavian RE
Economica e Sociale, Annali di Storia RE
Economies, Societes, Civilisations Annales. B, RE
Economique Sociale, Revue D' Histoire RE
Economisch Historisch Jaarboek RE
Economy, Review of Social CPLI
Ecumenica "Ut Unum Sint", Revista ETL
Ecumenical Notes IOB
Ecumenical Review GSSRPL, NTA, RE, RPI
Ecumenical Review, Polish IOB
Ecumenical Studies, Journal of CPLI, ETL, IRPL, IZBG, RE, RPI
Ecumenist CPLI, NTA
Ed Egeo-Anatolici, Studi Micenci IBHR
Education GSSRPL
Education, International Journal of Religious SISPL
Education, Journal of Christian B, SISPL
Education, Notre Dame Journal of CPLI
Education, Religious GSSRPL, IJP, RPI
Education, Theological IRPL, RPI
Education, Today's GSSRPL
Education Association Bulletin, National Catholic CPLI
Education Review, Catholic Business CPLI
Educator, Catholic CPLI
Educator, Jewish IJP, RTA
Educator, Southern Baptist SBPI
Educator, Theological GSSRPL, SBPI
Egeo-Anatolici, Studi Micenci Ed IBHR
Eglise D' Alsace, Archives de l' RE
Eglise de France, Revue D' Histoire de l' RE
Eglise et Mission ETL
Eglise et Theologie IZBG

Egykaz, Reformatus ICB
Egypt, Journal of American Research Center in B
Egypte, Annales du Service des Antiquites de l' B
Egypte, Chronique D' IZBG
Egyptisch Genootschap ex Oriente Lux, Jaarbericht van het Vooraziatisch IBHR
Egyptisch Genootschap ex Oriente Lux, Jarrbericht van het Vooraziatisch B
Egyptisch Genotschap ex Oriente Lux, Jaarbericht van het Vooraziatisch IZBG
Egyptological Bibliography, Annual B
Egyptologie, Bulletin de la Societe Francaise D' B
Egyptologie, Revue D' B, IBHR
Ehe. (Bern-Tubengen) IOB
Eigen Schoon en de Brabander RE
Ekklesia IOB
Elenchus Suppletorius ad Elenchum Bibliographe Biblicum B
Elenchum Bibliographe Biblicum, Elenchus Suppletorius ad B
Elenchus Bibliographicus Biblicus, Ipse hic B
Elfder Ure, Te ICB
Emulation de Bruges, Handeling van het Genootschap voor Geschiedenis Gesticht Onder de Benaming Societe D' RE
Emuna IOB
Encounter GSSRPL, IRPL, IZBG, RPI
Encounter, Study IRPL, RPI
Encounter Today B
Encyclopedia Judaica B
Engage RPI
Englische Philologie, Anglia. Zeitschrift fur RE
English and Germanic Philology, Journal of RE
English Historical Review RE
English Literature, Studies in RE
English Studies RE
English Studies, Review of RE
Entschluss, der Grosse IOB
Environment GSSRPI
Envoy CPLI
Ephemerides Carmelitica ETL, IZBG, NTA, RE
Ephemerides Juris Canonici ETL, RE
Ephemerides Liturgicae ETL, IZBG, NTA, RE
Ephemerides Mariologicae ETL, NTA, RE
Ephemerides Theologicae Lovanienses ETL, IZBG, NTA, RE
Ephemerides Thomisticae, Aquinas ETL
Epigraphica RE

Episcopal Church, Historical Magazine of the
Protestant RPI
Episcopal Overseas Mission Review IOB
Episcopal Recorder RPI
Episcopalian GSSRPL, RPI
Epworth Notes UMPI
Eranos RE
Eranos Jahrbuch IZBG
Erasmus. Speculum Scientiarum RE
Erbe und Auftrag ETL, IOB, IZBG, NTA
Eredienst, Jaarbock voor de IOB
Eretz Israel IZBG
Erforschung des Mittelalters, Deutsches Archiv
fur der B, RE
Erfurter Theologische Studien IZBG
Erneuerung, Tradition und IBHR, IOB
Erudiri, Sacris ETL, IZBG, NTA, RE
Erzahlforschung, Fabula. Zeitschrift fur RE
Erzieher, Katholische B
Erziekar, Evangelische IBHR
Escritos del Vedat B
Escuelas de Estudios Arabes, al Andalus. Revista
de las RE
Espana, Cuadernos de Historia de RE
Espanol, Anuario de Historia del Derecho RE
Espanol, Indice Historico RE
Espanol de Arqueologia, Archivo B
Espanol de Arte, Archivo RE
Espanola, Boletin de la Real Academia RE
Espanola, Revista de Filologia RE
Espanola, Semana Biblica B
Espanola de Derecho Canonico, Revista RE
Espanola de Historia, Hispania. Revista RE
Espanola de Teologia, Revista ETL, IZBG, NTA, RE
Espanola de Teologia, Semana B
Espiritual, Teologia B, IOB
Espiritualidad, Revista Agustiniana de B, ETL, NTA
Espiritualidad, Revista de RE
Esprit IOB
Esprit, Science et ETL, IZBG, NTA, RE
Esprit et Vie ETL, NTA
Est, Annales de l' RE
Estudio Augustiniano B
Estudios ETL
Estudios Arabes, al Andalus. Revista de las
Escuelas de RE
Estudios Arabes y Hebreos, Miscelanea de B
Estudios Biblicos ETL, IOB, NTA, RE

Estudios de Arte y Arqueologia, Boletin del Seminario de RE
Estudios de Filoscfia y Religion Orientales B
Estudios Eclesiasticos IZBG, RE
Estudics Franciscanos RE
Estudios Gallegos, Cuadernos de RE
Estudios Helenicos, Bcletin del Instituto de B
Estudios Josefiros B
Estudios Lulianos RE
Estudios Marianos B
Estudios Medievales, Anuario de RE
Estudios Trinitarios B
Etats, Anciens Pays et Assemblees D' RE
Eternity IZBG
Eternity Magazine CPI, GSSRPL, RPI
Ethiopia Observer IOB
Ethiopian Studies, Journal of B
Ethiopie, Annales de B
Ethnographica Academiae Scientiarum Hungaricae, Acta IBHR
Ethnographisch-Archaeologische Zeitschrift IBHT
Ethnomusicology IBHR
Ethclogcia IBHR
Etiopici, Rassegna di Studi B
Etranger, Revue Historique du Droit Francais et RE
Etranger, Revue Philosophique de la France et de l' RE
Etude des Religiones, Annales du Centre D' B
Etudes CPLI, ETL, IZBG, NTA, RE
Etudes, Buletin du Centre Protestant D' IOB
Etudes, Ecole Pratique des Hautes B, IBHR
Etudes Anciennes, Revue des B, IBHR
Etudes Armeniennes, Revue des B, IBHR, RE
Etudes Augustiniennes, Revue de ETL, NTA
Etudes Augustiniennes, Revue des RE
Etudes Byzantines, Actes du Congres International des B
Etudes Byzantines, Revue des B, IBHR, RE
Etudes Carmelitaines IZBG
Etudes Cathares, Cahiers D' RE
Etudes Celtiques RE
Etudes Chamitc-Semitiques, Comptes Rendus du Groupe Linguistique D' B
Etudes Classiques ETL, IZBG, RE
Etudes de Papyrclogie B
Etudes et de Documentation, Centre Prctestant D' IOB
Etudes et Travaux B

Etudes Franciscaines ETL, NTA, RE
Etudes Grecques, Revue des RE
Etudes Gregoriennes RE
Etudes Indochinoses, Bulletin de la Societe de IBHR
Etudes Islamiques, Revue des B, IBHR
Etudes Italiennes, Revue des RE
Etudes Juives, Revue des B, IBHR, IZBG, RE
Etudes Latines, Revue des RE
Etudes Litteraires, Scientifiques et Artistiques du Lot Bulletin de la Societe des RE
Etudes Marianles, Bulletin de la Societe Francaise D' B
Etudes Moriales B
Etudes Orientales, Melanges de l' Institut Dominicain D' B, IZBG
Etudes Orientales de Caire, Melanges de l' Instiut Domincain D' RE
Etudes Orientalis de Institut Francais, Bulletin D' IBHR
Etudes Philosophiques ETL, RE
Etudes Portugaises, Publie Par l' Institut Francais au Portugal Bulletin des RE
Etudes Slaves, Revue des RE
Etudes Sud-Est Europeenes, Revue des IBHR, RE
Etudes sur l' Evangelisation, Concept F. Documents du Department D' IOB
Etudes Teilhardiennes ETL
Etudes Theologiques et Religieuses ETL, IRPL, IZBG, NTA, RE
Eucharist RPI
Eucharistia, Santissima IOB
Euntes Docete ETL, NTA, RE
Euphorion. Zeitschrift fur Literaturgeschichte RE
Eure et Loir, Bulletin de la Societe Archeologique D' RE
Europe Occidentale, Messager de l' Exauchat de Patriarche Russe en Iob
European Churches, Current Developments in the Eastern IOB
European Judaism IJP
Europeenes, Revue des Etudes Sud-Est IBHR, RE
Evangel, Pentecostal GSSRPL
Evangelica, Studia IBHR
Evangelica, Theologia IZBG
Evangelical Action, United CPI, GSSRPL, RPI
Evangelical Quarterly CPI, IRPL, IZBG, RPI
Evangelical Theological Society, Journal of the B

Evangelicio, Predicador IOB
Evangelijus Flet IOB
Evangelisation, Concept F. Documents du Department D' Etudes sur l' IOB
Evangelisation, Information IOB
Evangelisation, Revue del' IOB
Evangelisch Katholischer Kommentar B
Evangelische Erziekar IBHR
Evangelische Kirche in Deutschland, Kirchliches Jahrbuch fur die ICB
Evangelische Kommentare B, IBHR, IZBG
Evangelische Theologie ETL, IZBG, NTA, RE, RTA
Evangelische Welt ICB
Evangelischen Kirche in Deutschland, Amtsblatt der IOB
Evangelischen Konsistoriums in Grerfswald, Amtsblatt des IOB
Evangelischen Theologie, Beitraege Zur B, IZBG
Evangelischer Kirchentag, Deutscher IOB
Evangelischer Mission, Jahrbuch IOB
Evangelisches Pfarrerblatt IOB
Evangelisch-Lutherischen Kirche in Thuringen, Amtsblatt der IOB
Evangeliser ETL
Evangelishas Missicnamagazin IOB
Evangelism, Concept E. Papers from the Department on Studies in IOB
Evangelism, Monthly Letter About IOB
Evangile IZBG
Event RPI
Evo e Archivic Muratoriano, Bullettino dell' Istitutc Storico Italiano per Il Medic RE
Exauchat de Patriarche Russe en Europe Occidentale, Messager de l' Iob
Exegese, Beitraege Zur Geschichte der Biblischen IZBG
Exegetisk Arsbok, Svensk ETL, IZBG, NTA, RE
Existenz Heute, Theologische B, IZBG
Expedition B, IZBG
Exploration Journal, Israel ETL, IZBG, NTA
Exploration Quarterly, Palestine ETL, IRPL, IZBG, NTA
Explore UMPI
Explore Resource Kit UMPI
Explore Teacher's Guide UMPI
Expositor, Review and ETL, IRPL, IZBG, NTA
Expository Times ETL, IRPL, IZBG, RTA
Extension Magazine CPII, RPI

Extranjeras, Misiones IOB
F. Documents du Department D' Etudes sur l' Evangelisation, Concept IOB
Fabula. Zeitschrift fur Erzahlforschung RE
Facalta di Letare e Filosafia dell' Universita degli Studi di Trieste, Annoli della IBHR
Face, Face to UMPI
Face to Face UMPI
Facolta di Filosofia e Letter di UN-Versita Statale de Milano, Annali del RE
Faculty of Arts, University of Libya Bulletin of the IBHR
Faith and Forum RPI
Faith and Order Trends IOB
Faith and Thought SISPL
Faith at Work RPI
Faith in Life-Supplement, Christian UMPI
Faith Study-Selected Reading, Foundation Studies in Christian UMPI
Family, Journal of Marriage and the GSSRPL, IOB
Family Digest, Today's CPLI
Far Eastern Antiquities, the Museum of IBHR
Fe, Mision Avierta al Servicio de al B
Fe, Razon y ETL, NTA, RE
Fede e Civilta ICB
Federation der Societes D' Histoire et D' Archeologie de l' Aisne, Memoires de la RE
Federation des Societes Historie et Archeologie de Paris et de l' Ile de France, Memoires de la RE
Fellowship RPI
Fenici, Rivista di Studi B
Fennicae, Annales Academiae Scientiarum IZBG
Festiva, la Parola per l' Assemblea B
Fides et Historici SISPL
Filologia, Giornali Italiano di B
Filologia, Rivista di ETL
Filologia e di Istruzione Classica, Rivista di RE
Filologia Espanola, Revista de RE
Filologiche Aevum. Rassegna di Scienze Storiche, Linguistiche e B, IZBG, RE
Filosafia dell' Universita degli Studi di Trieste, Annoli della Facalta di Letare e IBHR
Filosofia, Sophia. Rassegna Critica di Filosofia e Storia della RE
Filosofia de Diritto, Rivista Internazionale de ETL
Filosofia e di Cultura, Ribista Rosminiana di RE

Filosofia e Letter di UN-Versita Statale de Milano, Annali del Facolta di RE

Filosofia e Storia della Filosofia, Sophia. Rassegna Critica di RE
Filosofia Italiana, Giornale Critico della ETL, RE

Filosofia Neoscolastica, Rivista di RE
Filosofia y Religion Orientales, Estudios de B
Filosofie en Theologie, Bijdragen. Tijdschrift vcor RE
Fin de l' Antiquite, Synthronon Art et Archeclogie de la IBHR
Findsh Teclogisk Tidsskrift IOB
Firanze, Bollettino dell' Amiciza Ebraico-Cristiana di B
Five/Six UMPI
Fivista Italiana di Numismatica e Scienze Affini RE
Flet, Evangelijus IOB
Foi et Le Temps RE
Foi et Vie ETL, IRPI
Foi Vivante (Suisse) ETL
Folia, Classical RE
Foliu Orientalia IBHR
Folk Religion and the Worldview in the South Western Pacific IBHR
Folklore IZBG, RE
Folklore Studies, Asian IBHR
Fomenta Social IOB
Fondamentale D' Afrique Noire, Bulletin de l' Institut IBHR
Fondazione Italiana per la Storia Amministrativa, Annali della RE
For Biblisk Tro IOB
Forderung Christlicher Theologie, Beitraege Zur IZBG
Formation Bulletin, Sister CPLI
Forogiuliesi, Memcrie Storiche RE
Forschung, Theologische IZBG
Forschungen, Byzantinische RE
Forschungen, Indogermanische B
Forschungen, Romanische RE
Forschungen, Ugarit B
Forschungen aus Italienischen Archiven und Bibliotheken, Quellen und Re
Forschungen und Berichte IBHR
Forschungen und Fortschritte ETL
Forschungen Zur Osteuropaischen Geschichte RE

Forschungen Zur Religion und Literatur des Alten und Neuen Testaments B

Forschungen Zur Religion und Literatur des Alten und Neuen Testaments Izbg
Forschungsbeitrage der Cusanus Gesellschaft, Mitteilungen und RE
Fortschritte, Forschungen und ETL
Forum IOB
Forum, Christlich-Judisches IOB
Forum, Faith and RPI
Forum, Israel IZBG
Forum, Kristel ICB
Forum, Lutheran RPI
Forum, Natural Law CPLI
Forum, Neues IOB
Foundation Studies in Christian Faith Study-Selected Reading UMPI
Foundations IRPL, RPI
Fragen der Verkuendigung, Concept G. Arbeiten aus dem Referat fur Iob
Francais, Bulletin D' Etudes Orientalis de Institut IBHR
Francais, Bulletin de la Societe de l' Historie de l' Art RE
Francais, Bulletin de la Societe de l' Historie du Protestantisme ETL, RE
Francais, Recherches et Debats du Centre Catholiques des Intellectuals IOB
Francais au Portugal Bulletin des Etudes Portugaises, Publie Par l' Institut RE
Francais D' Archeologie Orientale, Bulletin de l' Institut IZBG
Francais D' Archeologie Orientale, Bulletin del' Institut B, IBHR
Francais et Etranger, Revue Historique du Droit RE
Francaise, Annales Historiques de la Revolution RE
Francaise, Bulletin de la Societe Prehistorique IBHR
Francaise, Revue D' Histoire de l' Amerique RE
Francaise D' Egyptologie, Bulletin de la Societe B
Francaise D' Etudes Marianles, Bulletin de la Societe B
Francaise de Rome, Melanges D' Archeologie et D' Historier de l' Ecole IBHR
France, Bibliographie de la RE
France, Bulletin de la Societe Nationale des Antiquaires de RE

France, Memoires de la Federation des Societes Historie et Archeolcgie de Paris et de l' Ile de RE
France, Monuments Historuques de la RE
France, Revue D' Histcire de l' Eglise de RE
France, Revue D' Histcire Litteraire de la RE
France, Revue du Louvre et des Musees de RE
France et de l' Etranger, Revue Philosophique de la RE
Francescani, Studi B, RE
Franciscaines, Etudes ETL, NTA, RE
Franciscan Herald RPI
Franciscan Message RPI
Franciscan Studies CPLI, ETL, IZBG, NTA, RE, RPI
Franciscana ETL, RE
Franciscana, Collectanea B, ETL, IZBG, RE
Franciscana, Miscellanea RE
Franciscani Liber Annuus, Studii Biblici ETL, IZBG, NTA
Franciscanos, Estudios RE
Franciscanum B
Franciscanum Historicum, Archivum ETL, RE
Franciskaans Leven ETL
Frankfurter Hefte IOB
Frankische Landesforschung, Jahrbuch fur RE
Franziskanische Studien ETL, IOB, IZBG, NTA, RE
Fratrum Minorum, Analecta Ordinis ETL
Fratrum Praedicatorum, Analecta Sacri Ordinis ETL
Fratrum Praedicatorum, Archivum ETL, RE
Free University Quarterly RTA
Freiburg (Dialog) IOB
Freiburger Diczesan Archiv RE
Freiburger Rundbrief IOB, IZBG
Freiburger Zeitschrift fur Philosophie und Theologie ETL, NTA, RE
Freide uber Israel IOB
French Review RE
French Studies RE
Friar RPI
Friends Journal RPI
Frcme, Revue du Louvre et des Museede B, IBHR
Frontier CPI, IRPI
Frontier, Jewish GSSRPI, IJP
Fruhmittelalrerliche Studien RE
Furrow CPLI, NTA
G. Arbeiten aus dem Referat fur Fragen der Verkuendigung, Concept Icb
Gallegos, Cuadernos de Estudios RE

Gandavenses, Collationes Brugenses et ETL, IOB, IZBG, NTA
Gateway SBPI
Gateway, Drew IRPL, RPI
Gazette des Beaus Arts RE
Geestelijk, Ons IOB
Geestelijk Leven, One B
Gegenwart, Heilige Land in Vergangenheit und IZBG
Gegenwart, Religion in Geschichte und ETL
Geist und Leben ETL, IZBG, NTA, RE
Geistegeschechte, Deutsche Vierteljahrsschrift fur Literaturwissenschaft und B, RE
Geistesgeschichte Osteruopas, Kyrios. Vierteljahresschrift fur Kirchen und RE
Geldgeschichte, Jahrbuch fur Numismatik und B, RE
Gelehrte Anzeigen, Gottingische B, RE
Gelre, Bijdragen en Mededelingen Uitger Door de Vereniging RE
Gemeenschap der Kerken IOB
Gemenskap, Kristen ICB
Generale, Revue RE
Generale, Studium ICB
Generde, Stimme der IOB
Geneva RE
Geneve, Musees de IBHR
Geneve-Afrique ICB
Genootschap ex Oriente Lux, Jaarbericht van het Vooraziatisch Egyptisch IBHR
Genootschap ex Oriente Lux, Jarrbericht van het Vooraziatisch Egyptisch B
Genootschap "ex Oriente Lux", Mededlingen en Verhandelingen van het Vooraziatisch-Egytisch ETL
Genootschap vocr Geschiedenis Gesticht Onder de Benaming Sciete D' Emulation de Bruges, Handeling van het RE
Genotschap ex Criente Lux, Jaarbericht van het Vooraziatisch Egyptisch IZBG
Gent, Handelingen der Maatschappij vocr Geschiedenis en Oudheidkunde Te RE
Gentse Bijdragen tct de Kunstgeschiedenis en de Oudheidkunde RE
Geografica Italianc, Bollettino della Societa B
Gecgraphic, National B
Gecgraphical Jcurnal B
Gecgraphical Review B
Gecgraphie Ecclesiastiques, Dictionnaire D' Historie et de B
Geographische Zeitschrift B

Geography of Israel, Studies in the IZBG

Gereformeerd Theologisch Tijdschrift ETL, IZBG, NTA, RE, RTA
Gereformeerde Teologiese Tydskrif, Nederduitse B, IBHR, IZBG
Germanic Philology, Journal of English and RE
Germanisch Romanische Monatsschrift RE
Geschichliche und Volkskunde. Beitrage Zur Heimantkunde, Carinthia I. KARNTENS RE
Geschichte, Archiv fur Osterreichische RE
Geschichte, Forschungen Zur Osteuropaischen RE
Geschichte, Hemecht. Zeitschrift fur Luxemburger RE
Geschichte, Historia. Zeitschrift fur Alte RE
Geschichte, Schweizerische Zeitschrift fur RE
Geschichte Berlin et Wiesbaden, Klio. Beitrage Zur Alten RE
Geschichte der Biblischen Exegese, Beitraege Zur IZBG
Geschichte der Deutschen Sprache und Literatur, Beitraege Zur RE
Geschichte der Philosophie, Archiv fur B, RE
Geschichte des Antiken Judentums und des Urchristentums, Arbeiten Zur B
Geschichte des Benediktiner Ordens und Seiner Zweige, Studien und Mitteilungen Zur RE
Geschichte Mittelingen und Ostdeutschlands, Jahrbuch fur die RE
Geschichte Osteuropas, Jahrbuch fur IOB
Geschichte Osteuropas, Jahrbucher fur RE
Geschichte und Altertumskunde, Basler Zeitschrift fur RE
Geschichte und Gegenwart, Religion in ETL
Geschichte und Kunst des Trierer Landes und Seiner Nachbargebiete, Trierer Zeitschrift fur RE
Geschichtliche Landeskunde RE
Geschichtsblatter, Bonner RE
Geschichtsblatter, Hansische RE
Geschichtsforschung, Mitteilungen des Instituts fur Osterreichesche Re
Geschichtsvereins, Jahrbuch des Kolnischen RE
Geschiedenis, Bijdragen tot de RE
Geschiedenis, Tijdschrift voor RE
Geschiedenis der Kruisheren, Clairlieu. Tijdschrift Gewijd Aan de RE
Geschiedenis der Nederlanden, Bijdragen en Mededelingen Betreffende de RE

Geschiedenis en Oudheidkunde Te Gent, Handelingen der Maatschappij voor RE
Geschiedenis en Oudheidkundige Kring voor Leuven en Omgeving, Mededlingen van de ETL, RE
Geschiedenis Gesticht Onder de Benaming Societe D' Emulation de Bruges, Handeling van het Genootschap voor RE
Geschiedenis van de Katholieke Kerk in Nederland, Archief voor de ETL, IOB, RE
Gesellschaft, Jahrbuch der Osterreichischen Byzantinistichen IOB
Gesellschaft, Mitteilungen und Forschungsbeitrage der Cusanus RE
Gesellschaft, Mitteilunger der Deutschen Orient B, IBHR
Gesellschaft fur Niedersachsische Kirchengeschichte, Jahrbuch der RE
Gesta RE
Gesticht Onder de Benaming Societe D' Emulation de Bruges, Handeling van het Genootschap voor Geschiedenis RE
Getuigenis B, IOB
Gewijd Aan de Geschiedenis der Kruisheren, Clairlieu. Tijdschrift RE
Gidoggyosasang IOB
Giornale Critico della Filosofia Italiana ETL, RE
Giornale Storico della Letteratura Italiana RE
Giornali Italiano di Filologia B
Giuridico "Filippo Serafini", Archivio ETL, RE
Giurisprudenza, Diritto e ETL
Giurisprudenza Italiana ETL
Glasgow University Oriental Society Transactions B
Glass, Stained RPI
Glass Studies, Journal of B, N
Glaube, Theologie und ETL, IZBG, NTA, RE
Glottologico Italiano, Archivio B
Gnomon ETL, NTA, RE
Good Work CPLI
Gorresgesellschaft, Historisches Jahrbuch der B, RE
Gorresgeuschaft, Histerisenes Jahrbuch der B
Gotoburgensis, Acta Universitatis IZBG
Gottingen, Nachrichten der Akademie der Wissenschaften in RE
Gottingen, Nachrichter der Akademie der Wissenschaften zu B
Gottingische Gelehrte Anzeigen B, RE
Goya. Revista de Arte RE

Gracia, Naturaleza y B
Graduate, Christian SISPL
Granadino, Archivo Teologico IZBG, RE
Grande Lessico del Neue Testamente B
Granville, Revue de l' Anranchin et du Pays de RE
Graz, Jahrbuch des Kunsthistorischen Instiutes der Universitat RE
Great Britain and Ireland, Journal of the Royal Asiatic Society of RE
Grèca di Grottaferrata, Bollettino di Badia RE
Grecques, Revue des Etudes RE
Greek, Roman, and Byzantine Studies RE
Greek Orthodox Theological Review IRPI, RPI
Greek, Roman, and Byzantine Studies RE
Gregoriana, Analecta ETL
Gregorianae, Pontificiae Universitatis B
Gregorianae, Pontificiae Universitatis B
Gregorianium ETL, IZBG, NTA, RE, RTA
Gregoriennes, Etudes RE
Gregorios o Palamas IOB
Grerfswald, Amtsblatt des Evangelischen Konsistoriums in IOB
Grosse Entschluss, der IOB
Grosse Entschluss, der IOB
Grottaferrata, Bollettino di Badia Greca di RE
Groupe Linguistique D' Etudes Chamito-Semitiques, Comptes Rendus du B
Guardian IOB
Guidance Conference Journal, National Catholic CPLI, RPI
Guide SBPI
Guide, Explore Teacher's UMPI
Guide, New Creation Leaders UMPI
Guide, Real Class UMPI
Guide, Religious Book UMPI
Guild of Catholic Psychiatrists Bulletin, National CPLI
Guillaume Bude, Bulletin de l' Association B, ETL, RE
Gulden Passer RE
Gymnasium B
Gymnasium, Siculorum B, RE
Hadassah Magazine IJP
Halle Wittenberg, Wissenschaftliche Zeitschrift der Martin Luther Universitat IBHR, IZBG
Halte Wittenberg, Wissenschaftliche Zeitschrift der Martin Luther Universitat RERE
Handbuch der Orientalistik B

Handeling van het Genootschap voor Geschiedenis Gesticht Onder de Benaming Societe D' Emulation de Bruges RE
Handelingen der Maatschappij voor Geschiedenis en Oudheidkunde Te Gent Re
Handes Amsorya B
Handworter zum Alten Testament, Theologisches B
Handworterbuch, Akkadusches B
Hansische Geschichtsblatter RE
Hartford Quarterly IRPL, RTA
Harvard Semitic Series B
Harvard Studies in Classical Philology B, IBHR
Harvard Theological Review B, ETL, IRPL, IZBG, NTA, RE, RPI, RTA
Harvard Theological Studies IZBG
Hasselt, Diocesaan Tijdschrift ETL
Haute Auvergne, Revue de la RE
Hautes Etudes, Ecole Pratique des B, IBHR
Health, Journal of Religion and IRPL, RPI
Hearthstone SISPL
Hebraic Studies, the Journal of B
Hebraique, Revue de l' Histoire de la Medicine IBHR, IZBG
Hebreos, Miscelanea de Estudios Arabes y B
Hebrew Union College Annual ETL, NTA
Hechos y Dichos ICB
Heerbaan IOB
Hefte, Calwer IZBG
Hefte, Frankfurter IOB
Hefte fur Geschichte, Kunst und Volkskunde Westfalen. RE
Heidelberger Akademie der Wissenschaften, Sitzungsberichte der IZBG, RE
Heidelberger Jahrbucher RE
Heilig Land B, IZBG
Heilige Land in Vergangenheit und Gegenwart IZBG
Heiliger Dienst ICB
Heimantkunde, Carinthia I. Geschichliche und Volkskunde. Beitrage Zur Karntens RE
Helenicos, Boletin del Instituto de Estudios B
Helenistic and Roman Periods, Journal for the Study of Judaism in the Persian B
Hellenique, Bulletin de Correspondance B
Helmantica RE
Helveticum, Museum B
Hemecht. Zeitschrift fur Luxemburger Geschichte RE
Herald, Baptist RPI
Herald, Christian GSSRPL, RPI

Herald, Church GSSRPI, RPI

Herald, Franciscan RPI
Herald of Holiness GSSRPL

Herder Correspondence CPLI, ETL, RPI
Herder Korrespondenz IZBG
Heritage, Baptist History and SBPI
Heritage, Jewish IJP
Hermeneutik, Beitraege Zur der Biblischen IZBG
Hermes. Zeitschrift fur Klassische Philologie RE
Hervormde Teologiese Studies B, IZBG
Hesperis Tamuda RE
Hessischen Kirchengeschichtlichen Vereinigung, Jahrbuch der IOB
Heute, Theologische Existenz B, IZBG
Hevrew Union Xollege Annual IZBG
Heythrop Journal CPLI, ETL, IZBG, RE
Hi Times UMPI
Hibbert Journal ETL, RTA
Hibernica, Studia RE
Hibernicum, Archivium RE
His CPI, GSSRPL
Hispalense, Archivo IZBG
Hispania. Revista Espanola de Historia RE
Hispania Sacra ETL, RE
Hispanic Review RE
Hispanica, Missionalia RE
Hispanique, Bulletin RE
Histerisenes Jahrbuch der Gorresgeuschaft B
Histoire, Bulletin de la Commission Royale D' RE
Histoire, Bulletin des Musees Royaux D' Art et D' RE
Histoire, Cahiers D' RE
Histoire, Melanges D' Archeologie et D' RE
Histoire, Revue Belge de Philologie et D' RE
Histoire, Revue Roumaine D' IZBG, RE
Histoire Anciennes Revue de Philologie, de Litterature et D' RE
Histoire de l' Amerique Francaise, Revue D' RE
Historie de l' Art, Revue Belge D' Archeologie et D' RE
Histoire de l' Eglise de France, Revue D' RE
Histoire de la Medicine Hebraique, Revue de l' IBHR, IZBG
Histoire de Philosophie et de Theologie, Revue D' ETL
Histoire des Religions, Revue D' RE

Histoire des Religions, Revue de l' ETL, IRPL, IZBG, NTA
Histoire des Sciences, Archives Internationales D' RE
Histoire des Sciences et de Leurs Applications, Revue D' RE
Histoire des Textes, Bulletin de l' Institut de Recherche et D' RE
Histoire des Textes, Revue D' B
Histoire Diplomatique, Revue D' RE
Histoire Doctrinale et Litteraire du Paris, Archives D' RE
Historie du Diocese de Liege, Bulletin de la Societe D' Art et D' RE
Histoire du Droit et des Institutions des Anciens Pays Bourguignons, Comtois et Romands Memoires de la Societe Pour l' RE
Histoire Ecclesiastique, Revue D' ETL, IRPL, IZBG, NTA, RE
Histoire Economique Sociale, Revue D' RE
Histoire et Civilisation Byzantines, Travaux et Memoires du Centre de Recherche D' RE
Histoire et D' Archeolcgie de l' Aisne, Memoires de la Federation der Societes D' RE
Histoire et D' Archeolcgie de la Lorraine, Annuaire de la Societe D' Re
Histoire et de Philosophie Religieuses, Revue D' ETL, IRPL, IZBG, NTA, RE
Histoire Liegeoise, Annuaire D' RE
Histoire Litteraire de la France, Revue D' RE
Histoire Mitteilungen, Revue D' RE
Histoire Moderne et Contemporaine, Revue D' RE
Historia B, RE
Historia, Boletin de la Real Academia de la RE
Historia, Hispania. Revista Espanola de RE
Historia de Espana, Cuadernos de RE
Historia del Derecho Espanol, Anuario de RE
Historia y Antiguedades, Boletin de RE
Historia. Zeitschrift fur Alte Geschichte RE
Historiae Conciliorum, Annuarium ETL, RE
Historiae et Iuris, Studia et Documenta B, RE
Historiae Neerlandica, Acta RE
Historiael, Spiegel RE
Historica RE
Historica, Acta RE
Historica, Acta Poloniae RE
Historica, Paedagogica RE
Historica Slovaca, Studia RE

Historical Institute Quarterly, Concordia ETL, RTA

Historical Journal RE
Historical Journal, University of Birmingham RE

Historical Magazine of the Protestant Episcopal Church RPI
Historical Quarterly, American Jewish IJP
Historical Records, American Catholic CPLI
Historical Research, Bulletin of the Institute of RE
Historical Review, American RE
Historical Review, Canadian RE
Historical Review, Catholic CPLI, ETL, GSSRPI, RE, RPI
Historical Review, English RE
Historical Review, Scottish RE
Historical Society, Transactions of the Royal RE
Historical Society of Philadelphia, Records of the American Catholic Re
Historical Society of the Church in Wales, Journal of the RE
Historical Studies, Irish RE
Historical Studies, Journal of ETL, IBHR, IZBG, NTA
Historical Studies, the Quarterly Review of IBHR
Historici, Fides et STSPI
Historicky, Ceskoslovensky Casopis RE
Historico Espanol, Indice RE
Historicum, Archivum Franciscanum ETL, RE
Historicum Congregationis Ssmi Redemptoris, Spicilegium RE
Historicum Societatis Iesu, Archivum ETL, RE
Historie Contemporaine, Revue Belge D' RE
Historie de l' Art Francais, Bulletin de la Societe de l' RE
Historie des Sciences, Archives de l' B
Historie Doctrinale et Litteraire du Moyen Age, Archives D' B
Historie du Protestantisme Francais, Bulletin de la Societe de l' ETL, RE
Historie et Archeologie de Paris et de l' Ile de France, Memoires de la Federation des Societes RE
Historie et de Geographie Ecclesiastiques, Dictionnaire D' B
Historie Instituut Te Rome, Mededlingen van het Nederlands RE

Historie Moderne et Contemperaine, Bulletin de la Section D' RE
Historie Mondiale, Cahiers D' B, IBHR, RE
Historie Orientales et Slaves, Annuaire de l' Institut de Philolcgie et D' B, IBHR
Historier de l' Ecole Francaise de Rome, Melanges D' Archecloqie et D' IBHR
Historii Sztuki, Biuletyn RE
Historique, Annales de Demographie RE
Historique, Information RE
Historique, Revue B, IZBG, RE
Historique Belge de Rome, Bulletin de l' Institut RE
Historique de l' Institut Ducal de Luxembourg, Publications de la Section RE
Historique de la Charente, Memoires de la Societe Archeologie et RE
Historique de Nantes et de Loire Atlantique, Bulletin de la Societe Archeologie et RE
Historique du Comite des Travaux Historiques et scientifiques, Bulletin Philologique et RE
Historique du Droit Francais et Etranger, Revue RE
Historique du Limousin, Bulletin de la Societe Archeologique et RE
Historique et Archeologique du Perigord, Bulletin de la Scciete RE
Historique et Archologique dans Le Limbourg a Maestricht, Publications de la Societe RE
Historiques de la Revolution Francaise, Annales RE
Historiques et scientifiques, Bulletin Philclogique et Historique du Comite des Travaux RE
Historisch Jaarboek, Economisch RE
Historische Mitteilungen, Romische RE
Historische Zeitschrift B, IOB, RE
Historischen Vereins fur der Niererrhein, Annalen der RE
Historisches Jahrbuch der Gorresgesellschaft B, RE
Historischin Vereins Bamberg, Bericht des RE
Historisk Tidsskrift (Oslo) RE
Historuques de la France, Monuments RE
History RE
History, American Journal of Legal RE
History, Bulletin of the Society for African Church IOB
History, Buried SISPL
History, Church CPI, ETL, IRPL, RE, RPI
History, Comparative Studies in Society and RE

History, International Review of Social RE
History, Journal of African IBHR, RE
History, Journal of Contemporary RE
History, Journal of Ecclesiastical ETL, GSSRPL, IRPL, IZBG, RE RPI
History, Journal of Ecomonic RE
History, Journal of Modern RE
History, Journal of Presbyterian IRPL, RPI
History, Journal of Religious ETL, IRPL, IZBG, RE
History, Methodist IRPL, RPI
History, Quaker IRPL, RPI
History, Recusant RE
History, Soviet Studies in RE
History, Studies in Medieval and Renaissance RE
History and Heritage, Baptist SBPI
History and Theory RE
History Association of India, Bulletin of the Church IOB
History of Ideas, Journal of the B, RE
History of Iran, Cambridge IBHR
History of Music, Musica Disciplina. a Yearbook of the RE
History of Philosophy, Journal of the RE
History of Religions ETL, GSSRPL, IBHR, IRPL, IZBG, RE, RPI
History of Religions, Studies in the B
History of Religions Numen, International Review for the ETL, IRPL, NTA
History of the Orient, Journal of Economic and Social B
History of the Orient, Journal of the Economic and Social RE
History Review, Economic RE
History Review, Scandinavian Economic RE
History Today RE
Historyczne, Roczniki RE
Historyczne, Zapiski RE
Historyczny, Kwartalnik RE
Historyczny, Przeglad RE
Hittite et Asianique, Revue B, IBHR
Hochland IOB, RE
Holiness, Herald of GSSRPL
Holland (Ministerium) B
Holland, Oud RE
Holsteinische Geschichte, Zeitschrift der Gesellschaft fur Schleswig Re
Home Life SBPI
Home Missions SBPI

Homelitica en Biblica ETL, IZBG
Homiletic and Pastoral Review CPLI, NTA
Homine Deo, de B
Hospital Progress CPLI
Hsientai Hsuehyuan B
Hsuehyuan, Hsientai B
Humaines, Revue des Sciences RE
Humanism, Arsbok for Kristen IOB
Humanism, Religious GSSRPL
Humanisme et Renaissance, Bibliotheque D' RE
Humanist RPI
Humanistica, Medievalia et RE
Humanistyczne, Roczniki RE
Humanities, Computers in the B
Humanities, Proceedings of the Israel Academy of Sciences and B
Humbolt Universitat zu Berlin, Wissenschaftliche Zeitschrift der RE
Hungaricae, Acta Antiqua Academiae Scientiarum IBHR
Hungaricae, Acta Ethnographica Academiae Scientiarum IBHR
Hymnologie, Jahrbuch fur Liturgik und B, IOB, RE
Ibero Americano, Archivo RE
Ideas, Journal of the History of B, RE
Iesu, Archivum Historicum Societatis ETL, RE
Iglesia Viva B
Igreja e Missao IOB
Ikonographie, Lexikon der Christichen B
Il Medio Evo e Archivio Muratoriano, Bullettino dell' Istituto Storico Italiano per RE
Ile de France, Memoires de la Federation des Societes Historie et Archeologie de Paris et de l' RE
Ille et Vilaine, Bulletin et Memoirs de la Societe Archeologique du Department D' RE
Illustrated London News B
Im Bistum Berlin, Wichmann Jahrbuch fur Kirchengeschichte RE
Im Osten, Kirche RE
Imago Mundi RE
In Lichte der Reformation IOB
Index Quaderri Camerti di Studi Romanistici B
India, Bulletin of the Church History Association of IOB
Indian Churchman, South IOB
Indian Ecclesiastical Studies B, NTA
Indian Journal of Theology IZBG, NTA, RTA

Indias, Revista de RE

Indice Historico Espanol RE
Indigena, America IBHR

Indochinoses, Bulletin de la Societe de Etudes IBHR
Indogermanische Forschungen B
Indogermanischer Sprachen, Zeitschrift fur Vergleichende Sprachforschung auf dem Gebiet der B
Indo-Iranian Journal B, IBHR
Informatie, Internationales Katholiche IOB
Information, Background IOB
Information Evangelisation IOB
Information Historique RE
Information Service (New York) IOB
Information Service, Secretariat for Promoting Christian Unity IOB
Information Service, Secretariat for Promoting Christian Unity IOB
Informations Catholiques Internationales ETL, IOB
Innsbrucker Beitraege Zur Kulturwissenschaft IBHR
Inscriptions et Belles Lettres, Comptes Rendus de l' Academie des IZbg
Inscriptions et Belles Lettres, Comptes Rendus des Seances de l' Academie des RE
Insight CPLI
Inspirada, Palabra ETL
Institut Archeologique du Luxembourg, Annales de l' RE
Institut de Philolcgie et D' Historie Orientales et Slaves, Annuaire de l' B, IBHR
Institut de Recherche et D' Histoire des Textes, Bulletin de l' RE
Institut des Belles Letters Arabes, Revue de l' B, IBHR
Institut Dominicain D' Etudes Orientales, Melanges de l' B, IZBG
Institut Ducal de Luxembourg, Publications de la Section Historique de l' RE
Institut Fondamentale D' Afrique Noire, Bulletin de l' IBHR
Institut Francais, Bulletin D' Etudes Orientalis de IBHR
Institut Francais au Portugal Bulletin des Etudes Portugaises, Publie Par l' RE
Institut Francais D' Archeclogie Orientale, Bulletin de l' IZBG

Institut Francais D' Archeclogie Orientale, Bulletin del' B, IBHR

Institut Historique Belge de Rome, Bulletin de l' RE
Institut Royal du Patrimoine Artistique, Bulletin de l' RE

Institute, Annual of the Swedish Theological B IBHR, IZBG, NTA
Institute China Academy, Buletin of the Catholic Research B
Institute Communications, Oriental B
Institute for Judaiistic Studies, Lown IZBG
Institute Man, the Journal of the Royal Anthropologist IBHR
Institute Narodov Azii, Kratkie Soobscenija IZBG
Institute of Archaeology, Bulletin of the B
Institute of Archaeology at Anakara, Anatolian Studies Journal of the British B, IBHR
Institute of Historical Research, Bulletin of the RE
Institute Quarterly, Concordia Historical ETL, RTA
Institutes, Journal of the Warburg and Courtauld RE
Institutions des Anciens Pays Bourguignons, Comtois et Romands Memoires de la Societe Pour l' Histoire du Droit et des RE
Instituto Caro y Cuervo, Boletin del IZBG
Instituto de Estudios Helenicos, Boletin del B
Instituts, Jahrbuch des Deutschen Archaelogischen B
Instituts, Materialdienst des Konfessionskundlichen B, IOB
Instituts, Mitteilunger des Deutschen Archaeolcgischen B, IBHR
Instituts fur Christliche Sozialwissenschaften, Jahrbuch des IOB
Instituts fur Orientforschung, Mitteilungen des B, IBHR, IZBG
Instituts fur Osterreichesche Geschichtsforschung, Mitteilungen des Re
Instituts fur Wissenschaftlishe Padogogik, Schriften des Deutschen Etl
Instituut Te Rome, Mededlingen van het Nederlands Historie RE
Instiut Domincain D' Etudes Orientales de Caire, Melanges de l' RE

Instiutes der Universitat Graz, Jahrbuch des Kunsthistorischen RE
Integraal, Missie IOB
Intellectuals Francais, Recherches et Debats du Centre Catholiques des IOB
International, IDOC CPLI, ETL
International de Numismatique, Actes du Congres B
International de Papyrclogie, Actes du Congres B
International des Etudes Byzantines, Actes du Congres B
International des Orientalistes, Actes du Congres B
International Journal for the Philosophy of Religion B
International Journal of Religious Education SISPL
International Reformed Bulletin IOB
International Review of Missions B, CPI, ETL, IBHR, IBPL, RPI, RTA
International Review of Social History RE
Internationale, Recontre Assyriologique B
Internationale de Philosophie, Revue RE
Internationale des Archives, Archivum. Revue RE
Internationale des Droits de l' Antiquite, Revue IZBG, RE
Internationale Kirchliche Zeitschrift ETL, IZBG, NTA, RE
Internationale Kongresses, Akten des B
Internationale Zeitschrift fur Kunst, Pantheon. RE
Internationale Zusammenarbeit, Dokumente. Zeitschrift fur IOB
Internationales, Informations Catholiques ETL, IOB
Internationales D' Histoire des Sciences, Archives RE
Internationales Jahrbuch fur Religions-Sociologie IOB
Internationales Katholiche Informatie IOB
Internationaux de Sociologie, Cahiers IBHR
Internazionale, Bollettino Bibliografiro B
Internazionale de Filosofia de Diritto, Rivista ETL
Internazionale dei Lincei, Academia ETL
Internazionale Scottista, Bollettino della Societa IZBG
Interpretation ETL, IBPL, IZBG, NTA, RE, RPI, RTA
Ipse hic Elenchus Bibliographicus Biblicus B
Iran, Archaeclogische Mitteilungen aus B
Iran, Cambridge History of IBHR
Iranica, Acta IBHR

Iranica Antiqua B
Iranistische Mittelungen IBHR
Iraq IZBG
Ireland, Journal of the Royal Asiatic Society of Great Britain and RE
Ireland, Journal of the Royal Society of Antiquaries of RE
Irenikon ETL, IRPL, IZBG, NTA, RE
Irish Ecclesiastical Record CPLI, ETL, IOB, RE
Irish Historical Studies RE
Irish Theological Quarterly CPLI, ETL, IZBG, RE
Isis RE
Islam RE
Islam, Studies in IBHR
Islamic Quarterly B
Islamica, Studia B, IBHR
Islamiques, Revue des Etudes B, IBHR
Islamologiques, Annales IBHR
Islams, Welt des IOB
Israel, Christian News from IOB, IZBG
Israel, Eretz IZBG
Israel, Freide uber IOB
Israel, Noticias Cristianas de IZBG
Israel, Nouvelles Chretiennes D' B
Israel, Rassegna Mensile di B, IBHR, IZBG
Israel, Studies in the Geography of IZBG
Israel Academy of Sciences and Humanities, Proceedings of the B
Israel Digest IJP
Israel Exploration Journal ETL, IZBG, NTA
Israel Forum IZBG
Israel Magazine IJP
Israelitisches Wochenblatt IZBG
Istina IRPL, NTA, RE
Istituto Lombardo di Scienze e Lettere, Rendiconti dell' RE
Istituto Nazionale D' Archeologia e Storia dell' Arte, Rendiconti dell' RE
Istituto Orientale di Napoli, Annali del' B, ETL, IBHR, IZBG
Istituto Storico Italiano per Il Medio Evo e Archivio Muratoriano, Bullettino dell' RE
Istituto Veneto di Scienze, Lettere di Arte Atti dell' RE
Istriana di Archeologia e Storia Patria, Atti e Memorie de Societa RE
Istruzione Classica, Rivista di Filologia e di RE
Italaia Medioevale e Umanistica RE

Italia, Accademie e Biblioteche D' B
Italia, Libri e Riviste D' B
Italia, Rivista di Storia della Chiesa in RE
Italiana, Bibliografia Nazionale RE
Italiana, Esegesi Biblica Associazione Biblica ETL
Italiana, Giornale Critico della Filosofia ETL, RE
Italiana, Giornale Storico della Letteratura RE
Italiana, Giurisprudenza ETL
Italiana (Revista Biblica) IZBG
Italiana, Rivista Storica RE
Italiana di Numismatica e Scienze Affini, Rivista RE
Italiana per la Storia Amministrativa, Annali della Fondazione RE
Italiano, Archivio Glottologico B
Italiano, Archivio Storico RE
Italiano, Bollettino della Societa Geografica B
Italiano, Rivista di Storia del Diritto RE
Italiano di Filologia, Giornali B
Italiano per Il Medio Evo e Archivio Muratoriano, Bullettino dell' Istituto Storico RE
Italiano per la Storia della Pieta, Archivio RE
Italienischen Archiven und Bibliotheken, Quellen und Forschungen aus Re
Italiennes, Revue des Etudes RE
Iuris, Studia et Documenta Historiae et B, RE
Iuris Canonici, Ephemerides ETL, RE
Ius Canonicum RE
Ius Commune RE
Iustitia ETL
Iv, Scuola Pasitiva Serie IBHR
Jaarbericht van het Vooraziatisch Egyptisch Genootschap ex Oriente Lux IBHR
Jaarbericht van het Vooraziatisch Egyptisch Genotschap ex Oriente Lux IZBG
Jaarbock voor de Eredienst IOB
Jaarboek, Economisch Historisch RE
Jaarboek, Nederlands Kunsthistorisch RE
Jaarboek Werkgenootschap van Katholieke Theologen in Nederland B
Jagdwissenshaft, Zeitschrift fur IBHR
Jahrbuch, Dusseldorfer RE
Jahrbuch, Eranos IZBG
Jahrbuch, Lateinamerika RE
Jahrbuch, Literaturwissenschaftliches RE
Jahrbuch, Liturgisches B, RE
Jahrbuch, Luther RE
Jahrbuch, Mittellanteinisches RE

Jahrbuch, Philosophisches B, RE
Jahrbuch, Romanistisches RE
Jahrbuch, Theologisches IZBG
Jahrbuch, Wallraf Richartz RE
Jahrbuch der Berliner Museen RE
Jahrbuch der Gesellschaft fur Niedersachsische Kirchengeschichte RE
Jahrbuch der Gorresgesellschaft, Historisches B, RE
Jahrbuch der Gorresgeuschaft, Histerisenes B
Jahrbuch der Hessischen Kirchengeschichtlichen Vereinigung IOB
Jahrbuch der Kunsthistorischen Sammlungen Wien RE
Jahrbuch der Osterreichischen Byzantinistichen Gesellschaft IOB
Jahrbuch der Osterreichischin Byzantinistik RE
Jahrbuch der Stallichen Kunstsammuluger in Baden-Wurttemberg IBHR
Jahrbuch des Deutschen Archaelogischen Instituts B
Jahrbuch des Instituts fur Christliche Sozialwissenschaften IOB
Jahrbuch des Kolnischen Geschichtsvereins RE
Jahrbuch des Kunsthistorischen Instiutes der Universitat Graz RE
Jahrbuch des Martin Luther-Bundes IOB
Jahrbuch des Museums fur Volkerbunder zu Leipzig IBHR
Jahrbuch Evangelischer Mission IOB
Jahrbuch fur Antike und Christentum IZBG, RE
Jahrbuch fur die Evangelische Kirche in Deutschland, Kirchliches IOB
Jahrbuch fur die Geschichte Mittelingen und Ostdeutschlands RE
Jahrbuch fur Frankische Landesforschung RE
Jahrbuch fur Geschichte Osteuropas IOB
Jahrbuch fur Kirchengeschichte Im Bistum Berlin, Wichmann RE
Jahrbuch fur Kunstgeschichte, Romisches RE
Jahrbuch fur Landesgeschichte, Niedersachsisches RE
Jahrbuch fur Landeskunde voor Niederosterreich RE
Jahrbuch fur Liturgik und Hymnologie B, IOB, RE
Jahrbuch fur Mystiche Theologie ETL
Jahrbuch fur Numismatik und Geldgeschichte B, RE
Jahrbuch fur Religions-Sociologie, Internationales IOB
Jahrbuch fur Wirtschaftsgeschichte RE
Jahrbucher, Heidelberger RE

Jahrbucher fur Geschichte Osteuropas RE
Japan, Contemporary Religions in SISPL
Japan Missionary Bulletin IOB
Japanese Religions IOB
Jaarbericht van het Vooraziatisch Egyptisch
Genootschap ex Oriente Lux B
Jean-Baptist, Bulletin Saint IBHR, IOB
Jena, Wissenschaftliche Zeitschrift der Friedrich
Schiller Universitat RE
Jena, Wissenschaftliche Zeitschrift der
Universitat IZBG
Jerusalem, Levant. Journal of the British
School of Archaeology in SISPL
Jewish Archives, American IJP
Jewish Communal Service, Journal of IJP
Jewish Digest IJP
Jewish Educator IJP, RTA
Jewish Frontier GSSRPL, IJP
Jewish Heritage IJP
Jewish Historical Quarterly, American IJP
Jewish Journal of Sociology B, IBHR
Jewish Life IJP, RPI
Jewish Lore and Philosophy, Journal of B
Jewish Monthly, National IJP
Jewish Observer and Middle East Review IJP
Jewish People Newsletter, National Council
of Churches Committee on the Church and IOB, SBPI
Jewish Quarterly Review ETL, IJP, IRPL, IZBG,
RE, RPI
Jewish Research, Proceedings of the American
Academy for B
Jewish Social Studies IZBG
Jewish Spectator GSSRPL, IJP, RPI
Jewish Studies, Journal of ETL, IZBG, NTA
Jewish Studies, Proceedings of the World Congress
of B
Jiskry, Kostnicke IOB
Johannesburg (African Studies) IBHR, IOB
John Rylands Library, Bulletin of the ETL,
IZBG, NTA, RE
Jordan, Annual of the Department of Antiquities
of B
Jordan Lectures in Comparative Religions ETL
Josefinos, Estudios B
Joseph, Melanges de l' Universite St. B, IBHR,
IZBG, RE
Josephologie, Cahiers de NTA, RTA
Journal, Africa Theological SISPL

Journal, Antiquaries B, RE

Journal, Archaeological RE
Journal, Art RE
Journal, Baptist Men's SBPI
Journal, Calvin Theological CPI, ETL, IRPL, IZBG, RE, RPI
Journal, Catholic School CPLI, RPI
Journal, Central Asiatic IBHR
Journal, Central Conference of American Rabbis B, IJP
Journal, Durham University IZBG
Journal, Friends RPI
Journal, Geographical B
Journal, Heythrop CPLI, ETL, IZBG, RE
Journal, Hibbert ETL, RTA
Journal, Historical RE
Journal, Indo-Iranian B, IBHR
Journal, Israel Exploration ETL, IZBG, NTA
Journal, Middle East GSSRPL
Journal, National Catholic Guidance Conference CPLI, RPI
Journal, Numismatic Chronicle and B
Journal, Perkins School of Theology NTA
Journal, Presbyterian SISPL
Journal, Religion Teacher's CPLI
Journal, University of Birmingham Historical RE
Journal, Weslyan Theological SISPL
Journal, Westminister Theological CPI, ETL, IRPL, IZBG, NTA, RPI, RTA
Journal Asiatique IZBG, RE
Journal de la Societe des Americanistes IBHR
Journal des Moskauer Patriarchats IZBG
Journal des Savants B, RE
Journal for the Philosophy of Religion, International B
Journal for the Scientific Study of Religion IRPL, RE, RPI
Journal for the Study of Judaism IZBG
Journal for the Study of Judaism in the Persian Helenistic and Roman Periods B
Journal for Theology and the Church IRPL, RPI
Journal of African History IBHR, RE
Journal of American Oriental Society IZBG
Journal of American Research Center in Egypt B
Journal of Ancient Near Eastern Society of Columbia B, SISPL
Journal of Applied Behavorial Science SISPL

Journal of Archaeology, American B, ETL, IBHR, IZBG, SISPL
Journal of Biblical Archaeology, Australian IZBG
Journal of Biblical Literature ETL, GSSRPL, IJP, IRPL, IZBG, NTA, RE, RPI, RTA
Journal of Christian Education B, SISPL
Journal of Church and State IRPL, RPI
Journal of Church Music RPI
Journal of Classical Studies B
Journal of Contemporary History RE
Journal of Cuneiform Studies IZBG
Journal of Ecclesiastical History ETL, GSSRPL, IRPL, IZBG, RE, RPI
Journal of Ecomonic History RE
Journal of Economic and Social History of the Orient B
Journal of Ecumenical Studies CPLI, ETL, IRPL, IZBG, RE, RPI
Journal of Education, Notre Dame CPLI
Journal of English and Germanic Philology RE
Journal of Ethiopian Studies B
Journal of Glass Studies B, N
Journal of Hebraic Studies, the B
Journal of Hebraic Studies, the B
Journal of Historical Studies ETL, IBHR, IZBG, NTA
Journal of Jewish Communal Service IJP
Journal of Jewish Lore and Philosophy B
Journal of Jewish Studies ETL, IZBG, NTA
Journal of Jurisprudence, American CPLI
Journal of Juristic Papyrology B
Journal of Legal History, American RE
Journal of Linguistics SISPL
Journal of Marriage and the Family GSSRPL, IOB
Journal of Modern African Studies GSSRPL
Journal of Modern History RE
Journal of Near Eastern Studies ETL, IZBG, NTA, RPI
Journal of Pastoral Care IRPL, RPI
Journal of Philology, American B, IBHR
Journal of Presbyterian History IRPL, RPI
Journal of Religion GSSRPL, IRPL, IZBG, RE, RPI
Journal of Religion and Health IRPL, RPI
Journal of Religion in Africa RE, SISPL
Journal of Religious Education, International SISPL
Journal of Religious History ETL, IRPL, IZBG, RE
Journal of Religious Thought IRPL, RPI
Journal of Roman Studies B, RE
Journal of Semitic Studies ETL, IRPL, IZBG, NTA

Journal of Social Psychology IBHR
Journal of Sociology, American GSSRPL
Journal of Sociology, British IBHR
Journal of Sociology, Jewish B, IBHR
Journal of the American Academy of Religion
ETL, GSSRPL, IRPL, IZBG, NTA, RE, RPI
Journal of the British Archaeological Association
RE
Journal of the British Institute of Archaeology
at Anakara, Anatolian Studies B, IBHR
Journal of the British School of Archaeology
in Jerusalem, Levant. Sispl
Journal of the Economic and Social History of
the Orient RE
Journal of the Evangelical Theological Society B
Journal of the Historical Society of the Church
in Wales RE
Journal of the History of Ideas B, RE
Journal of the History of Philosophy RE
Journal of the Linguistic Society of America,
Language.
Ibhr
Iob
Izbg
Journal of the Northwest Semitic Languages B
Journal of the Polynesian Society IBHR
Journal of the Royal Anthropologist Institute
Man, the IBHR
Journal of the Royal Asiatic Society of Great
Britain and Ireland RE
Journal of the Royal Society of Antiquaries
of Ireland RE
Journal of the University of Bombay IBHR
Journal of the Warburg and Courtauld Institutes RE
Journal of Theological Studies ETL, IRPL, IZBG,
RE, RTA
Journal of Theology, Canadian ETL, IRPL, IZBG, RTA
Journal of Theology, Indian IZBG, NTA, RTA
Journal of Theology, Scottish ETL, IRPL, IZBG, RTA
Journal of Theology, South East Asia IRPL, NTA
Journal of Theology, Southwestern CPI, ETL,
IRPL, IZBG, NTA, RPI, RTA, SBPI
Jours, Travaux et IOB
Jubliee, US Catholic and CPLI, GSSRPL, RPI
Judaean, Young IJP
Judaean Desert, Discoveries in the B
Judah, Studies on the Texts of the Desert of ETL
Judaica IZBG

Judaica, Encyclopedia B

Judaiistic Studies, Lown Institute for IZBG
Judaism ETL, IBHR, IJP, IOB, IRPL, IZBG, RPI

Judaism, Conservative IJP
Judaism, Dimensions in American RPI
Judaism, European IJP
Judaism, Journal for the Study of IZBG
Judaism in the Persian Helenistic and Roman Periods, Journal for the Study of B
Judentums, Zeitschrift fur Geschichte des B
Judentums und des Urchristentums, Arbeiten Zur Geschichte des Antiken B
Juie. la Revue du Centre de Documentation Juife Contemporaine, Monde IZBG
Juife Contemporaine, Monde Juie. la Revue du Centre de Documentation IZBG
Juives, Revue des Etudes B, IBHR, IZBG, RE
Junge Kirche IOB
Junior Hi Times UMPI
Jurisprudence, American Journal of CPLI
Jurist RE
Juristic Papyrology, Journal of B
Jus ETL
Justice, World CPLI, IOB
Justice dans de Monde ETL
Justice Review, Social CPLI, RPI
Kairos ETL, IZBG, NTA, RE
Kanoniczne, Prawo RE
Kanoniczne, Roczniki Reologiczno ETL, NTA
Kanoniczne, Roczniki Teologiczno IZBG, RE
Kant Studien ETL, RE
Karl Marx Universitat, Wissenschaftliche Zeitschrift der
Re IZBG
Katallagete B, IRPL, RPI
Katechetische Blatter IZBG
Katholiche Informatie, Internationales IOB
Katholiek Archief ETL
Katholieke Kerk in Nederland, Archief voor de Geschiedenis van de ETL, IOB, RE
Katholieke Theologen in Nederland, Jaarboek Werkgenootschap van B
Katholieke Theologen in Nederland, Werkgenootschap voor ETL, IOB
Katholische Erzieher B
Katholische Stemmen, Nederlands ETL

Katholische Theologie, Zeitschrift fur ETL, IZBG, NTA

Katholischen Missionen IOB
Katholischer Kommentar, Evangelisch B
Katholisches Kirchenrecht, Archiv fur ETL, IBHR, RE
Katholisches Missionejahrbuch der Schweiz IOB
Katolickiego Uniwersytetu Lubelskiego, Zeszyty Naukowe B, RE
Keeping Posted IJP
Kerk en Missie ETL
Kerk en Theologie B, IOB
Kerk in Nederland, Archief voor de Geschiedenis van de Katholieke ETL, IOB, RE
Kerkelijk Leven IOB
Kerken, Gemeenschap der IOB
Kerkgeschiedenis, Nederlands Archief voor IOB, RE
Kerygma und Dogma ETL, IRPL, IZBG, RE, RTA
Kindergarten UMPI
Kirche, Bibel und ETL, IZBG, NTA
Kirche, Junge IOB
Kirche, Kunst und IOB
Kirche, Musik und IOB
Kirche, Tidsskrift for Teologi og ETL, IZBG
Kirche, Zeitschrift fur Theologie und ETL, IRPL, IZBG, RE, RTA
Kirche Im Osten RE
Kirche in Deutschland, Amtsblatt der Evangelischen IOB
Kirche in Deutschland, Kirchliches Jahrbuch fur die Evangelische IOB
Kirche in Thuringen, Amtsblatt der Evangelisch-Lutherischen IOB
Kirche und Gesellschaft, Wissenschaft UN Prozis in B
Kirchen der Tschechoslowakei, Protestantischen IZBG
Kirchen und Geistesgeschichte Osteruopas, Kyrios. Vierteljahresschrift fur RE
Kirchenblatt fur die Reformierte Schweiz B
Kircheneschichte, Zeitschrift fur Bayerische RE
Kirchengeschichte, Archiv fur Mittelrheinische IOB, RE
Kirchengeschichte, Archiv fur Schlesische RE
Kirchengeschichte, Beitraege Zur Altbayerischen RE
Kirchengeschichte, Jahrbuch der Gesellschaft fur Niedersachsische RE

Kirchengeschichte, Romanische Quartalschrift
 fur Christliche Alterumskunde und RE
Kirchengeschichte, Zeitschrift fur RE
Kirchengeschichte, Zeitschrift fur Schweizerische
 IOB, RE
Kirchengeschichte Im Bistum Berlin, Wichmann
 Jahrbuch fur RE
Kirchengeschichtlichen Vereinigung, Jahrbuch
 der Hessischen IOB
Kirchenrecht, Archiv fur Katholisches ETL,
 IBHR, RE
Kirchenrecht, Oesterreichisches Archiv fur
 ETL, IOB, RE
Kirchentag, Deutscher Evangelischer IOB
Kirchenzeitung, Reformierte IOB
Kirchliche Zeitschrift, Internationale ETL,
 IZBG, NTA, RE
Kirchlichen Dienst IOB
Kirchliches Jahrbuch fur die Evangelische Kirche
 in Deutschland IOB
Kirjath Sepher IZBG
Kirke og Luther IOB
Kirkehistorike Samlinger RE
Kit, Explore Resource UMPI
Klassische Altertum, Philologus. Zeitschrift
 fur das RE
Klassische Philologie, Hermes. Zeitschrift fur RE
Klerusblatt, Oesterreichisches ETL
Kliene Pauly B
Klio. Beitrage Zur Alten Geschichte Berlin et
 Wiesbaden RE
Kolnischen Geschichtsvereins, Jahrbuch des RE
Kommentar, Evangelisch Katholischer B
Kommentare, Evangelische B, IBHR, IZBG
Kommentare und Beitrage zum Alten und Neuen
 Testament (Dusseldorf) B
Kommunist IOB
Konfessionskundlichen Instituts, Materialdienst
 des B, IOB
Kongresses, Akten des Internationale B
Konsistoriums in Greifswald, Amtsblatt des
 Evangelischen IOB
Korrespondenz, Herder IZBG
Korrespondenz, Ordens B
Koscielne Archiwa, Biblioteki Muzea RE
Kosmos en Oecumene IOB
Kostnicke Jiskry IOB
Kratkie Soobscenija Institute Narodov Azii IZBG

Krestanska Revue IOB, IZBG

Krestanske Revue, Theologicka Priloha IZBG
Kring voor Leuven en Omgeving, Mededlingen van de Geschiedenis en Oudheidkundige ETL, RE

Kristel Forum IOB
Kristen Gemenskap IOB
Kristen Humanism, Arsbok for IOB
Kronika, Sprawozdania Z Czynnosci Wydawniczej i Posiedzen Naukoeych Oraz RE
Kruisheren, Clairlieu. Tijdschrift Gewijd Aan de Geschiedenis der RE
Kultur Religion, Wissenschaft, IZBG
Kultura, Duchovna IOB
Kulturarbeit IOB
Kulturgeschichte, Archiv fur B, IOB, RE
Kulturwissenschaft, Innsbrucker Beitraege Zur IBHR
Kultuurleven IOB
Kunde des Morgenlandes, Wiener Zeitschrift fur B, ETL, IZBG
Kunst, Pantheon. Internationale Zeitschrift fur RE
Kunst des Trierer Landes und Seiner Nachbargebiete, Trierer Zeitschrift fur Geschichte und RE
Kunst und Denkmalpflege, Oesterreichische Zeitschrift fur RE
Kunst und Denkmalpflete, Deutsche RE
Kunst und Kirche IOB
Kunst und Kunstwissenschaft Munster, Zeitschrift fur Christliche IOB, RE
Kunstblatter, Aachener RE
Kunstgeschichte, Niederdeutsche Beitrage Zur RE
Kunstgeschichte, Romisches Jahrbuch fur RE
Kunstgeschichte, Zeitschrift fur Schweizerische Archaologie und RE
Kunstgeschiedenis en de Oudheidkunde, Gentse Bijdragen tot de RE
Kunsthistorisch Jaarboek, Nederlands RE
Kunsthistorischen Instiutes der Universitat Graz, Jahrbuch des RE
Kunsthistorischen Sammlungen Wien, Jahrbuch der RE
Kunstsammulugen in Baden-Wurttemberg, Jahrbuch der Stallichen IBHR
Kunstwissenschaft Munster, Zeitschrift fur Christliche Kunst und IOB, RE
Kunstwisswenschaft, Zeitschrift des Deutschen Vereins fur RE

Kvartalskrift, Svensk Teologisk ETL, IRPL, IZBG, NTA, RE

Kwartalnik Historyczny RE
Kyrios. Vierteljahresschrift fur Kirchen und Geistesgeschichte Osteruopas RE
Kyrklig Tidsskrift, Ny ETL, IZBG
Kyrkohistorisk Arsskrift RE
L' Osservatore CPLI
Laennec, Cahiers ETL
Laity, Documents from the Department for the IOB
Lajsja, Reformatasok IOB
Land, Heilig B, IZBG
Land in Vergangenheit und Gegenwart, Heilige IZBG
Land van Loon, Oude RE
Landergerchichte, Zeitschrift fur Bayerische RE
Landes und Seiner Nachbargebiete, Trierer Zeitschrift fur Geschichte und Kunst des Trierer RE
Landesforschung, Jahrbuch fur Frankische RE
Landesgeschichte, Blatter fur Deutsche RE
Landesgeschichte, Niedersachsisches Jahrbuch fur RE
Landeskunde, Geschichtliche RE
Landeskunde voor Niederosterreich, Jahrbuch fur RE
Language. Journal of the Linguistic Society of America IDHR, IOB, IZBG
Language Association, Publications of the Modern RE
Language Notes, Modern IZBG, RE
Language Quarterly, Modern RE
Language Review, Modern RE
Languages, Journal of the Northwest Semitic B
L' Art Francais, Bulletin de la Societe de l' Historie de RE
Lateinamerika Jahrbuch RE
Latina, Patrologia B
Latina, Revue du Moyen Age RE
Latines, Revue des Etudes RE
Latinitatis Medii Aevi. Bulletin du Cange, Archivum RE
Latomus ETL, RE
Laurentianum RE
Laval Theologique et Philosophique ETL, NTA
Law Forum, Natural CPLI
Lawyer, Catholic CPLI
Le Antiche Provincie Modenesi, Atti e Memorie de Deputazione di Storia Patria per RE

Le Limbourg a Maestricht, Publications de la Societe Historique et Archologique dans RE
Le Province di Romagna, Atti e Memorie de Deputazione di Storia Patria per RE
Le Province Napoletane, Archivio Storico per RE
Le Province Parmensi, Archivio Storico per RE
Le Temps, Foi et RE
Leader, Adult UMPI
Leader, Baptist BPI
Leader, Youth UMPI
Leaders Guide, New Creation UMPI
Leadership, Adult SBPI
Leadership, Childrens SBPI
Leadership, Preschool SBPI
Leadership, Youth SBPI
League Bulletin, Anti-Defamation IJP
League Quarterly, Bible SISPL
Learning for Living RTA
Leben, Bibel und ETL, NTA, RE
Leben, Geist und ETL, IZBG, NTA, RE
Lebendige Seelsorge ICB
Lebendiges Zeugnis ICB
Lecciones Cristianas UMPI
Lectures in Comparative Religions, Jordan ETL
Legal History, American Journal of RE
Legionense, Studium B
Leiegouw, Verslagen en Mededelingen van de RE
Leipzig, Berichte uber die Verhandlugn der Sachsischen Akademie der Wissenschaften zu RE
Leipzig, Jahrbuch des Museums fur Volkenbunder zu IBHR
Leipzig, Sitzungsberichte der Sachsischen Adademie der Wissenschaften zu RE
Lelkopasztor IOB
Leodium RE
Leoneses, Archivos RE
Leopold Delisle, Cahiers RE
Leshonenu IZBG
Lessico del Neue Testamente, Grande B
Lessons for Adults, Bible UMPI
Lessons for Youth, Bible UMPI
Letare e Filosafia dell' Universita degli Studi di Trieste, Annoli della Facalta di IBHR
Letopis IZBG
Letter About Evangelism, Monthly IOB
Letter di UN-Versita Statale de Milano, Annali del Facolta di Filoscfia e RE
Letteratura Italiana, Giornale Storico della RE

Letteratura Religiosa, Rivista di Storia e RE

Letteratura Studi Urbinati di Storia, Filosofia e RE

Letteratura Tomistica, Rassegna di RE

Lettere, Rendiconti dell' Istituto Lombardo di Scienze e RE

Letterkunde, Tijdschrift voor Nederlandse Tall en RE

Letters Arabes, Revue de l' Institut des Belles E, IBHR

Lettres, Bulletin de la Classe des IZBG

Lettres, Comptes Rendus de l' Academie des Inscriptions et Belles Izbg

Lettres, Comptes Rendus des Seances de l' Academie des Inscriptions et Belles RE

Lettres et des Sciences Morales et Politiques, Academie Revue de Belgique. Bulletin de la Classe des RE

Lettres Romanis RE

Leurs Applications, Revue D' Histoire des Sciences et de RE

Leuven en Omgeving, Mededlingen van de Geschiedenis en Oudheidkundige Kring voor ETL, RE

Leuvense Bijdragen RE

Levant. Journal of the British School of Archaeology in Jerusalem Sispl

Leven, Franciskaans ETL

Leven, Kerkelijk IOB

Leven, One Geestelijk B

Lexikon der Christichen Ikonographie B

Lexington Theological Quarterly ETL, IRPL, NTA, RPI

Liber Annuus, Studii Biblici Franciscani ETL, IZBG, NTA

Librarian, Christian CPI

Library, Bulletin of the John Rylands ETL, IZBG, NTA, RE

Library, Bulletin of the New York Public RE

Library, Missionary Research IOB, RE

Library Magazine, Church RPI

Library Record, Bodleian RE

Library World, Catholic CPLI, RPI

Libri e Riviste D' Italia B

Libros, Selecciones de B

Libya Bulletin of the Faculty of Arts, University of IBHR

Lichte der Reformation, in IOB

Liege, Bulletin de la Societe D' Art et D' Historie du Diccese de RE

Liegeoise, Annuaire D' Histoire RE
Life, Christian CPI, GSSRPL, RPI
Life, Doctrine and ETL, NTA
Life, Home SEPI
Life, Jewish IJP, RPI
Life, Orthodox RPI
Life, Pastoral RPI
Life, Presbyterian GSSRPL, RPI
Life, Quaker RPI
Life, Spiritual CPLI, RPI
Life, Theology and RTA
Life and Thought, Brethern ETL, IRPL, RPI, RTA
Life-Supplement, Christian Faith in UMPI
Light, Living CPLI
Light, True RPI
Liguorian CPLI, RPI
Ligure di Storia Patria, Atti di Societa RE
Ligustico per la Storia e la Cultura Regionale, Bollettinc RE
Limbourg a Maestricht, Publications de la Societe Historique et Archologique dans Le RE
Limburg RE
Limousin, Bulletin de la Societe Archeologique et Historique du RE
Lincei, Academia Internazionale dei ETL
Lincei, Rendiconti della Academia Nazionale dei IBHR
Linguietique de Paris, Bulletin de la Societe de B
Linguistic Society of America, Language. Journal of the IBHR, IOB, IZBG
Linguistica Biblica IZBG
Linguistics, Journal of SISPL
Linguisticum, Archivum IZBG
Linguistique D' Etudes Chamito-Semitiques, Comptes Rendus du Groupe B
Linguistische Berichte IZBG
Lingusitica Biblica B
Link GSSRPL, RPI
Literary Supplement, Times B
Literatur, Beitraege Zur Geschichte der Deutschen Sprache und RE
Literatur, Zeitschrift fur Deutsches Altertum und Deutsche RE
Literatur, Zeitschrift fur Franzosische Sprache und RE

Literatur des Alten und Neuen Testaments, Forschungen Zur Religion und B, IZBG
Literaturanzeiger, Philosophischer B, RE
Literature, Comparative RE
Literature, Journal of Biblical ETL, GSSRPL, IJP, IRPL, IZBG, NTA, RE, RPI, RTA
Literature, Studies in English RE
Literaturen, Archiv fur das Studium der Neueren Sprachen und RE
Literaturgeschichte, Euphorion. Zeitschrift fur RE
Literaturwissenschaft und Geistegeschechte, Deutsche Vierteljahrsschrift fur B, RE
Literaturwissenschaftliches Jahrbuch RE
Literaturzeitung, Deutsche B, IBHR, IZBG, RE
Literaturzeitung, Orientalistische ETL, IZBG, NTA, RE
Literaturzeitung, Theologische Izbg ETL, IRPL, NTA, RE
Litteraire de la France, Revue D' Histoire RE
Litteraire du Moyen Age, Archives D' Historie Doctrinale et B
Litteraire du Paris, Archives D' Histoire Doctrinale et RE
Litteraires, Scientifiques et Artistiques du Lot Bulletin de la Societe des Etudes RE
Litteratur Comparee, Revue de RE
Litterature Ecclesiastique, Bulletin de ETL, IZBG, NTA, RE
Litterature et D' Histoire Anciennes Revue de Philologie, de RE
Liturgia, Rivista di B
Liturgica, Revista di Pastorale B
Liturgica, Studia IRPL, IZBG, NTA, RE
Liturgica Pericdica de Re Morali, Canonica, RE
Liturgicae, Ephemerides ETL, IZBG, NTA, RE
Liturgical Arts CPLI, RPI
Liturgical Studies, Yearbook of B
Liturgical Week, North American CPLI
Liturgiczny, Ruch Biblijny i ETL, IZBG, NTA
Liturgie, Bibel und ETL, NTA
Liturgie, Paroisse et IZBG
Liturgie, Tijdschrift voor IZBG
Liturgie und Monchtum ETL, IZBG
Liturgiewissenschaft, Archiv fur B, ETL, IBHR, IZBG, RE
Liturgik und Hymnologie, Jahrbuch fur B, IOB, RE
Liturgiques, Questions RE
Liturgisches Jahrbuch B, RE

Liv, Tro och IOB
Living, Learning for RTA
Living, Psychology for UMPI
Living, Studies in Christian UMPI
Living Light CPLI
Living Word CPLI
Ljubliana, Acta Archaeologica IZBG
Logos RPI
Loir, Bulletin de la Societe Archeologique D' Eure et RE
Loire Atlantique, Bulletin de la Societe Archeologie et Historique de Nantes et de RE
Lois et Ordonnances de Belgique, Bulletin de la Commission Royale de Anciennes RE
Lombarda, Arte RE
Lombardo, Archivio Storico RE
Lombardo di Scienze e Lettere, Rendiconti dell' Istituto RE
London (Africa) IOB
London (Sobornost) IOB, NTA
London (Tablet) CPLI
London News, Illustrated B
Loon, Oude Land van RE
Lore and Philosophy, Journal of Jewish B
Lorrain, Pays RE
Lorraine, Annuaire de la Societe D' Histoire et D' Archeologie de la
Losen, Var IOB
Lot Bulletin de la Societe des Etudes Litteraires, Scientifiques et Artistiques du RE
Louvain, Revue Philosophique de CPLI, ETI, RE
Louvain, Revue Theologique de RE
Louvain Studies CPLI, NTA
Louvre et des Museede Frome, Revue du B, IBHP
Louvre et des Musees de France, Revue du RE
Lovanienses, Ephemerides Theologicae ETL, IZBG, NTA, RE
Lovaniensia, Orientalia et Biblica B, IZBG
Lovaniensia Biblica et Orientalia, Analecta B, IZBG
Lovaniensia Periodica, Orientalia B
Lown Institute for Judaiistic Studies IZBG
Lubelskiego, Zeszyty Naukowe Katolickiego Uniwersytetu B, RE
Lulianos, Estudios RE
Lumen ETI, IOB
Lumen (Madrid) IOB
Lumen Vitae CPLI, ETL, IZBG

Lumiere et Vie CPLI, ETL, IZBG, RE

Lumiere et Vie, Collection IZBG
Lund Coniectanea Biblica, New Testament Series IZBG
Lunds Universitets Arsskrift IZBG
Lund, Coniectanea Biblica B
Lusitania Sacra RE
Luther, Kirke og ICB
Luther Jahrbuch RE
Luther Universitat Halle Wittenberg, Wissenschaftliche Zeitschrift der Martin IBHR, IZBG
Luther Universitat Halte Wittenberg, Wissenschaftliche Zeitschrift der Martin RERE
Lutheran GSSRPL, RPI
Lutheran Forum RPI
Lutheran Quarterly ETL, IRPL, IZBG, RPI
Lutheran Standard GSSRPL, RPI
Lutheran Theological Seminary Review SISPL
Lutheran Witness GSSRPL, RPI
Lutheran World IRPI, IRPL
Luther-Bundes, Jahrbuch des Martin IOB
Lutheriennes, Positions B, IOB, IZBG
Lutherische Monatshefte ETL, IZBG, NTA
Lutherische Rundschau ETL, NTA
Lutherischen Weltbundes, Offizieller Bericht der Vollversammlung des Iob
Lux, Jaarbericht van het Vooraziatisch Egyptisch Genootschap ex Oriente IBHR
Lux, Jaarbericht van het Vooraziatisch Egyptisch Genotschap ex Oriente IZBG
Lux, Jarrbericht van het Vooraziatisch Egyptisch Genootschap ex Oriente B
Lux", Mededlingen en Verhandelingen van het Vooraziatisch-Egytisch Genootschap "ex Oriente ETL
Luxembourg, Annales de l' Institut Archeologique du RE
Luxembourg, Publications de la Section Historique de l' Institut Ducal de RE
Luxemburger Geschichte, Hemecht. Zeitschrift fur RE
Maasfouw RE
Maatschappij voor Geschiedenis en Oudheidkunde Te Gent, Handelingen der RE
Mabillon, Revue RE
Madrid (Augustinus) B, ICB
Madrid (Lumen) ICB

Maestricht, Publications de la Societe Historique et Archologique dans Le Limbourg a RE

Magazine, Center GSSRPL
Magazine, Church Library RPI
Magazine, Church Recreation SBPI
Magazine, Eternity CPI, GSSRPL, RPI
Magazine, Extension CPLI, RPI
Magazine, Hadassah IJP
Magazine, Israel IJP
Magazine, Self-Realization RPI
Magazine of the Protestant Episcopal Church, Historical RPI
Magizine, Burlington RE
Mahrebini, Studi IBHR
Maine, Province du RE
Mainzer Zeitschrift RE
Maison Dieu ETL, NTA, RE
Malte, Annales de l' Ordre Souverain Militaire de RE
Man, Church IRPL, RPI
Man, the Journal of the Royal Anthropologist Institute IBHR
Man, the Journal of the Royal Anthropologist Institute IBHR
Manresa (Bibbas) NTA
Manuscripta CPLI, RE
Marburger Theologische Studien IZBG
Maria, Ave CPLI, RPI
Maria, Studi Storici dell' Ordine dei Servi di RE
Marian Studies B, CPLI
Marianles, Bulletin de la Societe Francaise D' Etudes B
Marianos, Estudios B
Marianum ETL, NTA, RE
Marinie, Bulletin Trimestriel de la Societe Academique des Antiquaires de la RE
Mariologicae, Ephemerides ETL, NTA, RE
Mariologische Studien B
Marne Memoires de la Societe D' Agriculture, Commerce, Sciences et
Marriage CPLI, RPI
Marriage and the Family, Journal of GSSRPL, IOB
Martin Luther Universitat Halle Wittenberg, Wissenschaftliche Zeitschrift der IBHR, IZBG
Martin Luther Universitat Halte Wittenberg, Wissenschaftliche Zeitschrift der RERE
Martin Luther-Bundes, Jahrbuch des IOB

Marx Universitat, Wissenschaftliche Zeitschrift der Karl
Re IZBG

Masses Ouvrieres IOB
Materialdienst des Konfessionskundlichen Instituts B, IOB
Materiali di Storia della Religioni, Studi e B, ETL, IBHR, IZBG, RE
Matrimoniale e Dello Stato Delle Persone, Rivista del Diritto ETL
Mature Years UMPI
McCormick Quarterly IBPL, RPI
Mechliniensia, Collectanea ETL, IOB, IZBG, NTA
Mededeelingen der Vereeniging tot Uitgaff der Bronnen van het Oud Vaderlandsche Recht, Verslagen en RE
Mededelingen Betreffende de Geschiedenis der Nederlanden, Bijdragen en RE
Mededelingen Uitger Docr de Vereniging Gelre, Bijdragen en RE
Mededelingen van de Leiegouw, Verslagen en RE
Mededlingen en Verhandelingen van het Vooraziatisch-Egytisch Genootschap "ex Oriente Lux" ETL
Mededlingen van de Geschiedenis en Oudheidkundige Kring voor Leuven en Omgeving ETL, RE
Mededlingen van het Nederlands Historie Instituut Te Rome RE
Mediaeval and Renaissance RE
Mediaeval Scandinavia RE
Mediaeval Studies RE
Mediaeval Studies, Nottingham RE
Mediaevale, Annuale RE
Mediaevalia, Classica et RE
Medicine Hebraique, Revue de l' Histoire de la IBHR, IZBG
Medieval and Renaissance History, Studies in RE
Medieval Archaeology RE
Medieval Studies B, IBHR
Medievale, Bulletin de Theologie Ancienne et IZBG, RE
Medievale, Cahiers de Civilisation B, RE
Medievale, Recherches de Theclogie Ancienne et ETL, IZBG, NTA, RE
Medievales, Anuario de Estudios RE
Medievali, Studi RE
Medievalia et Humanistica RE

Medii Aevi. Bulletin du Cange, Archivum Latinitatis RE

Medio Evo e Archivio Muratoriano, Bullettino dell' Istituto Storico Italiano per Il RE
Medioevale, Rivista di Cultura Classica e RE

Medioevale e Umanistica, Italaia RE
Mediolatini e Volgari, Studi RE
Mediterranee, Revue de l' Occident Musulman et de la IBHF
Medium Aevum RE
Melanges D' Archeologie et D' Histoire RE
Melanges D' Archeologie et D' Historier de l' Ecole Francaise de Rome IBHR
Melanges de l' Institut Dominicain D' Etudes Orientales E, IZBG
Melanges de l' Instiut Domincain D' Etudes Orientales de Caire RE
Melanges de l' Universite St. Joseph E, IBHR, IZBG, RE
Melanges de la Casa de Velazquez RE
Melanges de Science Religieuse ETL, IZBG, NTA, RE
Melita Theologica ETL, IZBG, NTA
Memoires de la Federation der Societes D' Histoire et D' Archeologie de l' Aisne RE
Memoires de la Federation des Societes Historie et Archeologie de Paris et de l' Ile de France RE
Memoires de la Societe Archeologie et Historique de la Charente RE
Memoires de la Societe D' Agriculture, Commerce, Sciences et Arts, du Departement de la Marne RE
Memoires de la Societe D' Agriculture, Commerce, Sciences et Arts, du Departement de la Marne RE
Memoires de la Societe Pour l' Histoire du Droit et des Institutions des Anciens Pays Bourguignons, Comtois et Romands RE
Memoires de la Societe Pour l' Histoire du Droit et des Institutions des Anciens Pays Bourguignons, Comtois et Romands RE
Memoires du Centre de Recherche D' Histoire et Civilisation Byzantines, Travaux et RE
Memoirs de la Societe Archeologique du Department D' Ille et Vilaine, Bulletin et RE
Memorie de Deputazione di Storia Patria per Le Antiche Provincie Modenesi, Atti e RE
Memorie de Deputazione di Storia Patria per Le Province di Romagna, Atti e RE

Memorie de Societa Istriana di Archeologia e Storia Patria, Atti e RE
Memorie Storiche Forogiuliesi RE
Mennonite GSSRPL, ICB, RPI
Mennonite Quarterly Review IRPL, RPI
Mens, Nieuwe IOB
Men's Journal, Baptist SBPI
Menschen, Wege zum ETL, IOB
Mensile di Israel, Rassegna B, IBHR, IZBG
Mercaturae, Scripta RE
Message, Franciscan RPI
Messager de l' Exauchat de Patriarche Russe en Europe Occidentale ICB
Messager Orthodoxe IOB
Messenger GSSRPL, RPI
Messenger, Church RPI
Messenger, St. Anthony CPLI, RPI
Messenger, Toledo Archdiocesan RPI
Metaphysiqye et de Morale, Revue de RE
Methodist History IRPL, RPI
Methodist Story UMPI
Methodist Student UMPI
Methodist Student, United (Series) UMPI
Methodist Teacher UMPI
Methodist Teacher, United (Series) UMPI
Methodist Woman UMPI
Metodista, Accion UMPI
Metonoia GSSRPL, RPI
Metropolis, Church in IOB
Metropolitan Museum of Art Bulletin RE
Mhacha, Seanchas Ard RE
Micenci Ed Egec-Anatolici, Studi IBHR
Mid America CPLI, RE
Middle East Journal GSSRPL
Middle East Review, Jewish Observer and IJP
Middle East Studies Association Bulletin IBHR
Midi, Annales du RE
Migration Today ICB
Migrations ICB
Mikra, Beth B
Milano, Annali del Facolta di Filosofia e Letter di UN-Versita Statale de RE
Milarbeit IOB
Militaire de Malte, Annales de l' Ordre Souverain RE
Ministerium (Holland) B
Ministry IOB
Ministry, Christian GSSRPL, RPI

Ministry, Music SISPL, UMPI

Minorum, Analecta Ordinis Fratrum ETL
Misao, Pravoslavna IBHR, IOB
Miscelanea Comillas ETL, IZBG, NTA, RE
Miscelanea de Estudios Arabes y Hebreos B
Miscellanea Franciscana RE
Mision Avierta al Servicio de al Fe B
Misiones Extranjeras IOB
Misjon, Norsk Tidsskrift for IOB
Missao, Igreja e IOB
Missie, Kerk en ETL
Missie Integraal IOB
Missiewerk IOB
Mission, Eglise et ETL
Mission, Jahrbuch Evangelischer IOB
Mission, Parole et B, IBHR
Mission, World CPLI, IOB
Mission Review, Episcopal Overseas IOB
Missionalia, Studia RE
Missionalia Hispanica RE
Missionamagazin, Evangelishas IOB
Missionary Bulletin, Japan IOB
Missionary Research Library IOB, RE
Missionejahrbuch der Schweiz, Katholisches IOB
Missionen, Katholischen IOB
Missioni Cattoliche IOB
Missions, Home SBPI
Missions, International Review of B, CPI, ETL, IBHR, IRPL, RPI, RTA
Missionswissenschaft, Neue Zeitschrift fur IZBG, RE
Missionwissenschaft und Religionswissenschaft, Zeitschrift fur ETL, IRPL, RE
Mistica, Rassegna di Ascetica e B
Mistica, Rivista di Ascetica e ETL, NTA
Mitropolia Ardealului IOB
Mitropolia Banatului IOB
Mitropolia Moldavei si Sucevei IOB, RE
Mitropolia Oltenici IOB, RE
Mitteilungen, Baghader B, IBHR
Mitteilungen, Neuphilologische RE
Mitteilungen, Revue D' Histoire RE
Mitteilungen, Romische Historische RE
Mitteilungen aus Iran, Archaeologische B
Mitteilungen der Deutschen Orient-Gesellschaft IZBG
Mitteilungen des Instituts fur Orientforschung B, IBHR, IZBG

Mitteilungen des Instituts fur Osterreichesche Geschichtsforschung RE
Mitteilungen des Oesterreichischen Staatsarchivs RE
Mitteilungen und Forschungsbeitrage der Cusanus Gesellschaft RE
Mitteilungen Zur Geschichte des Benediktiner Ordens und Seiner Zweige, Studien und RE
Mitteilunger der Deutschen Orient Gesellschaft B, IBHR
Mitteilunger des Deutschen Archaeologischen Instituts B, IBHR
Mittelalters, Deutsches Archiv fur der Erforschung des B, RE
Mittelingen und Ostdeutschlands, Jahrbuch fur die Geschichte RE
Mittellanteinisches Jahrbuch RE
Mittelrheinische Kirchengeschichte, Archiv fur IOB, RE
Mittelungen, Iranistische IBHR
Mnemosyne RE
Modenesi, Atti e Memorie de Deputazione di Storia Patria per Le Antiche Provincie RE
Modern African Studies, Journal of GSSRPL
Modern Churchman B, ETL, IRPI, NTA
Modern History, Journal of RE
Modern Language Association, Publications of the RE
Modern Language Notes IZBG, RE
Modern Language Quarterly RE
Modern Language Review RE
Modern Philology RE
Modern Schoolman CPLI, RE
Modern Society CPLI
Modern Studies, Renaissance and RE
Moderna, Arte Antica e RE
Moderne et Contemporaine, Bulletin de la Section D' Historie RE
Moderne et Contemporaine, Revue D' Histoire RE
Moderno, Oriente IBHR
Molad IZBG
Moldavei si Sucevei, Mitropolia IOB, RE
Momentum CPLI
Monastic Studies CPLI
Monastica, Studia RE
Monatshefte, Lutherische ETL, IZBG, NTA
Monatsschrift, Germanisch Romanische RE
Monchtum, Liturgie und ETL, IZBG
Monde, Justice dans de ETL

Monde Juie. la Revue du Centre de Documentation Juife Contemporaine IZBG

Mondiale, Cahiers D' Historie B, IBHR, RE
Monitor Ecclesiasticus ETL
Monographien, Stuttgarter Biblische IZBG
Monographien zum Alten und Neuen Testament, Wissenschaftliche ETL, IZBG
Month CPLI, ETL, NTA, RE
Monthly, Clergy NTA, RTA
Monthly, Concordia Theological CPI, ETL, IRPL, IZBG, NTA, RPI, RTA
Monthly, Moody CPI, GSSRPL
Monthly, National Jewish IJP
Monthly Letter About Evangelism IOB
Montis Reglii, Studia ETL
Monumental, Bulletin RE
Monuments Histcruques de la France RE
Moody Monthly CPI, GSSRPL
Morale, Revista di Teologia B
Morale, Revue de Metaphysiqye et de RE
Morales et Politiques, Academie Revue de Belgique. Bulletin de la Classe des Lettres et des Sciences RE
Morali, Canonica, Liturgica Periodica de Re RE
Morali, Rendiconti de Scienze IZBG
Moralia, Studia B
More, Moreana. Bulletin Theomas RE
Moreana. Bulletin Theomas More RE
Morgenlandes, Wiener Zeitschrift fur Kunde des B, ETL, IZBG
Morgenlandischen Gesellschaft, Zeitschrift der Deutschen ETL, IZBG, NTA, RE
Moriales, Etudes B
Moskauer Patriarchats, Journal des IZBG
Moskovskoj Patriarchii, Zurnal B, IBHR
Motive GSSPRL, RPI
Moyen Age RE
Moyen Age, Archives D' Historie Doctrinale et Litteraire du B
Moyen Age Cahiers Archeologiques, Fin de l' Antiquite et RE
Moyen Age Latina, Revue du RE
Munchener Studien Zur Sprachwissenschaft B, IBHR
Munchener Theologische Zeitschrift ETL, IZBG, NTA, RE
Mundi, Imago RE
Munster (Catholica) ETL, NTA

Munster, Zeitschrift fur Christliche Kunst und Kunstwissenschaft IOB, RE

Munster, Zeitschrift fur Christliche Kunst und Kunstwissenschaft IOB, RE
Munus, Perfice ETL
Muratoriano, Bullettino dell' Istituto Storico Italiano per Il Medio Evo e Archivio RE
Musart CPLI
Musee de Beyrouth, Bulletin du B
Museede Frome, Revue du Louvre et des B, IBHR
Museen, Jahrbuch der Berliner RE
Musees de France, Revue du Louvre et des RE
Musees de Geneve IBHR
Musees de Poitiers, Bulletin de la Societe des Antiquaires de l' Ouest et des RE
Musees Royaux D' Art et D' Histoire, Bulletin des RE
Musees Royaux des Beaus Arts de Belgique, Bulletin des RE
Museon ETL, IZBG, NTA, RE
Museos Revista de Archivos, Bibliotecas y RE
Museum fur Philologie, Rheinisches IZBG
Museum fur Volkunde in Dresden, Abhandlungen und Berichte des Staatlichen IBHR
Museum Helveticum B
Museum of Art Bulletin, Metropolitan RE
Museum of Far Eastern Antiquities, the IBHR
Museum of Far Eastern Antiquities, the IBHR
Museums fur Volkenbunder zu Leipzig, Jahrbuch des IBHR
Music, Journal of Church RPI
Music, Musica Disciplina. a Yearbook of the History of RE
Music, Sacred CPLI, RPI
Music Ministry SISPL, UMPI
Music the Acts, Response in Worship IOB
Musica Disciplina. a Yearbook of the History of Music RE
Musicologie, Revue Belge de RE
Musik und Altar IOB
Musik und Kirche IOB
Muslim World IFPL, RPI
Musulman et de la Mediterranee, Revue de l' Occident IBHR
Muzea Koscielne Archiwa, Biblioteki RE
Mysterium ETL, IZBG, NTA
Mystiche Theologie, Jahrbuch fur ETL

Mystique, Revue D' Ascetique et de ETL, IZBG, NTA, RE
Nabozenska Revue IOB
Nachbargebiete, Trierer Zeitschrift fur Geschichte und Kunst des Trierer Landes und Seiner RE
Nachrichten der Akademie der Wissenschaften in Gottingen RE
Nachrichten der Akademie der Wissenschaften zu Gottingen B
Namenforschung, Beitraege Zur B
Namur, Annales de la Societe Archeologique de RE
Namur, Revue Diocesaine de ETL
Namurcum RE
Nantes et de Loire Atlantique, Bulletin de la Societe Archeologie et Historique de RE
Napoletane, Archivio Storico per Le Province RE
Napoli, Annali del' Istituto Orientale di B, ETL, IBHR, IZBG
Narodov Azii, Kratkie Soobscenija Institute IZBG
Nasza Przeszlosc RE
National Catholic Education Association Bulletin CPLI
National Catholic Guidance Conference Journal CPLI, RPI
National Catholic Reporter CPLI
National Christian Council Review IOB
National Geographic B
National Guild of Catholic Psychiatrists Bulletin CPLI
National Jewish Monthly IJP
Nationale des Antiquaires de France, Bulletin de la Societe RE
Natural Law Forum CPLI
Naturaleza y Gracia B
Naturforschenden Gesleischaft in Basel, Verhandlungen der IBHR
Naukoeych Oraz Kronika, Sprawozdania Z Czynnosci Wydawniczej i Posiedzen RE
Naukowe Katolickiego Uniwersytetu Lubelskiego, Zeszyty B, RE
Nazionale D' Archeologia e Storia dell' Arte, Rendiconti dell' Istituto RE
Nazionale dei Lincei, Rendiconti della Academia IBHR
Nazionale Italiana, Bibliografia RE
Near East Council of Churches IOB
Near East Reporter IJP

Near Eastern Society of Columbia, Journal of Ancient B, SISPL

Near Eastern Studies, Journal of ETL, IZBG, NTA, RPI
Nederduitse Gereformeerde Teologiese Tydskrif B, IBHR, IZBG
Nederland, Archief voor de Geschiedenis van de Katholieke Kerk in ETL, IOB, RE
Nederland, Jaarboek Werkgenootschap van Katholieke Theologen in B
Nederland, Werkgenootschap voor Katholieke Theologen in ETL, IOB
Nederlanden, Bijdragen en Mededelingen Betreffende de Geschiedenis der RE
Nederlands Archief voor Kerkgeschiedenis IOB, RE
Nederlands Archievenblad RE
Nederlands Historie Instituut Te Rome, Mededlingen van het RE
Nederlands Katholische Stemmen ETL
Nederlands Kunsthistorisch Jaarboek RE
Nederlands Theologisch Tijdschrift ETL, IRPL, IZBG, NTA, RE
Nederlands Tijdschrift voor Wijsbegeerte en Psychologie, Algemeen ETL
Nederlandse Tall en Letterkunde, Tijdschrift voor RE
Neerlandica, Acta Historiae RE
Neolatina, Cultura RE
Neophilologica, Studia RE
Neophilologus RE
Neoscolastica, Rivista di Filosofia RE
Neotestamentica, Coniectanea IZBG
Neotestamentici Upsaliensis, Acta Seminarii ETL, IZBG
Neotestamentici Upsaliensis, Nuntius Sodalicii IZBG
Neue Ordnung ETL, IOB
Neue Rundschau IOB
Neue Testament, Theologisches Worterbuch zum B
Neue Testament, Wissenschafliche Untersuchungen zum B
Neue Testamente, Grande Lessico del B
Neue Zeitschrift fur Missionswissenschaft IZBG, RE
Neue Zeitschrift fur Systematische Theologie und Religionsphilosophie ETL, IRPL
Neue Zeitschrift fur Systematische Theologie und Religionsphilosophie Re

Neue Zeitschrift fur Systematische Theologie und Religionsphilosophie RTA
Neuen Testament, Beitraege Zur Wissenschaft Vom Alten und IZBG
Neuen Testament, Butraege Zur Wissenschaft von Alten und B
Neuen Testament, Kommentare und Beitrage zum Alten und (Dusseldorf) B
Neuen Testament, Studien zum Alten und IZBG
Neuen Testament, Wissenschaftliche Monographien zum Alten und ETL, IZBG
Neuen Testament, Wissenschaftliche Untersuchungen zum IZBG
Neuen Testaments, Abhandlungen Zur Theologie des Alten und B, IZBG
Neuen Testaments, Forschungen Zur Religion und Literatur des Alten und B, IZBG
Neuen Testaments, Studien Zur Umwelt des IZBG
Neueren Sprachen und Literaturen, Archiv fur das Studium der RE
Neues Forum IOB
Neukirchener Studienbucher ETL
Neuphilologische Mitteilungen RE
Neutestamentliche Abhandlungen IBHR, IZBG
Neutestamentliche Wissenschaft, Zeitschrift fur die ETL, IRPL, IZBG, NTA, RE, RTA
Neutestamentlichen Textforschung, Arbeiten Zur IZBG
New Blackfriars CPLI, ETL
New Book Review RPI
New Christian IOB
New City CPLI
New Creation UMPI
New Creation Leaders Guide UMPI
New Creation Resource Packet UMPI
New Scholasticism CPLI, ETL, RE
New Testament, Theological Dictionary of the B
New Testament Abstracts IZBG
New Testament Studies CPI, ETL, IRPL, IZBG, NTA, RE, RPI
New World Outlook RPI
New York (Dialog) ETL, IOB, IRPL, RPI
New York (Information Service) IOB
New York Public Library, Bulletin of the RE
Newman-Studien IOB
News, Illustrated London B
News, Southwestern SBPI
News Digest, Official RPI

News from Israel, Christian IOB, IZBG
Newsletter, Accrediting Association of Bible Colleges SISPL
Newsletter, Bible Science SISPL
Newsletter, National Council of Churches Committee on the Church and Jewish People IOB, SBPI
Newsletter, West African Archaeolcgical IBHR
Newsletter, National Council of Churches Committee on the Church and Jewish People IOB, SBPI
Newton Quarterly, Andover B, ETL, IBHR, IRPL, IZBG, NTA, RTA, SISPL
Niederdeutsche Beitrage Zur Kunstgeschichte RE
Niederosterreich, Jahrbuch fur Landeskunde voor RE
Niedersachsische Kirchengeschichte, Jahrbuch der Gesellschaft fur RE
Niedersachsisches Jahrbuch fur Landesgeschichte RE
Niererrhein, Annalen der Historischen Vereins fur der RE
Nieuwe Mens IOB
Night, Sunday UMPI
Noire, Bulletin de l' Institut Fondamentale D' Afrique IBHR
Nomata, St. NTA
Non Christianis, Bulletin Secretariatus pro B, IOB
Nord, Revue du RE
Nordisk Tidsskrift for Bok och Biblioteksvasen RE
Normale Superiore di Pisa, Annali della Scuola B, RE
Normandie, Bulletin de la Societe des Antiquaires de RE
Norsk Teologisk Tidsckrift ETL
Norsk Teologisk Tidsskrift ETL, IRPL, IZBG, NTA
Norsk Tidsskrift for Misjon IOB
Norsk Videnskaps Akademi i Oslo, Avhandlinger Utgitt Av Det IZBG
Norske Videnskaps Akademie i Oslo, Skrifter Utgitt Av Det IZBG
North American Liturgical Week CPLI
Northwest Semitic Languages, Journal of the B
Notes, Ecumenical IOB
Notes, Epworth UMPI
Notes, Modern Language IZBG, RE
Notes Africaines IBHR
Notes on Translation SISPL
Noticias Cristianas de Israel IZBG
Notre Catechese IZBG
Notre Dame Journal of Education CPLI

Nottingham Mediaeval Studies RE

Nouva Rivista Storica RE
Nouvelle Revue Theologique CPLI, ETL, IZBG, NTA, RE

Nouvelles Chretiennes D' Israel B
Nova et Vetera ETL, IZBG, NTA
Nova et Vetera (Suisse) B, ETL
Novare RE
Novum Testamentum ETL, IRPL, IZBG, NTA, RE, RTA
Numen IZBG, RE
Numen, International Review for the History of Religions ETL, IRPL, NTA
Numen, International Review for the History of Religions ETL, IRPL, NTA
Numismatic Chronicle RE
Numismatic Chronicle and Journal B
Numismatica e Scienze Affini, Rivista Italiana di RE
Numismatik und Geldgeschichte, Jahrbuch fur B, RE
Numismatique, Actes du Congres International de B
Numismatique, Revue B, RE
Numismatique et de Sigillographie, Revue Belge de RE
Nunc et Senyser IOB
Nuntius Sodalicii Neotestamentici Upsaliensis IZBG
Nuovo Testamento, Commenti Spirituali dell' Antico Testamento del B
Nursery Days UMPI
Ny Kyrklig Tidsskrift ETL, IZBG
Oaks Papers, Dumbarton B
Oberbayerisches Archiv RE
Oberrheins, Zeitschrift fur die Geschichte des RE
Observer, Ethiopia IOB
Observer and Middle East Review, Jewish IJP
Occasional Bulletin SISPL
Occident Musulman et de la Mediterranee, Revue de l' IBHR
Occidentale, Messager de l' Exauchat de Patriarche Russe en Europe Iob
Occidentalis, Slavia RE
Odrodzenie i Reformacja W Polsce RE
Oecumene IOB
Oecumene, Kosmos en IOB
Oecumenica B
Oecumenique, Recontre IOB
Oekumenische Diskussion IOB
Oekumenische Rundschau B, IOB

Oestereichischen Akademie der Wissenschaften, Anzeiger der RE

Oesterreicheschen Akademie der Wissenschaften, Sitzungsberichte der IZBG
Oesterreichische Bibliographie RE

Oesterreichische Zeitschrift fur Kunst und Denkmalpflege RE
Oesterreichischen Akademie der Wissenschaften, Sitzungsberichte der Re
Oesterreichischen Staatsarchivs, Mitteilungen des RE
Oesterreichisches Archiv fur Kirchenrecht ETL, ICB, RE
Oesterreichisches Klerusblatt ETL
Official News Digest RPI
Offizieller Bericht der Vollversammlung des Lutherischen Weltbundes Iob
Oikoumenikon ICB
Oltenici, Mitropolia IOB, RE
Omgeving, Mededlingen van de Geschiedenis en Oudheidkundige Kring voor Leuven en ETL, RE
Onder de Benaming Societe D' Emulation de Bruges, Handeling van het Genootschap voor Geschiedenis Gesticht RE
One Church RPT
One Geestelijk Ieven B
One/Two UMPI
Ons Geestelijk IOB
Oosten, Christelijk B, IOB, RE
Op het Oude Testament, Commentaar B
Opinion, American GSSRPL
Opuscula Atheniensia IBHR
Oratorium RE
Oraz Kronika, Sprawozdania Z Czynnosci Wydawniczej i Posiedzen Naukoeych RE
Orbis Catholicus IZBG
Ordens Korrespondenz B
Ordens und Seiner Zweige, Studien und Mitteilungen Zur Geschichte des Benediktiner RE
Order, World RPI
Order Trends, Faith and IOB
Ordine dei Servi di Maria, Studi Storici dell' RE
Ordinis Cistercienis, Analecta Sacri ETL
Ordinis Fratrum Minorum, Analecta ETL
Ordinis Fratrum Praedicatorum, Analecta Sacri ETL
Ordnung, Neue ETL, IOB

Ordonnances de Belgique, Bulletin de la Commission Royale de Anciennes Lois et RE
Ordre Souverain Militaire de Malte, Annales de l' RE
Oridinis Cistericciensium Reformatorum, Collectanea ETL
Oriens IZBG, RE
Oriens Antiquus IZBG
Oriens Christianus IZBG, RE
Orient, Journal of Economic and Social History of the B
Orient, Journal of the Economic and Social History of the RE
Orient, Parole de l' B, IZBG, RE
Orient Chretien, Proche RE
Orient Gesellschaft, Mitteilunger der Deutschen B, IBHR
Orient Syrien ETL, IZBG, NTA
Orient und Altes Testament, Alter B, IZBG
Oriental and African Studies, Bulletin of the School of RE
Oriental Institute Communications B
Oriental Research, Annual of the American School of IZBG
Oriental Research, Bulletin of the American Schools of B, ETL, IBHR, IZBG, NTA, SISPL
Oriental Society, Journal of American IZBG
Oriental Society Transactions, Glasgow University B
Oriental Studies, Pretoria ETL
Orientale, Archivio Storico per la Sicilia RE
Orientale, Bulletin de l' Institut Francais D' Archeologie IZBG
Orientale, Bulletin del' Institut Francais D' Archeologie B, IBHR
Orientale di Napoli, Annali del' Istituto B, ETL, IBHR, IZBG
Orientales, Estudios de Filosofia y Religion B
Orientales, Melanges de l' Institut Dominicain D' Etudes B, IZBG
Orientales de Caire, Melanges de l' Instiut Domincain D' Etudes RE
Orientales et Slaves, Annuaire de l' Institut de Philologie et D' Historie B, IBHR
Orientali, Revista degli Studi IZBG
Orientali, Rivista degli Studi B, ETL, IBHR, RE
Orientali, Studi Classici e B, IBHR
Orientalia ETL, IZBG, NTA, RE

Orientalia, Analecta IZBG
Orientalia, Analecta Lovaniensia Biblica et B, IZBG
Orientalia, Folia IBHR
Orientalia, Studia B, IBHR, IZBG
Orientalia Budapest, Acta IZBG
Orientalia Christiana, Studia B, RE
Orientalia Christiana Periodica ETL, NTA, RE, RTA
Orientalia et Biblica Lovaniensia B, IZBG
Orientalia Lovaniensia Periodica B
Orientalia Suecana B, IBHR
Orientalias, Biblica et B
Orientalis, Ars IBHR
Orientalis, Bibliotheca ETL, IZBG, NTA
Orientalis de Institut Francais, Bulletin D' Etudes IBHR
Orientalistes, Actes du Congres International des B
Orientalistik, Handbuch der B
Orientalistische Literaturzeitung ETL, IZBG, NTA, RE
Orientalistyczny, Przeglad B, IZBG
Orientalistyczny, Roczniki IZBG
Orientalium, Corpus Scriptorum Christianorum B
Orientalni, Archiv B, ETL, IBHR, IZBG, RE
Oriente, Bibbia e ETL, IZBG, NTA
Oriente Christiano IOB
Oriente Lux, Jaarbericht van het Vooraziatisch Egyptisch Genootschap ex IBHR
Oriente Lux, Jaarbericht van het Vooraziatisch Egyptisch Genctschap ex IZBG
Oriente Lux, Jarrbericht van het Vooraziatisch Egyptisch Genootschap ex B
Oriente Lux", Mededlingen en Verhandelingen van het Vooraziatisch-Egytisch Genootschap "ex ETL
Oriente Moderno IBHR
Orientforschung, Archiv fur B, ETL, IZBG
Orientforschung, Mitteilungen des Instituts fur B, IBHR, IZBG
Orient-Gesellschaft, Mitteilungen der Deutschen IZBG
Orientierung ETL, NTA
Orients, Welt des IZBG
Orpheus. Rivista di Umanita Classica e Cristiana RE
Orthodox Church RPI
Orthodox Life RPI
Orthodox Theological Review, Greek IRPL, RPI
Orthodox Word RPI

Orthodox Work, Ukrainian RPI
Orthodoxe, Messager IOB
Orthodoxe, Presence B
Orthodoxia IOB
Orthodoxie, Stimme der B, IOB
Ortodoxa Romana, Biserica IOB
Oslo, Avhandlinger Utgitt Av Det Norsk Videnskaps Akademi i IZBG
Oslo (Historisk Tidsskrift) RE
Oslo, Skrifter Utgitt Av Det Norske Videnskaps Akademie i IZBG
Osloenses, Symbolae B, IBHR, IZBG
Osservatore, l' CPLI
Ostdeutschlands, Jahrbuch fur die Geschichte Mittelingen und RE
Osten, Kirche Im RE
Osterreichesche Geschichtsforschung, Mitteilungen des Instituts fur Re
Osterreichische Geschichte, Archiv fur RE
Osterreichische Zeitschrift fur Volkskunde IBHR
Osterreichischen Byzantinistichen Gesellschaft, Jahrbuch der IOB
Osterreichischin Byzantinistik, Jahrbuch der RE
Osteruopas, Kyrios. Vierteljahresschrift fur Kirchen und Geistesgeschichte RE
Osteuropa IOE
Osteuropaischen Geschichte, Forschungen Zur RE
Osteuropas, Jahrbuch fur Geschichte IOB
Osteuropas, Jahrbucher fur Geschichte RE
Ostforschung, Zeitschrift fur RE
Ostkirchliche Studien ETL, NTA, RE
Other Side SISPL
Ottawa, Revue de l' Universite D' CPLI, ETL, IZBG, RE
Oud Holland RE
Oud Vaderlandsche Recht, Verslagen en Mededeelingen der Vereeniging tot Uitgaff der Bronnen van het RE
Oude Land van Loon RE
Oude Tectament, Boeken van het B
Oude Testament, Commentaar op het B
Oudheidkunde, Gentse Bijdragen tot de Kunstgeschiedenis en de RE
Oudheidkunde Te Gent, Handelingen der Maatschappij voor Geschiedenis en RE
Oudheidkundige Kring voor Leuven en Omgeving, Mededlingen van de Geschiedenis en ETL, RE
Oud-Katholiek IOB

Oudtestamentische Studien B, IZBG

Ouest et des Musees de Poitiers, Bulletin de la Societe des Antiquaires de l' RE
Ou-Testamentiese Werkgemeenskap van Suid-Afrika IZBG
Outlook SBPI
Outlook, New World RPI
Outlook, Presbyterian RPI
Outlook, World IOB
Outreach SBPI
Ouvrieres, Masses IOB
Overseas Mission Review, Episcopal IOB
Oxoniensia RE
Pacific, Folk Religion and the Worldview in the South Western IBHR
Packet, New Creation Resource UMPI
Packet, Real Resource UMPI
Padogogik, Schriften des Deutschen Instituts fur Wissenschaftlishe
Paedagogica Historica RE
Pages Documentaires IOB
Pain, Parole et ETL
Palabra de Clero ETL, NTA
Palabra Inspirada ETL
Palamas, Gregorios o IOB
Palastina Vereins, Zeitschrift des Deutschen ETL, NTA, RE
Palastinavereins, Zeitschrift Deutschen IZBG
Palestine Exploration Quarterly ETL, IRPL, IZBG, NTA
Palestinskii Sbaornik IZBG
Palestra del Clero IZBG
Palladia. Rivista di Storia dell' Architettura RE
Pantheon. Internationale Zeitschrift fur Kunst RE
Papers, Dumbarton Oaks B
Papers from the Department on Studies in Evangelism, Concept E. IOB
Papyrologica, Studia B, IBHR
Papyrologie, Actes du Congres International de B
Papyrologie, Etudes de B
Papyrologie und Epigraphik, Zeitschrift fur B
Papyrology, American Studies in B
Papyrology, Journal of Juristic B
Papyrusforschung, Archiv fur B
Par l' Institut Francais au Portugal Bulletin des Etudes Portugaises, Publie RE
Paris, Annales de l' Universite de RE

Paris, Archives D' Histoire Doctrinale et
Litteraire du RE

Paris, Bulletin de la Societe de Linguietique de B
Paris et de l' Ile de France, Memoires de la
Federation des Societes Historie et Archeologie
de RE
Parmensi, Archivio Storico per Le Province RE
Paroisse et Liturgie IZBG
Parola del Passato B, IBHR
Parola per l' Assemblea Festiva, la B
Parola per l' Assemblea Festiva, la B
Parole de l' Orient B, IZBG, RE
Parole di Vita B
Parole et Mission B, IBHR
Parole et Pain ETL
Pasitiva Serie Iv, Scuola IBHR
Passato, Parola del B, IBHR
Passer, Gulden RE
Past and Present RE
Pastor Bonus ETL
Pastoral, Collationes Vlaoms Tijdschaft voor
Theologie en B
Pastoral Blatter ETL, NTA
Pastoral Care, Journal of IRPL, RPI
Pastoral Counselor SISPL
Pastoral Life RPI
Pastoral Psychology CPI, GSSRPL, IRPL, RPI, RTA
Pastoral Review, Homiletic and CPLI, NTA
Pastorale au Rwanda et Burundi, Theologie B
Pastorale et Spiritualite, Theologie. ETL
Pastorale Liturgica, Revista di B
Pastoraltheologie, Wissenschaft und Pranxis IOB
Pastoraltheologie, Wissenschaft und Pranxis IOB
Patavina, Studia ETL, NTA, RE
Pathways, Sighted GSSRPL
Patria, Archivio di Societa Romana di Storia RE
Patria, Atti di Societa Ligure di Storia RE
Patria, Atti e Memorie de Societa Istriana
di Archeologia e Storia RE
Patria per Le Antiche Provincie Modenesi, Atti
e Memorie de Deputazione di Storia RE
Patria per Le Province di Romagna, Atti e Memorie
de Deputazione di Storia RE
Patriarchats, Journal des Moskauer IZBG
Patriarche Russe en Europe Occidentale, Messager
de l' Exauchat de Icb
Patriarchii, Zurnal Moskovskoj B, IBHR

Patrimoine Artistique, Bulletin de l' Institut Royal du RE
Patristica, Studia B
Patrologia Latina B
Patterns of Prejudice IJP
Paul and Qumran IBHR
Pauly, Kliene B
Pays Bourguignons, Comtois et Romands Memoires de la Societe Pour l' Histoire du Droit et des Institutions des Anciens RE
Pays de Granville, Revue de l' Anranchin et du RE
Pays et Assemblees D' Etats, Anciens RE
Pays Lorrain RE
Pazmaveb IZBG
Peace Conference, Christian IOB
Pedagogia e Scienze Religiose, Rivista di B
Pedagogic Reporter IJP
Pensamiento RE
Pensamiento Cristiano STSPL
Pensee Catholique, la B
Pensee Catholique, la B
Pentecostal Evangel GSSRPL
People Newsletter, National Council of Churches Committee on the Church and Jewish IOB, SBPI
Perfice Munus ETL
Perigord, Bulletin de la Societe Historique et Archeologique du RE
Periodica, Orientalia Christiana ETL, NTA, RE, RTA
Periodica, Orientalia Lovaniensia B
Periodica de Re Morali, Canonica, Liturgica RE
Periodica de Re Morali, Canonica, Liturgica RE
Periods, Journal for the Study of Judaism in the Persian Helenistic and Roman B
Perkins School of Theology Journal NTA
Persian Helenistic and Roman Periods, Journal for the Study of Judaism in the B
Persone, Rivista del Diritto Matrimoniale e Dello Stato Delle ETL
Perspectiva Teologica B
Perspective IBPL, RPI
Perspectives de Catholicite IOB
Perspektive der Zukunft B
Pfarrerblatt, Deutsches B, IBHR
Pfarrerblatt, Evangelisches IOB
Philadelphia, Records of the American Catholic Historical Society of Re
Philippiana Sacra B
Philippine Studies B, IBHR

Philological Association, Transactions and Proceedings of the American RE

Philological Association Transaction Proceeding, American B
Philological Quarterly RE

Philologie, Anglia. Zeitschrift fur Englische RE
Philologie, de Litterature et D' Histoire Anciennes Revue de RE
Philologie, Hermes. Zeitschrift fur Klassische RE
Philologie, Rheinisches Museum fur IZBG
Philologie, Zeitschrift fur Celtische RE
Philologie, Zeitschrift fur Deutsche RE
Philologie, Zeitschrift fur Slavische RE
Philologie et D' Histoire, Revue Belge de RE
Philologie et D' Historie Orientales et Slaves, Annuaire de l' Institut de B, IBHR
Philologique, Annee B
Philologique et Historique du Comite des Travaux Historiques et scientifiques, Bulletin RE
Philologus. Zeitschrift fur das Klassische Altertum RE
Philology, American Journal of B, IBHR
Philology, Harvard Studies in Classical B, IBHR
Philology, Journal of English and Germanic RE
Philology, Modern RE
Philology, Romance RE
Philology, Studies in RE
Philology, University of California Publications in Classical Archaelogy and Semitic IZBG
Philosophia Reformata IOB, RE
Philosophical Association Proceedings, American Catholic CPLI
Philosophical Review RE
Philosophical Society, Proceedings of the American B
Philosophical Studies CPLI
Philosophie, Archiv fur Geschichte der B, RE
Philosophie, Archives de ETL, RE
Philosophie, Deutsche Zeitschrift fur RE
Philosophie, Revue de Theologie et de ETL, IZBG, NTA, RE
Philosophie, Revue Internationale de RE
Philosophie, Theologie und ETL, IZBG, NTA, RE
Philosophie, Tijdschrift voor RE
Philosophie, Wiener Zeitschrift fur ETL
Philosophie du Droit, Archives de RE

Philosophie et de Theologie, Revue D' Histoire de ETL

Philosophie Religieuses, Revue D' Histoire et de ETL, IFPL, IZBG, NTA, RE
Philosophie und Theologie, Freiburger Zeitschrift fur ETL, NTA, RE

Philosophique, Laval Theologique et ETL, NTA
Philosophique de la France et de l' Etranger, Revue RE
Philosophique de Louvain, Revue CPLI, ETL, RE
Philosophiques, Etudes ETL, RE
Philosophiques et Theologiques, Revue des Sciences B, ETL, IBHR, IZBG, NTA, RE
Philosophische Forschung, Zeitschrift fur ETL, RE
Philosophische Rundschau IBHR
Philosophischer Literaturanzeiger B, RE
Philosophisches Jahrbuch B, RE
Philosophy, Journal of Jewish Lore and B
Philosophy, Journal of the History of RE
Philosophy of Religion, International Journal for the B
Philosophy Today CPLI
Phoenix ETL
Phoibos ETL
Phylon GSSRPI
Piacentino, Bollettino Storico RE
Picardie, Bulletin Trimestriel de la Societe des Antiquaires de RE
Picena, Studia RE
Pieta, Archivio Italiano per la Storia della RE
Pisa, Annali della Scuola Normale Superiore di B, RE
Plain Truth SISPL
Planbook for Adults UMPI
Poitiers, Bulletin de la Societe des Antiquaires de l' Ouest et des Musees de RE
Polish Ecumenical Review IOB
Politics, Review of CPLI, RE
Politiques, Academie Revue de Belgique. Bulletin de la Classe des Iettres et des Sciences Morales et RE
Poloniae Historica, Acta RE
Polsce, Odrodzenie i Reformacja W RE
Polynesian Society, Journal of the IBHR
Pontifica Accademia Romana de Archaeologia, Rendiconti della IBHR

Pontifica Accademia Romana di Archeologia, Reniconti della RE
Pontificia Accademia Romana di Archeologia, Atti della B
Pope Speaks CPLI, RPI
Populaires, Arts et Traditions RE
Porefthendes IOB
Portugaises, Publie Par l' Institut Francais au Portugal Bulletin des Etudes RE
Portugal Bulletin des Etudes Portugaises, Publie Par l' Institut Francais au RE
Posiedzen Naukceych Craz Kronika, Sprawozdania Z Czynnosci Wydawniczej i RE
Positions Lutheriennes B, IOB, IZBG
Posted, Keeping IJP
Pour l' Histoire du Droit et des Institutions des Anciens Pays Bourguignons, Comtois et Romands Memoires de la Societe RE
Practica, Theologia B, ICB
Practical Anthropology CPI, IRPL
Praedicatorum, Analecta Sacri Ordinis Fratrum ETL
Praedicatorum, Archivum Fratrum ETL, RE
Praemonstratensia, Analecta ETL, RE
Praktijk, Theologie in IOB
Praktische Quartalschrift, Theologisch IZBG, RE
Praktische Seelsorge Anima, Vierteljahrsschrift fur IZBG
Pranxis Pastoraltheologie, Wissenschaft und IOB
Pratique des Hautes Etudes, Ecole B, IBHR
Pravoslavna Misao IBHR, ICB
Prawo Kanoniczne RE
Preaching CPLI
Predicador Evangelicio IOB
Prehistorique Francaise, Bulletin de la Societe IBHR
Preistorici, Bollettino del Centro Camuno di Studi IZBG
Prejudice, Patterns of IJP
Presbyterian Alliance and the World Alliance of Reformed Churches, Bulletin of the Department of Theology of the World IOB
Presbyterian History, Journal of IRPL, RPI
Presbyterian Journal SISPI
Presbyterian Life GSSPL, RPI
Presbyterian Outlock RPI
Presbyterian Survey RPI
Presbyterian World, Reformed and IRPL, RPI
Preschool Leadership SBPI

Presence Orthodoxe B
Present, Past and RE
Presente, Teclogia del B
Pretoria Oriental Studies ETL
Priest CPLI
Priloha Krestanske Revue, Theologicka IZBG
Princeton Seminary Bulletin ETL, IRPL, IZBG, RPI
Prism IOB
Probe SBPI
Proceeding, American Philological Association Transaction B
Proceedings, American Catholic Philosophical Association CPLI
Proceedings, Catholic Theological Society of America CPLI
Proceedings of the American Academy for Jewish Research B
Proceedings of the American Philological Association, Transactions and RE
Proceedings of the American Philosophical Society B
Proceedings of the British Academy RE
Proceedings of the College Theology Society CPLI
Proceedings of the Israel Academy of Sciences and Humanities B
Proceedings of the World Congress of Jewish Studies B
Proche Orient Chretien RE
Proclaim SBPI
Program Quarterly UMPI
Progress, Hospital CPLI
Project IOB
Promoting Christian Unity Information Service, Secretariat for IOB
Protestant D' Etudes, Buletin du Centre IOB
Protestant D' Etudes et de Documentation, Centre IOB
Protestant Episcopal Church, Historical Magazine of the RPI
Protestante, Cahiers Theologiques de l' Actualite IZBG
Protestantesimo IZBG
Protestantischen Kirchen der Tschechoslowakei IZBG
Protestantisme Francais, Bulletin de la Societe de l' Historie du ETL, RE
Province di Romagna, Atti e Memorie de Deputazione di Storia Patria per Le RE
Province du Maine RE
Province Napoletane, Archivio Storico per Le RE

Province Parmensi, Archivio Storico per Le RE
Provincie Modenesi, Atti e Memorie de Deputazione di Storia Patria per Ie Antiche RE
Prczdor IZBG
Prczis in Kirche und Gesellschaft, Wissenschaft UN B
Przeglad Historyczny RE
Przeglad Orientalistyczny B, IZBG
Przeszlosc, Nasza RE
Psychiatrists Bulletin, National Guild of Catholic CPLI
Psychologie, Algemeen Nederlands Tijdschrift voor Wijsbegeerte en ETL
Psychology, Journal of Social IBHR
Psychology, Pastoral CPI, GSSRPL, IRPL, RPI, RTA
Psychology for Living UMPI
Psychology Today GSSRPL
Public Library, Bulletin of the New York RE
Publications de la Section Historique de l' Institut Ducal de Luxembourg RE
Publications de la Societe Historique et Archeologique dans Le Limbourg a Maestricht RE
Publications in Classical Archaelogy and Semitic Philology, University of California IZBG
Publications of the Modern Language Association RE
Quadermi di Semiliatica B
Quaderni Storici RE
Quaderri Camerti di Studi Romanistici, Index B
Quadrivium RE
Quaerendo RE
Quaestiones Disputatae ETL, IZBG
Quaker History IRPL, RPI
Quaker Life RPI
Quartalschrift, Romische ETL, IOB, NTA
Quartalschrift, Theologisch Praktische IZBG, RE
Quartalschrift, Theologische ETL, IBHR, NTA, RE
Quartalschrift, Tubinger Theologische ETL, IZBG
Quartalschrift fur Christliche Alterumskunde und Kirchengeschichte, Romanische RE
Quartelschrift, Theologisch-Praktische B
Quarterly, American IRPL
Quarterly, American Church NTA
Quarterly, American Jewish Historical IJP
Quarterly, Andover Newton B, ETL, IBHR, IRPL, IZBG, NTA, RTA, SISPL
Quarterly, Anthropological CPLI, IBHR
Quarterly, Baptist IRPL, IZBG, RTA
Quarterly, Bible League SISPL

Quarterly, Catholic Biblical ETL, IRPL, IZBG, NTA, RE, RPI

Quarterly, Central Bible SISPL
Quarterly, Christian Council IOB

Quarterly, Church ETL, IRPL, NTA, RPI
Quarterly, Classical B, RE
Quarterly, Concordia Historical Institute ETL, RTA
Quarterly, Creation Research Society SISPL
Quarterly, Evangelical CPI, IRPL, IZBG, RPI
Quarterly, Free University RTA
Quarterly, Hartford IRPL, RTA
Quarterly, Irish Theological CPLI, ETL, IZBG, RE
Quarterly, Islamic B
Quarterly, Lexington Theological ETL, IRPL, NTA, RPI
Quarterly, Lutheran ETL, IRPL, IZBG, RPI
Quarterly, McCormick IRPL, RPI
Quarterly, Modern Language RE
Quarterly, Palestine Exploration ETL, IRPL, IZBG, NTA
Quarterly, Philological RE
Quarterly, Program UMPI
Quarterly, Renaissance RE
Quarterly, St. Vladimir's Theological ETL, IRPL, IZBG, NTA, RPI
Quarterly, Synagogue School IJP
Quarterly, Wesley UMPI
Quarterly Review RPI
Quarterly Review, Jewish ETL, IJP, IRPL, IZBG, RE, RPI
Quarterly Review, Mennonite IRPL, RPI
Quarterly Review, Union Seminary ETL, IRPL, RPI, RTA
Quarterly Review of Historical Studies, the IBHR
Quarterly Review of Historical Studies, the IBHR
Quatember IOB
Quellen und Forschungen aus Italienischen Archiven und Bibliotheken RE
Questions Bulletin, Social RPI
Questions de Vida Cristia B
Questions Liturgiques RE
Qumran, Paul and IBHR
Qumran, Revue de ETL, IRPL, IZBG, RE, RTA
Quran, Bible und IBHR
Rabbis Journal, Central Conference of American B, IJP

Rassegna Critica di Filosofia e Storia della Filosofia, Sophia. RE

Rassegna di Ascetica e Mistica B
Rassegna di Letteratura Tomistica RE

Rassegna di Scienze Storiche, Linguistiche e Filologiche Aevum. B, IZBG, RE
Rassegna di Studi Etiopici B
Rassegna Mensile di Israel B, IBHR, IZBG
Rassegna Storica del Risorgimento RE
Rassegna Storica Toscana RE
Ravennate e Bizantina, Corsi di Cultura Sull' Arte RE
Razon y Fe ETL, NTA, RE
Re Morali, Canonica, Liturgica Periodica de RE
Reader, Christian GSSRPL
Reading, Foundation Studies in Christian Faith Study-Selected UMPI
Real UMPI
Real Academia, Burgense. Collectanea Scientifica de la IZBG, NTA
Real Academia de la Historia, Boletin de la RE
Real Academia Espanola, Boletin de la RE
Real Class Guide UMPI
Real Resource Packet UMPI
Reallexikon fur Antike und Christentum B
Recherche D' Histoire et Civilisation Byzantines, Travaux et Memoires du Centre de RE
Recherche et D' Histoire des Textes, Bulletin de l' Institut de RE
Recherches Augustiniennes B, RE
Recherches Bibliques B
Recherches de Science Religieuse ETL, IRPL, IZBG, NTA, RE
Recherches de Theologie Ancienne et Medievale ETL, IZBG, NTA, RE
Recherches et Debats du Centre Catholiques des Intellectuals Francais IOB
Recht, Verslagen en Mededeelingen der Vereeniging tot Uitgaff der Bronnen van het Oud Vaderlandsche RE
Rechts und Sozialphilosophie, Archiv fur ETL
Rechtsforshung Zeitschrift fur Vergleichinde Rechtsgeschichte,
Rechtsforshung Zeitschrift fur Vergleichinde Rechtsgeschichte, Einschliesslich der Ethnologischen B

Rechtsgeschichte, Einschliesslich der Ethnologischen Rechtsforshung Zeitschrift fur Vergleichinde B, IBHR

Rechtsgeschichte Romanische Abteilung, Zeitschrift der Gavigny Stiftung fur RE
Rechtsgeschiedenis, Tijdschrift voor B, RE
Reconciliation IOB
Reconstructionist IJP
Recontre Assyriologique Internationale B
Recontre Oecumenique IOB
Record, Australasian Catholic ETL, NTA, RTA
Record, Bible Society IZBG, RPI
Record, Bodleian Library RE
Record, Irish Ecclesiastical CPLI, ETL, IOB, RE
Recorder, Episcopal RPI
Records, American Catholic Historical CPLI
Records of the American Catholic Historical Society of Philadelphia RE
Recreation Magazine, Church SBPI
Recueil Dalloz ETL
Recusant History RE
Redemptoris, Spicilegium Historicum Congregationis Ssmi RE
Referat fur Fragen der Verkuendigung, Concept G. Arbeiten aus dem Iob
Reformacja W Polsce, Odrodzenie i RE
Reformata, Philosophia IOD, RE
Reformata, Vox NTA
Reformatasok Lajsja IOB
Reformation, in Lichte der IOB
Reformation Review IOB
Reformationsgeschichte, Archiv fur ETL, IRPL, RE, RTA
Reformatorum, Collectanea Oridinis Cistericciensium ETL
Reformatus Egykaz IOB
Reforme IOB
Reformed and Presbyterian World IRPL, RPI
Reformed Bulletin, International IOB
Reformed Churches, Bulletin of the Department of Theology of the World Presbyterian Alliance and the World Alliance of IOB
Reformed Review IRPL, IZBG, RPI
Reformed Theological Review ETL, IRPL, IZBG, NTA
Reformierte Kirchenzeitung IOB
Reformierte Schweiz, Kirchenblatt fur die B
Regelrecht IOB

Regionale, Bollettino Ligustico per la Storia e la Cultura RE

Register, Chicago Theological Seminary B, SISPL
Reglii, Studia Montis ETL

Regnum Dei ETL, RE
Religieuse, Melanges de Science ETL, IZBG, NTA, RE
Religieuse, Recherches de Science ETL, IRPL, IZBG, NTA, RE
Religieuse et Sociale, Cahiers D' Action IOB
Religieuses, Etudes Theologiques et ETL, IRPL, IZBG, NTA, RE
Religieuses, Revue D' Histoire et de Philosophie ETL, IRPL, IZBG, NTA, RE
Religieuses, Revue des Communautes ETL
Religieuses, Revue des Sciences ETL, IRPL, IZBG, NTA
Religieuses de l' Universite de Strasbourg, Revue des Sciences RE
Religion, Bulletin of the American Academy of IZBG
Religion, International Journal for the Philosophy of B
Religion, Journal for the Scientific Study of IRPL, RE, RPI
Religion, Journal of GSSRPL, IRPL, IZBG, RE, RPI
Religion, Journal of the American Academy of ETL, GSSRPL, IRPL, IZBG, NTA, RE, RPI
Religion, Review of SISPL
Religion, Studies in IZBG
Religion, Studies in Comparative B, IBHR
Religion, Temenos. Studies in Comparative RE
Religion, Wesleyan Studies in IZBG, SISPL
Religion, Wissenschaft, Kultur IZBG
Religion and Health, Journal of IRPL, RPI
Religion and Society IOB
Religion and the Worldview in the South Western Pacific, Folk IBHR
Religion in Africa, Journal of RE, SISPL
Religion in Geschichte und Gegenwart ETL
Religion Orientales, Estudios de Filosofia y B
Religion Teacher's Journal CPLI
Religion und Literatur des Alten und Neuen Testaments, Forschungen Zur B, IZBG
Religion, Wissenschaft, Kultur IZBG
Religion y Cultura B, IOB
Religiones, Annales du Centre D' Etude des B
Religiones Africaines, Cahiers des IBHR

Religioni, Studi e Materiali di Storia della
B, ETL, IBHR, IZBG, RE
Religions, Archives de Sociologie de B, ETL,
IBHR, RE
Religions, History of ETL, GSSRPL, IBHR, IRPL,
IZBG, RE, RPI
Religions, Japanese IOB
Religions, Jordan Lectures in Comparative ETL
Religions, Revue D' Histoire des RE
Religions, Revue de l' Histoire des ETL, IRPL,
IZBG, NTA
Religions, Studies in the History of B
Religions in Japan, Contemporary SISPL
Religions Numen, International Review for the
History of ETL, IRPL, NTA
Religions und Geistesgeschichte, Zeitschrift
fur ETL, IRPL, IZBG, NTA, RE, RTA
Religionsphilosophie, Neue Zeitschrift fur
Systematische Theologie und ETL, IRPL, RE, RTA
Religions-Sociologie, Internationales Jahrbuch
fur IOB
Religionswissenschaft, Zeitschrift fur
Missionwissenschaft und ETL, IRPL, RE
Religiosa, Rivista di Storia e Letteratura RE
Religiosa, Sociologia IBHR
Religiosa, Vita ETL
Religiose, Ricerche Bibliche e ETL
Religiose, Rivista di Pedagogia e Scienze B
Religious, Review for CPLI, ETL, NTA, RPI
Religious and Theological Abstracts IZBG
Religious Book Guide UMPI
Religious Education GSSRPL, IJP, RPI
Religious Education, International Journal
of SISPL
Religious History, Journal of ETL, IRPL, IZBG, RE
Religious Humanism GSSRPL
Religious Research, Review of IRPL, RE, RPI
Religious Studies IRPL, RPI
Religious Thought, Journal of IRPL, RPI
Renaiscence CPLI
Renaissance, Bibliotheque D' Humanisme et RE
Renaissance, Mediaeval and RE
Renaissance, Studies in the RE
Renaissance and Modern Studies RE
Renaissance History, Studies in Medieval and RE
Renaissance Quarterly RE
Renan, Bulletin E. IZBG
Renan, Cahiers IZBG

Rendiconti de Scienze Morali IZBG
Rendiconti dell' Istituto Lombardo di Scienze e Lettere RE
Rendiconti dell' Istituto Nazionale D' Archeolcgia e Storia dell' Arte Re
Rendiconti della Academia Nazionale dei Lincei IBHR
Rendiconti della Pontifica Accademia Romana de Archaeclogia IBHR
Rendus, Comptes B, IBHR
Rendus de l' Academie des Inscriptions et Belles Lettres, Comptes Izbg
Rendus des Seances de l' Academie des Inscriptions et Belles Lettres, Comptes RE
Rendus du Groupe Linguistique D' Etudes Chamito-Semitiques, Comptes B
Renewal IRPL, RPI
Reniconti della Pontifica Accademia Romana di Archeologia RE
Renovation ETL
Reologiczno Kanoniczne, Roczniki ETL, NTA
Report from the Capital SBPI
Reporter, National Catholic CPLI
Reporter, Near East IJP
Reporter, Pedagogic IJP
Reporter for Conscience's Sake RPI
Research, Annual of the American School of Oriental IZBG
Research, Biblical IZBG
Research, Bulletin of the American Schools of Oriental B, ETL, IBHR, IZBG, NTA, SISPL
Research, Bulletin of the Institute of Historical RE
Research, Proceedings of the American Academy for Jewish B
Research, Review of Religious IRPL, RE, RPI
Research Center in Egypt, Journal of American B
Research Institute China Academy, Buletin of the Catholic B
Research Library, Missionary IOB, RE
Research Society Quarterly, Creation SISPL
Resonance CPLI
Resource Kit, Explore UMPI
Resource Packet, New Creation UMPI
Resource Packet, Real UMPI
Response RTA, SBPI, UMPI
Response in Worship Music the Acts IOB
Review, American Benedictine NTA, RPI
Review, American Ecclesiastical RE

Review, American Historical RE
Review, American Sciological GSSRPL
Review, Anglican Theological B, ETL, IBHR, IRPL, IZBG, NTA, SISPL
Review, Australian Biblical ETL, IZBG, NTA
Review, Calvary SISPL
Review, Canadian Historical RE
Review, Catholic Business Education CPLI
Review, Catholic Charities CPLI, RPI
Review, Catholic Historical CPLI, ETL, GSSRPL, RE, RPI
Review, Christian Scholar's NTA
Review, Church Theological RPI
Review, Classical B, RE
Review, Clergy CPLI, ETL, RE
Review, Downside ETL, IRPL, IZBG, RE , RTA
Review, Dublin CPLI, ETL
Review, Duke Divinity School IRPL, RPI
Review, Dunwoodie IZBG
Review, Economic History RE
Review, Ecumenical GSSRPL, NTA, RE, RPI
Review, English Historical RE
Review, Episcopal Overseas Mission IOB
Review, French RE
Review, Geographical B
Review, Greek Orthodox Theological IRPL, RPI
Review, Harvard Theological B, ETL, IRPL, IZBG, NTA, RE, RPI, RTA
Review, Hispanic RE
Review, Homiletic and Pastoral CPLI, NTA
Review, Jewish Observer and Middle East IJP
Review, Jewish Quarterly ETL, IJP, IRPL, IZBG, RE, RPI
Review, Lutheran Theological Seminary SISPL
Review, Mennonite Quarterly IRPL, RPI
Review, Modern Language RE
Review, National Christian Council IOB
Review, New Book RPI
Review, Philosophical RE
Review, Polish Ecumenical IOB
Review, Quarterly RPI
Review, Reformation IOB
Review, Reformed IRPL, IZBG, RPI
Review, Reformed Theological ETL, IRPL, IZBG, NTA
Review, Romanic RE
Review, Scandinavian Economic History RE
Review, Scottish Historical RE
Review, Social Justice CPLI, RPI

Review, Teilhard CPLI
Review, Union Seminary Quarterly ETL, IRPL, RPI, RTA
Review, United Church IOB
Review, United Synagogue CPLI, RPI
Review and Expositor ETL, IRPL, IZBG, NTA
Review for Religious CPLI, ETL, NTA, RPI
Review for the History of Religions Numen, International ETL, IRPL, NTA
Review of Archaeology, Turkish IBHR
Review of English Studies RE
Review of Historical Studies, the Quarterly IBHR
Review of Missions, International B, CPI, ETL, IBHR, IRPL, RPI, RTA
Review of Politics CPLI, RE
Review of Religion SISPL
Review of Religious Research IRPL, RE, RPI
Review of Social Economy CPLI
Review of Social History, International RE
Revista Agustiniana de Espiritualidad B, ETL, NTA
Revista Biblica (Argentina) B
Revista Biblica (Buenos Aires) IZBG
Revista Biblica (Italiana) IZBG
Revista de Archivos, Bibliotecas y Museos RE
Revista de Archivos, Bibliotecas y Museos RE
Revista de Arte, Goya. RE
Revista de Cultura Biblica ETL, IZBG, NTA
Revista de Cultura Teologica ETL, NTA
Revista de Espiritualidad RE
Revista de Filologia Espanola RE
Revista de Indias RE
Revista de las Escuelas de Estudios Arabes, al Andalus. RE
Revista degli Studi Orientali IZBG
Revista di Cultura Tehologica IZBG
Revista di Pastorale Liturgica B
Revista di Teologia Morale B
Revista Eclesiastica Brasileria ETL, IZBG, NTA, RE
Revista Ecumenica "Ut Unum Sint" ETL
Revista Espanola de Derecho Canonico RE
Revista Espanola de Historia, Hispania. RE
Revista Espanola de Teologia ETL, IZBG, NTA, RE
Revolution Francaise, Annales Historiques de la RE
Revue, Krestanska IOB, IZBG
Revue, Nabozenska IOB
Revue, Theologicka Priloha Krestanske IZBG
Revue, Theologische ETL, IZBG, NTA, RE
Revue Archeologique RE

Revue Belge D' Archeologie et D' Historie de l' Art RE

Revue Belge D' Historie Contemporaine RE
Revue Belge de Musicologie RE

Revue Belge de Numismatique et de Sigillographie RE
Revue Belge de Philologie et D' Histoire RE
Revue Benedictine ETL, NTA, RE
Revue Biblique ETL, IRPL, IZBG, NTA, RE
Revue Biblique, Cahiers de la IZBG
Revue D' Archeologique B
Revue D' Ascetique et de Mystique ETL, IZBG, NTA, RE
Revue D' Auvergne RE
Revue D' Egyptologie B, IBHR
Revue D' Histoire de l' Amerique Francaise RE
Revue D' Histoire de l' Eglise de France RE
Revue D' Histoire de Philosophie et de Theologie ETL
Revue D' Histoire des Religions RE
Revue D' Histoire des Sciences et de Leurs Applications RE
Revue D' Histoire des Textes B
Revue D' Histoire Diplomatique RE
Revue D' Histoire Ecclesiastique ETL, IRPL, IZBG, NTA, RE
Revue D' Histoire Economique Sociale RE
Revue D' Histoire et de Philosophie Religieuses ETL, IRPL, IZBG, NTA, RE
Revue D' Histoire Litteraire de la France RE
Revue D' Histoire Mitteilungen RE
Revue D' Histoire Moderne et Contemporaine RE
Revue de Belgique. Bulletin de la Classe des Beaux Arts, Academie RE
Revue de Belgique. Bulletin de la Classe des Lettres et des Sciences Morales et Politiques, Academie RE
Revue de Droit Canonique RE
Revue de Etudes Augustiniennes ETL, NTA
Revue de l' Anranchin et du Pays de Granville RE
Revue de l' Art RE
Revue de l' Histoire de la Medicine Hebraique IBHR, IZBG
Revue de l' Histoire des Religions ETL, IRPL, IZBG, NTA
Revue de l' Institut des Belles Letters Arabes B, IBHR

Revue de l' Occident Musulman et de la Mediterranee IBHR
Revue de l' Universite D' Ottawa CPLI, ETL, IZBG, RE
Revue de la Haute Auvergne RE
Revue de Litteratur Comparee RE
Revue de Metaphysigye et de Morale RE
Revue de Philclogie, de Litterature et D' Histcire Anciennes RE
Revue de Philologie, de Litterature et D' Histoire Anciennes RE
Revue de Qumran ETL, IRPL, IZBG, RE, RTA
Revue de Synthese RE
Revue de Theolcgie et de Philosophie ETL, IZBG, NTA, RE
Revue del' Evangelisation IOB
Revue des Communautes Religieuses ETL
Revue des Etudes Anciennes B, IBHR
Revue des Etudes Armeniennes B, IBHR, RE
Revue des Etudes Augustiniennes RE
Revue des Etudes Byzantines B, IBHR, RE
Revue des Etudes Grecques RE
Revue des Etudes Islamiques B, IBHR
Revue des Etudes Italiennes RE
Revue des Etudes Juives B, IBHR, IZBG, RE
Revue des Etudes Latines RE
Revue des Etudes Slaves RE
Revue des Etudes Sud-Est Europeenes IBHR, RE
Revue des Sciences Humaines RE
Revue des Sciences Philosophiques et Theologiques B, ETL, IBHR, IZBG, NTA, RE
Revue des Sciences Religieuses ETL, IRPL, IZBG, NTA
Revue des Sciences Religieuses de l' Universite de Strasbourg RE
Revue Diocesaine de Namur ETL
Revue Diocesaine de Tournai ETL
Revue Diocesaine de Tournai, Confrontations. Etl B
Revue du Centre de Documentation Juife Contemporaine, Monde Juie. la Izbg
Revue du Droit Canonique ETL, IOB
Revue du Louvre et des Museede Frome B, IBHR
Revue du Louvre et des Musees de France RE
Revue du Moyen Age Latina RE
Revue du Nord RE
Revue du Vivarais RE
Revue Generale RE
Revue Historique B, IZBG, RE

Revue Historique du Droit Francais et Etranger RE

Revue Hittite et Asianique B, IBHR
Revue Internationale de Philosophie RE

Revue Internationale des Archives, Archivum. RE
Revue Internationale des Droits de l' Antiquite IZBG, RE
Revue Mabillon RE
Revue Numismatique B, RE
Revue Philosophique de la France et de l' Etranger RE
Revue Philosophique de Louvain CPLI, ETL, RE
Revue Roumaine D' Histoire IZBG, RE
Revue Theologique, Nouvelle CPLI, ETL, IZBG, NTA, RE
Revue Theologique de Louvain RE
Revue Thomiste ETL, IZBG, NTA, RE
Revuo, Biblia IZBG
Rheinische Vierteljahrsblatter RE
Rheinisches Museum fur Philologie IZBG
Ribista Rosminiana di Filosofia e di Cultura RE
Ricerche Bibliche e Religiose ETL
Richartz Jahrbuch, Wallraf RE
Rider, Circuet UMPI
Rinascimento RE
Risk IOB
Risorgimento RE
Risorgimento, Rassegna Storica del RE
Rivista Biblica ETL, NTA, RE
Rivista degli Studi Orientali B, ETL, IBHR, RE
Rivista del Diritto Matrimoniale e Dello Stato Delle Persone ETL
Rivista di Archeologia Cristiana RE
Rivista di Ascetica e Mistica ETL, NTA
Rivista di Cultura Classica e Medioevale RE
Rivista di Diritto Civile ETL
Rivista di Filologia ETL
Rivista di Filologia e di Istruzione Classica RE
Rivista di Filosofia Neoscolastica RE
Rivista di Liturgia B
Rivista di Pedagogia e Scienze Religiose B
Rivista di Storia del Diritto Italiano RE
Rivista di Storia dell' Architettura, Palladia. RE
Rivista di Storia della Chiesa in Italia RE
Rivista di Storia e Letteratura Religiosa RE
Rivista di Studi Classici ETL
Rivista di Studi Fenici B

Rivista di Umanita Classica e Cristiana, Orpheus. RE

Rivista Internazionale de Filosofia de Diritto ETL
Rivista Storica, Nouva RE

Rivista Storica Italiana RE
Riviste D' Italia, Libri e B
Roczniki Historyczne RE
Roczniki Humanistyczne RE
Roczniki Orientalistyczny IZBG
Roczniki Reologiczno Kanoniczne ETL, NTA
Roczniki Teologiczne Chrzescijanskiej Akademii Teologicznej IZBG
Roczniki Teologiczno Kanoniczne IZBG, RE
Romagna, Atti e Memorie de Deputazione di Storia Patria per Le Province di RE
Roman Periods, Journal for the Study of Judaism in the Persian Helenistic and B
Roman Studies, Journal of B, RE
Romana, Biserica Ortodoxa IOB
Romana de Archaeologia, Rendiconti della Pontifica Accademia IBHR
Romana di Archeologia, Atti della Pontificia Accademia B
Romana di Archeologia, Reniconti della Pontifica Accademia RE
Romana di Storia Patria, Archivio di Societa RE
Romance Philology RE
Romands Memoires de la Societe Pour l' Histoire du Droit et des Institutions des Anciens Pays Bourguignons, Comtois et RE
Romani, Studi B, RE
Romania RE
Romanic Review RE
Romanis, Lettres RE
Romanische Abteilung, Zeitschrift der Gavigny Stiftung fur Rechtsgeschichte RE
Romanische Forschungen RE
Romanische Monatsschrift, Germanisch RE
Romanische Quartalschrift fur Christliche Alterumskunde und Kirchengeschichte RE
Romanistici, Index Quaderri Camerti di Studi B
Romanistisches Jahrbuch RE
Rome, Bulletin de l' Institut Historique Belge de RE
Rome, Mededlingen van het Nederlands Historie Instituut Te RE

Rome, Melanges D' Archeologie et D' Histcrier de l' Ecole Francaise de IBHR
Romische Historische Mitteilungen RE
Romische Quartalschrift ETL, IOB, NTA
Romisches Jahrbuch fur Kunstgeschichte RE
Rosminiana di Filosofia e di Cultura, Ribista RE
Rostock, Wissenschaftliche Zeitschrift der Universitat RE
Roumaine D' Histoire, Revue IZBG, RE
Roundtable UMEI
Royal Anthropologist Institute Man, the Journal of the IBHR
Royal Asiatic Society of Great Britain and Ireland, Journal of the RE
Royal du Patrimoine Artistique, Bulletin de l' Institut RE
Royal Historical Society, Transactions of the RE
Royal Service SBPI
Royal Society of Antiquaries of Ireland, Journal of the RE
Royale D' Histoire, Bulletin de la Commission RE
Royale de Anciennes Lois et Ordonnances de Belgique, Bulletin de la Commission RE
Royale de Belgique, Academie B
Royaux D' Art et D' Histoire, Bulletin des Musees RE
Royaux des Beaus Arts de Belgique, Bulletin des Musees RE
Ruch Biblijny i Liturgiczny ETL, IZBG, NTA
Rundbrief, Freiburger IOB, IZBG
Rundschau, Lutherische ETL, NTA
Rundschau, Neue IOB
Rundschau, Oekumenische B, IOB
Rundschau, Philosophische IBHR
Rundschau, Schweizer IOB
Rundschau, Theologische ETL, IRPL, IZBG, RE, RTA
Russe en Europe Occidentale, Messager de l' Exauchat de Patriarche Iob
Rwanda et Burundi, Theologie Pastorale au B
Rylands Library, Bulletin of the John ETL, IZBG, NTA, RE
Sacerdos ETL
Sacerdotal, Apostclado IZBG
Sachsischen Adademie der Wissenschaften zu Leipzig, Sitzungsberichte der RE
Sachsischen Akademie der Wissenschaften zu Leipzig, Berichte uber die Verhandlugn der RE
Saciolcgia, Studi di IBHR

Sacra, Bibliotheca CPI, ETL, IRPL, IZBG, NTA, RE, RTA

Sacra, Hispania ETL, RE
Sacra, Lusitania RE

Sacra, Philippiana B
Sacra Doctrina ETL, NTA, RE
Sacra Tarraconensia, Analecta RE
Sacred Music CPLI, RPI
Sacri Ordinis Cistercienis, Analecta ETL
Sacri Ordinis Fratrum Praedicatorum, Analecta ETL
Sacris Erudiri ETL, IZBG, NTA, RE
Saeculum IZBG, RE
Saint Jean-Baptist, Bulletin IBHR, ICB
Sainte, Bible et Terre IZBG
Sainte, Terre IZBG
Sake, Reporter for Conscience's RPI
Salesianum IZBG, RE
Salmanticensis ETL, IZBG, NTA, RE
Samlinger, Kirkehistorike RE
Sammlungen Wien, Jahrbuch der Kunsthistorischen RE
Sanatu Arastermalan, Anadolu IBHR
Sancta, Una ETL, IRPL, IZBG, NTA, RPI
Sanctam, Unam IZBG
Santa, Terra B
Santissima Eucharistia ICB
Sapienza ETL, NTA, RE
Savants, Journal des B, RE
Sbaornik, Palestinskii IZBG
Scandinavia, Mediaeval RE
Scandinavian Economic History Review RE
Schema XIII CPLI
Schiller Universitat Jena, Wissenschaftliche Zeitschrift der Friedrich RE
Schlesische Kirchengeschichte, Archiv fur RE
Schleswig Holsteinische Geschichte, Zeitschrift der Gesellschaft fur Re
Scholar, American GSSRPL
Scholar, Christian ICB
Scholar's Review, Christian NTA
Scholasticism, New CPLI, ETL, RE
School, Church UMPI
School Journal, Catholic CPLI, RPI
School of Archaeology in Jerusalem, Levant. Journal of the British SISPL
School of Oriental and African Studies, Bulletin of the RE

School of Oriental Research, Annual of the American IZBG

School of Theology Journal, Perkins NTA
School Quarterly, Synagogue IJP
School Review, Duke Divinity IRPL, RPI
Schoolman, Modern CPLI, RE
Schools of Oriental Research, Bulletin of the American B, ETL, IBHR, IZBG, NTA, SISPL
Schoon en de Brabander, Eigen RE
Schriften des Deutschen Instituts fur Wissenschaftlishe Padogogik ETL
Schriftgeschichte, Siegel und Wappenkunde Archiv fur Diplomatik RE
Schweiz, Katholisches Missionejahrbuch der IOB
Schweiz, Kirchenblatt fur die Reformierte B
Schweizer Buchhandel RE
Schweizer Rundschau IOB
Schweizerische Archaologie und Kunstgeschichte, Zeitschrift fur RE
Schweizerische Kirchengeschichte, Zeitschrift fur IOB, RE
Schweizerische Theologische Umschau IOB
Schweizerische Zeitschrift fur Geschichte RE
Schweizerisches Archiv fur Volkskunde IBHR, RE
Science, Journal of Applied Behavorial SISPL
Science et Esprit ETL, IZBG, NTA, RE
Science Newsletter, Bible SISPL
Science Religieuse, Melanges de ETL, IZBG, NTA, RE
Science Religieuse, Recherches de ETL, IRPL, IZBG, NTA, RE
Sciences, Archives de l' Historie des B
Sciences, Archives Internationales D' Histoire des RE
Sciences and Humanities, Proceedings of the Israel Academy of B
Sciences Ecclesiastiques ETL, RTA
Sciences et Arts, du Departement de la Marne Memoires de la Societe D' Agriculture, Commerce, RE
Sciences et de Leurs Applications, Revue D' Histoire des RE
Sciences Humaines, Revue des RE
Sciences Morales et Politiques, Academie Revue de Belgique. Bulletin de la Classe des Lettres et des RE
Sciences Philosophiques et Theologiques, Revue des B, ETL, IBHR, IZBG, NTA, RE

Sciences Religieuses, Revue des ETL, IRPL, IZBG, NTA

Sciences Religieuses de l' Universite de Strasbourg, Revue des RE
Scientiarum, Erasmus. Speculum RE
Scientiarum Fennicae, Annales Academiae IZBG
Scientiarum Hungaricae, Acta Antiqua Academiae IBHR
Scientiarum Hungaricae, Acta Ethnographica Academiae IBHR
Scientific Study of Religion, Journal for the IRPL, RE, RPI
Scientifica de la Real Academia, Burgense. Collectanea IZBG, NTA
Scienze, Lettere di Arte Atti dell' Istituto Veneto di RE
Scienze Affini, Rivista Italiana di Numismatica e RE
Scienze e Lettere, Rendiconti dell' Istituto Lombardo di RE
Scienze Morali, Rendiconti de IZBG
Scienze Religiose, Rivista di Pedagogia e B
Scienze Storiche, Linguistiche e Filologiche Aevum. Rassegna di B, IZBG, RE
Sciological Review, American GSSRPL
Scottish Historical Review RE
Scottish Journal of Theology ETL, IRPL, IZBG, RTA
Scottista, Bollettino della Societa Internazionale IZBG
Scripta Mercaturae RE
Scripta Theologica B
Scriptorium RE
Scriptorium Victoriense RE
Scriptorum Christianorum Orientalium, Corpus B
Scripture CPLI, ETL
Scripture Bulletin CPLI, ETL, IZBG, NTA
Scuola, Cultura e B, IBHR
Scuola Cattolica ETL, IZBG, NTA, RE
Scuola Normale Superiore di Pisa, Annali della B, RE
Scuola Pasitiva Serie Iv IBHR
Seances de l' Academie des Inscriptions et Belles Lettres, Comptes Rendus des RE
Seanchas Ard Mhacha RE
Search IOB, SEPI
Secretariado Trinitario ETL
Secretariatus pro Non Christianis, Bulletin B, IOB

Section D' Historie Moderne et Contemperaine, Bulletin de la RE
Section Historique de l' Institut Ducal de Luxembourg, Publications de la RE
Sedis, Acta Apostalicae CPLI, ETL
Seelscrge, Lebendige IOB
Seelsorge Anima, Vierteljahrsschrift fur Praktische IZBG
Sefarad ETL, IZBG, NTA, RE
Seigneur, Assemblees die B
Sein und Sendung B
Seiner Nachbargebiete, Trierer Zeitschrift fur Geschichte und Kunst des Trierer Landes und RE
Seiner Zweige, Studien und Mitteilungen Zur Geschichte des Benediktiner Ordens und RE
Selecciones de Libros B
Self-Realization Magazine RPI
Semana Biblica Espancla B
Semana Espanola de Teologia B
Semeur IOB
Semiliatica, Quadermi di B
Seminarii Neotestamentici Upsaliensis, Acta ETL, IZBG
Seminario Conciliar IZBG
Seminario de Estudios de Arte y Arqueologia, Boletin del RE
Seminarios ETL
Seminarium ETL
Seminary Bulletin, Princeton ETL, IRPL, IZBG, RPI
Seminary Quarterly Review, Union ETL, IRPL, RPI, RTA
Seminary Register, Chicago Theological B, SISPL
Seminary Review, Lutheran Theological SISPL
Seminary Studies, Andrews University B, ETL, IBHR, IRPL, IZBG, NTA, SISPL
Semitic Languages, Journal of the Northwest B
Semitic Philology, University of California Publications in Classical Archaelogy and IZBG
Semitic Series, Harvard B
Semitic Studies, Journal of ETL, IRPL, IZBG, NTA
Semitica IZBG
Semitici, Studi IZBG
Sendung, Sein und B
Senesi, Studi RE
Senyser, Nunc et IOB
Sepher, Kirjath IZBG
Serafini", Archivio Giuridico "Filippo ETL, RE
Serie Iv, Scuola Pasitiva IBHR

Series, Harvard Semitic B

Series (United Methodist Student) UMPI
Series (United Methodist Teacher) UMPI
Series Lund Coniectanea Biblica, New Testament IZBG
Serran RPI
Servi di Maria, Studi Storici dell' Ordine dei RE
Service, Information (New York) IOB
Service, Journal of Jewish Communal IJP
Service, Royal SBPI
Service, Secretariat for Promoting Christian Unity Information IOB
Service des Antiquites de l' Egypte, Annales du B
Servicio de al Fe, Mision Avierta al B
Settimana Biblica, Atti della B
Shenhsueh Yu Cjiaohui B
Sicilia Archeclogica IBHR
Sicilia Orientale, Archivio Storico per la RE
Siculorum Gymnasium B, RE
Side, Other SISPL
Siecle, Christianisme au 20e IOB
Sighted Pathways GSSRPL
Sigillographie, Revue Belge de Numismatique et de RE
Sign CPLI, RPI
Signaletique, Bulletin B
Signes du Temps IOB
Signos de los Tiempos B
Sinhagbondan IOB
Sinhagyeicgu IOB
Sint", Revista Ecumenica "Ut Unum ETL
Sint, Ut Unum IOB
Sister Formaticn Bulletin CPLI
Sisters Today CPLI, RPI
Sitzungsberichte der Bayerischen Akademie der Wissenschaften RE
Sitzungsberichte der Deutschen Akademie der Wissenschaften IZBG, RE
Sitzungsberichte der Heidelberger Akademie der Wissenschaften IZBG, RE
Sitzungsberichte der Oesterreicheschen Akademie der Wissenschaften Izbg
Sitzungsberichte der Oesterreichischen Akademie der Wissenschaften RE
Sitzungsberichte der Sachsischen Adademie der Wissenschaften zu Leipzig RE
Sjaloom IOB

Skrifter Utgitt Av Det Norske Videnskaps Akademie i Oslo IZBG

Slaven, Welt der IOB
Slaves, Annuaire de l' Institut de Philologie et D' Historie Orientales et B, IBHR
Slaves, Revue des Etudes RE
Slavia RE
Slavia Antiqua RE
Slavia Occidentalis RE
Slavische Philolcgie, Zeitschrift fur RE
Slcavica, Byzantino IBHR, RE
Slcva, Sluzba IZBG
Slcvaca, Studia Historica RE
Sluzba Slcva IZBG
Smotra, Bogoslcvska B
Sobornost (London) IOB, NTA
Social, Christianisme IOB
Social, Fomenta IOB
Social Action IRPI, RPI
Social Compass ETL, RE, RTA
Social Economy, Review of CPLI
Social History, International Review of RE
Social History of the Orient, Journal of Economic and B
Social History of the Orient, Journal of the Economic and RE
Social Justice Review CPLI, RPI
Social Psychology, Journal of IBHR
Social Questions Bulletin RPI
Social Studies, Jewish IZBG
Social und Wirtschaftsgeschishte, Vierteljahrsschrift fur RE
Sociale, Annali di Storia Economica e RE
Sociale, Cahiers D' Action Religieuse et IOB
Sociale, Revue D' Histoire Economique RE
Societa Geografica Italiano, Bollettino della B
Societa Internazionale Scottista, Bollettino della IZBG
Societa Istriana di Archeologia e Storia Patria, Atti e Memorie de RE
Societa Ligure di Storia Patria, Atti di RE
Societa Romana di Storia Patria, Archivio di RE
Societatis Iesu, Archivum Historicum ETL, RE
Societe Academique des Antiquaires de la Marinie, Bulletin Trimestriel de la RE
Societe Archeologie et Historique de la Charente, Memoires de la RE

Societe Archeclogie et Historique de Nantes et de Loire Atlantique, Bulletin de la RE

Societe Archeologique D' Eure et Loir, Bulletin de la RE
Societe Archeclogique de Namur, Annales de la RE
Societe Archeologique de Touraine, Bulletin Trimestriel de la RE
Societe Archeclogique du Department D' Ille et Vilaine, Bulletin et Memoirs de la RE
Societe Archeclogique et Historique du Limousin, Bulletin de la RE
Societe D' Agriculture, Commerce, Sciences et Arts, du Departement de la Marne Memoires de la RE
Societe D' Archeolcgie Copte, Bulletin de la IZBG, RE
Societe D' Archeologie et de Statistique de la Drome, Bulletin de la Re
Societe D' Art et D' Historie du Diocese de Liege, Bulletin de la RE
Societe D' Emulaticn de Bruges, Handeling van het Genootschap voor Geschiedenis Gesticht Onder de Benaming RE
Societe D' Histcire et D' Archeologie de la Lorraine, Annuaire de la Re
Societe de Etudes Indochinoses, Bulletin de la IBHR
Societe de l' Historie de l' Art Francais, Bulletin de la RE
Societe de l' Historie du Protestantisme Francais, Bulletin de la ETL, RE
Societe de Linguietique de Paris, Bulletin de la B
Societe de'Archeclogie Copte, Bulletin de la B
Societe des Americanistes, Journal de la IBHR
Societe des Antiquaires de l' Ouest et des Musees de Poitiers, Bulletin de la RE
Societe des Antiquaires de Normandie, Bulletin de la RE
Societe des Antiquaires de Picardie, Bulletin Trimestriel de la RE
Societe des Etudes Litteraires, Scientifiques et Artistiques du Lot Bulletin de la RE
Societe Francaise D' Egyptclogie, Bulletin de la B
Societe Francaise D' Etudes Marianles, Bulletin de la B
Societe Historique et Archeologique du Perigord, Bulletin de la RE

Societe Historique et Archologique dans Le Limbourg a Maestricht, Publications de la RE

Societe Nationale des Antiquaires de France, Bulletin de la RE
Societe Pour l' Histoire du Droit et des Institutions des Anciens Pays Bourguignons, Comtois et Romands Memoires de la RE

Societe Prehistorique Francaise, Bulletin de la IBHR
Societes D' Histoire et D' Archeologie de l' Aisne, Memoires de la Federation der RE
Societes Historie et Archeologie de Paris et de l' Ile de France, Memoires de la Federation des RE
Societies, Bulletin of the United Biblical IZBG
Societies Bulletin, United Bible B
Society, Ancient B
Society, Church and IRPL, RPI
Society, Journal of American Oriental IZBG
Society, Journal of the Evangelical Theological B
Society, Journal of the Polynesian IBHR
Society, Modern CPLI
Society, Proceedings of the American Philosophical B
Society, Proceedings of the College Theology CPLI
Society, Religion and ICB
Society, Transactions of the Royal Historical RE
Society and History, Comparative Studies in RE
Society for African Church History, Bulletin of the IOB
Society of America, Language. Journal of the Linguistic IBHR, ICB, IZBG
Society of America Proceedings, Catholic Theological CPLI
Society of Antiquaries of Ireland, Journal of the Royal RE
Society of Columbia, Journal of Ancient Near Eastern B, SISPL
Society of Great Britain and Ireland, Journal of the Royal Asiatic RE
Society of Philadelphia, Records of the American Catholic Historical Re
Society of the Church in Wales, Journal of the Historical RE
Society Quarterly, Creation Research SISPL
Society Record, Bible IZBG, RPI

Society Transactions, Glasgow University Oriental
B

Sociologia, Annali di IBHR
Sociologia Religiosa IBHR

Sociological Analysis IBHR
Sociologie, Annales de IBHR
Sociologie, Cahiers Internationaux de IBHR
Sociologie de Religions, Archives de B, ETL,
IBHR, RE
Sociologisch Bulletin IOB
Sociology, American Journal of GSSRPL
Sociology, British Journal of IBHR
Sociology, Jewish Journal of B, IBHR
Sodalicii Neotestamentici Upsaliensis, Nuntius
IZBG
Solia RPI
Soobscenija Institute Narodov Azii, Kratkie IZBG
Sophia. Rassegna Critica di Filosofia e Storia
della Filosofia RE
Soundings IRPI, RPI
South East Asia Journal of Theology IRPL, NTA
South Indian Churchman IOB
South Western Pacific, Folk Religion and the
Worldview in the IBHR
Southern Baptist Educator SBPI
Southwestern Journal of Theology CPI, ETL,
IRPL, IZBG, NTA, RPI, RTA, SBPI
Southwestern News SBPI
Souverain Militaire de Malte, Annales de l'
Ordre RE
Soviet Studies in History RE
Sozialphilosophie, Archiv fur Rechts und ETL
Sozialwissenschaften, Jahrbuch des Instituts
fur Christliche IOB
Span SBPI
Speaks, Pope CPLI, RPI
Spectator, Jewish GSSRPL, IJP, RPI
Spectrum RPI
Speculum B, RE, SISPL
Speculum Scientiarum, Erasmus. RE
Spicilegium Historicum Congregationis Ssmi
Redemptoris RE
Spiegel Historiael RE
Spire SBPI
Spirit CPLI
Spiritual Life CPLI, RPI

Spirituali dell' Antico Testamento del Nuovo Testamento, Commenti B

Spiritualite, Theologie. Pastorale et ETL
Spirituelle, Vie IZBG
Spiritus IOB
Sprache und Alterumskunde, Zeitschrift fur Agypitsche IZBG
Sprache und Alterumskunde, Zeitschrift fur Agyptische B
Sprache und Literatur, Beitraege Zur Geschichte der Deutschen RE
Sprache und Literatur, Zeitschrift fur Franzosische RE
Sprachen, Zeitschrift fur Vergleichende Sprachforschung auf dem Gebiet der Indogermanischen B
Sprachen und Literaturen, Archiv fur das Studium der Neueren RE
Sprachforschung auf dem Gebiet der Indogermanischen Sprachen, Zeitschrift fur Vergleichende B
Sprachwissenschaft, Munchener Studien Zur B, IBHR
Sprawozdania Z Czynnosci Wydawniczej i Posiedzen Naukoeych Oraz Kronika RE
Springfielder IRPI, RPI
Ssmi Redemptoris, Spicilegium Historicum Congregationis RE
St. Anthony Messenger CPLI, RPI
St. Joseph, Melanges de l' Universite B, IBHR, IZBG, RE
St. Nomata NTA
St. Vladimir's Theological Quarterly ETL, IRPL, IZBG, NTA, RPI
Staatlichen Museum fur Volkunde in Dresden, Abhandlungen und Berichte des IBHR
Staatsarchivs, Mitteilungen des Oesterreichischen RE
Stained Glass RPI
Stallichen Kunstsammulugen in Baden-Wurttemberg, Jahrbuch der IBHR
Standard, Christian GSSRPL
Standard, Lutheran GSSRPL, RPI
Starinár RE
Start SBPI
Statale de Milano, Annali del Facolta di Filosofia e Letter di UN-Versita RE
State, Journal of Church and IRPL, RPI

Statistique de la Drome, Bulletin de la Societe D' Archeologie et de RE
Stato Delle Persone, Rivista del Diritto Matrimoniale e Dello ETL
Stemmen, Nederlands Katholische ETL
Stiftung fur Rechtsgeschichte Romanische Abteilung, Zeitschrift der Gavigny RE
Stimme der Generde IOB
Stimme der Orthodoxie B, IOB
Stimmen der Zeit CPLI, ETL, IZBG, NTA, RE
Storia, Economia e RE
Storia, Filosofia e Letteratura Studi Urbinati di RE
Storia Amministrativa, Annali della Fondazione Italiana per la RE
Storia Contemporanea RE
Storia del Diritto, Annali di RE
Storia del Diritto Italiano, Rivista di RE
Storia dell' Architettura, Palladia. Rivista di RE
Storia della Chiesa in Italia, Rivista di RE
Storia della Filosofia, Sophia. Rassegna Critica di Filosofia e RE
Storia della Pieta, Archivio Italiano per la RE
Storia della Religioni, Studi e Materiali di B, ETL, IBHR, IZBG, RE
Storia dell' Arte, Rendiconti dell' Istituto Nazionale D' Archeologia e RE
Storia e la Cultura Regionale, Bollettino Ligustico per la RE
Storia e Letteratura Religiosa, Rivista di RE
Storia Economica e Sociale, Annali di RE
Storia Patria, Archivio di Societa Romana di RE
Storia Patria, Atti di Societa Ligure di RE
Storia Patria, Atti e Memorie de Societa Istriana di Archeologia e RE
Storia Patria per Le Antiche Provincie Modenesi, Atti e Memorie de Deputazione di RE
Storia Patria per Le Province di Romagna, Atti e Memorie de Deputazione di RE
Storica, Nouva Rivista RE
Storica Bolognese, Strenna RE
Storica del Risorgimento, Rassegna RE
Storica Italiana, Rivista RE
Storica Toscana, Rassegna RE
Storiche, Linguistiche e Filologiche Aevum. Rassegna di Scienze B, IZBG, RE
Storiche Forogiuliesi, Memorie RE
Storici, Quaderni RE

Storici, Studi RE
Storici dell' Ordine dei Servi di Maria, Studi RE
Storico Bibliografico Subalpino, Bollettino RE
Storico della Letteratura Italiana, Giornale RE
Storico Italiano, Archivio RE
Storico Italiano per Il Medio Evo e Archivio Muratoriano, Bullettino dell' Istituto RE
Storico Lombardo, Archivio RE
Storico per la Sicilia Orientale, Archivio RE
Storico per le Province Napoletane, Archivio RE
Storico per Le Province Parmensi, Archivio RE
Storico Piacentino, Bollettino RE
Story, Methodist UMPI
Strasbourg, Revue des Sciences Religieuses de l' Universite de RE
Streeven B, ICB, IZBG, RE
Strenna Storica Bolognese RE
Stromata IOB, IZBG, RE
Student SBPI
Student, Adult SBPI
Student, Methodist UMPI
Student, United Methodist (Series) UMPI
Studi Biblici IZBG
Studi Classici, Rivista di ETL
Studi Classici e Orientali B, IBHR
Studi Danteschi RE
Studi di Saciclogia IBHR
Studi di Trieste, Anncli dclla Facalta di Letare e Filosafia dell' Universita degli IBHR
Studi e Materiali di Storia della Religioni B, ETL, IBHR, IZBG, RE
Studi Ebraici, Annuario di B
Studi Etiopici, Rassegna di B
Studi Fenici, Rivista di B
Studi Francescani B, RE
Studi Mahrebini IBHR
Studi Medievali RE
Studi Mediolatini e Volgari RE
Studi Micenci Ed Egeo-Anatolici IBHR
Studi Orientali, Revista degli IZBG
Studi Orientali, Rivista degli B, ETL, IBHR, RE
Studi Preistorici, Bollettino del Centro Camuno di IZBG
Studi Romani B, RE
Studi Romanistici, Index Quaderni Camerti di B
Studi Semitici IZBG
Studi Senesi RE
Studi Storici RE

Studi Storici dell' Ordine dei Servi di Maria RE
Studi Urbinati di Storia, Filosofia e Letteratura
RE
Studi Urbinati di Storia, Filosofia e Letteratura
RE
Studia et Documenta Historiae et Iuris B, RE
Studia Evangelica IBHR
Studia Hibernica RE
Studia Historica Slovaca RE
Studia Islamica B, IBHR
Studia Liturgica IRPL, IZBG, NTA, RE
Studia Missionalia RE
Studia Monastica RE
Studia Montis Reglii ETL
Studia Moralia B
Studia Neophilologica RE
Studia Orientalia B, IBHR, IZBG
Studia Orientalia Christiana B, RE
Studia Papyrologica B, IBHR
Studia Patavina ETL, NTA, RE
Studia Patristica B
Studia Picena RE
Studia Theologica ETL, IRPL, IZBG, NTA, RE
Studia Theologica Varsaviensia RE
Studia Warminkie B
Studia Zrodloznawcze RE
Studien, Asiatische ETL, IZBG
Studien, Biblische IZBG
Studien, Erfurter Theologische IZBG
Studien, Franziskanische ETL, IOB, IZBG, NTA, RE
Studien, Fruhmittelalrerliche RE
Studien, Kant ETL, RE
Studien, Marburger Theologische IZBG
Studien, Mariologische B
Studien, Ostkirchliche ETL, NTA, RE
Studien, Oudtestamentische B, IZBG
Studien, Theologische ETL, IZBG
Studien, Trierer Theologische IZBG
Studien und Mitteilungen Zur Geschichte des
Benediktiner Ordens und Seiner Zweige RE
Studien zum Alten und Neuen Testament IZBG
Studien Zur Sprachwissenschaft, Munchener B, IBHR
Studien Zur Umwelt des Neuen Testaments IZBG
Studienbucher, Neukirchener ETL
Studies CPLI
Studies, Adult Bible UMPI
Studies, African IBHR
Studies, African (Johannesburg) IBHR, ICB

Studies, Andrews University Seminary B, ETL, IBHR, IRPL, IZBG, NTA, SISPL
Studies, Asian Folklore IBHR
Studies, Augustinian RE
Studies, Bulletin of the School of Oriental and African RE
Studies, Chicago CPLI, ETL, NTA, RPI
Studies, English RE
Studies, Franciscan CPLI, ETL, IZBG, NTA, RE, RPI
Studies, French RE
Studies, Harvard Theological IZBG
Studies, Hervormde Teologiese B, IZBG
Studies, Indian Ecclesiastical B, NTA
Studies, Irish Historical RE
Studies, Jewish Social IZBG
Studies, Journal of Classical B
Studies, Journal of Cuneiform IZBG
Studies, Journal of Ecumenical CPLI, ETL, IRPL, IZBG, RE, RPI
Studies, Journal of Ethiopian B
Studies, Journal of Glass B, N
Studies, Journal of Historical ETL, IBHR, IZBG, NTA
Studies, Journal of Jewish ETL, IZBG, NTA
Studies, Journal of Modern African GSSRPL
Studies, Journal of Near Eastern ETL, IZBG, NTA, RPI
Studies, Journal of Roman B, RE
Studies, Journal of Semitic ETL, IRPL, IZBG, NTA
Studies, Journal of Theological ETL, IRPL, IZBG, RE, RTA
Studies, Louvain CPLI, NTA
Studies, Lown Institute for Judaiistic IZBG
Studies, Marian B, CPLI
Studies, Mediaeval RE
Studies, Medieval B, IBHR
Studies, Monastic CPLI
Studies, New Testament CPI, ETL, IRPL, IZBG, NTA, RE, RPI
Studies, Nottingham Mediaeval RE
Studies, Philippine B, IBHR
Studies, Philosophical CPLI
Studies, Pretoria Oriental ETL
Studies, Proceedings of the World Congress of Jewish B
Studies, Religious IRPL, RPI
Studies, Renaissance and Modern RE
Studies, Review of English RE

Studies, the Journal of Hebraic B

Studies, the Quarterly Review of Historical IBHR
Studies, Theological CPLI, ETL, IRPL, IZBG, NTA, RE, RPI, RTA
Studies, Yearbook of Liturgical B
Studies Association Bulletin, Middle East IBHR
Studies Greek, Roman, and Byzantine RE
Studies in Biblical Theology IZBG
Studies in Bibliography and Booklore IJP
Studies in Christian Faith Study-Selected Reading, Foundation UMPI
Studies in Christian Living UMPI
Studies in Classical Philology, Harvard B, IBHR
Studies in Comparative Religion B, IBHR
Studies in Comparative Religion, Temenos. RE
Studies in English Literature RE
Studies in Evangelism, Concept E. Papers from the Department on IOB
Studies in History, Soviet RE
Studies in Islam IBHR
Studies in Medieval and Renaissance History RE
Studies in Papyrology, American B
Studies in Philology RE
Studies in Religion IZBG
Studies in Religion, Wesleyan IZBG, SISPL
Studies in Society and History, Comparative RE
Studies in the Geography of Israel IZBG
Studies in the History of Religions B
Studies in the Renaissance RE
Studies Journal of the British Institute of Archaeology at Anakara, Anatolian B, IBHR
Studies on the Texts of the Desert of Judah ETL
Studies on Voltaire and the XVIIIth Century RE
Studii Biblici Franciscani Liber Annuus ETL, IZBG, NTA
Studii Teologice B, RE
Studium ETL, NTA
Studium der Neueren Sprachen und Literaturen, Archiv fur das RE
Studium Generale IOB
Studium Legionense B
Study Encounter IRPL, RPI
Study of Judaism, Journal for the IZBG
Study of Judaism in the Persian Helenistic and Roman Periods, Journal for the B
Study of Religion, Journal for the Scientific IRPL, RE, RPI

Study-Selected Reading, Foundation Studies in Christian Faith UMPI

Stuttgarter Bibelstudien B, IZBG
Stuttgarter Biblische Monographien IZBG

Subalpino, Bollettino Storico Bibliografico RE
Sucevei, Mitropolia Moldavei si IOB, RE
Suchness RPI
Sud-Est Europeenes, Revue des Etudes IBHR, RE
Sudost-Forschungen IBHR
Suecana, Orientalia B, IBHR
Suid-Afrika, Ou-Testamentiese Werkgemeenskap van IZBG
Suisse (Foi Vivante) ETL
Suisse (Nova et Vetera) B, ETL
Sull' Arte Ravennate e Bizantina, Corsi di Cultura RE
Sumer B, ETL, IZBG
Summit RPI
Sunday Night UMPI
Superiore di Pisa, Annali della Scuola Normale B, RE
Supplement RE
Supplement, Times Literary B
Suppletorius ad Elenchum Bibliographe Biblicum, Elenchus B
Survey, Presbyterian RPI
Svensk Exegetisk Arsbok ETL, IZBG, NTA, RE
Svensk Teologisk Kvartalskrift ETL, IRPL, IZBG, NTA, RE
Swedish Theological Institute, Annual of the B IBHR, IZBG, NTA
Symbolae Osloenses B, IBHR, IZBG
Synagogue Review, United CPLI, RPI
Synagogue School Quarterly IJP
Synthese, Revue de RE
Synthronon Art et Archeologie de la Fin de l' Antiquite IBHR
Syria IZBG
Syrien, Orient ETL, IZBG, NTA
Syriennes, Annales Archeologiques Arabe B, IBHR
Systemantische Theologie, Zeitschrift fur IZBG
Systematische Theologie und Religionsphilosophie, Neue Zeitschrift fur ETL, IRPL, RE, RTA
Sztuki, Biuletyn Historii RE
Taal-Land en Volkenkunde, Bijdragen tot de IBHR
Tablet (London) CPLI

Tall en Letterkunde, Tijdschrift voor Nederlandse RE

Tamuda, Hesperis RE
Tanulmanyck, Antik IBHR

Tarbiz ETL, IZBG, RTA
Tarraconensia, Analecta Sacra RE
Taxandria RE
Te Elfder Ure IOB
Te Gent, Handelingen der Maatschappij voor Geschiedenis en Oudheidkunde RE
Te Rome, Mededlingen van het Nederlands Historie Instituut RE
Teacher, Adult UMPI
Teacher, Methodist UMPI
Teacher, United Methodist (Series) UMPI
Teacher and Ccunselor, Youth UMPI
Teacher for Adults, Bible UMPI
Teacher's Guide, Explcre UMPI
Teacher's Journal, Religion CPLI
Technik, Umschau in Wissenschaft und B
Tectament, Bceken van het Oude B
Teholoqica, Revista di Cultura IZBG
Teilhard Review CPLI
Teilhardiennes, Etudes ETL
Temenos. Studies in Comparative Religion RE
Tempc RPI
Temps, Foi et Le RE
Temps, Signes du ICB
Teclcgi og Kirche, Tidsskrift for ETL, IZBG
Teologia, Revista Espanola de ETL, IZBG, NTA, RE
Teologia, Semana Espanola de B
Teclcgia del Presente B
Teologia Espiritual B, IOB
Teclcgia Morale, Revista di B
Teologica, Perspectiva B
Teclogica, Revista de Cultura ETL, NTA
Teclogice, Studii B, RE
Teologico Agustiniano, Archivo ETL
Teclcgico Granadinc, Archivo IZBG, RE
Teolcgicos, Cuadernos IOB
Teologiczne Chrzescijanskiej Akademii Teologicznej, Roczniki IZBG
Teologicznej, Roczniki Teologiczne Chrzescijanskiej Akademii IZBG
Teologicznc Kanoniczne, Roczniki IZBG, RE
Teologiese Studies, Hervormde B, IZBG

Teologiese Tydskrif, Nederduitse Gereformeerde B, IBHR, IZBG
Teologinen Aikakauskirja B, IZBG
Teologisk Kvartalskrift, Svensk ETL, IRPL, IZBG, NTA, RE
Teologisk Tidsckrift, Norsk ETL
Teologisk Tidsskrift, Dansk ETL, IRPL, IZBG, NTA
Teologisk Tidsskrift, Findsh IOB
Teologisk Tidsskrift, Norsk ETL, IRPL, IZBG, NTA
Terra Santa B
Terre Sainte IZBG
Terre Sainte, Bible et IZBG
Testament, Alter Orient und Altes B, IZBG
Testament, Beitraege Zur Wissenschaft Vom Alten und Neuen IZBG
Testament, Butraege Zur Wissenschaft von Alten und Neuen B
Testament, Commentaar op het Oude B
Testament, Kommentare und Beitrage zum Alten und Neuen (Dusseldorf) B
Testament, Studien zum Alten und Neuen IZBG
Testament, Theological Dictionary of the New B
Testament, Theologisches Handworter zum Alten B
Testament, Theologisches Worterbuch zum Alten B
Testament, Theologisches Worterbuch zum Neue B
Testament, Wissenschafliche Untersuchungen zum Neue B
Testament, Wissenschaftliche Monographien zum Alten und Neuen ETL, IZBG
Testament, Wissenschaftliche Untersuchungen zum Neuen IZBG
Testament Abstracts, New IZBG
Testament Series Lund Coniectanea Biblica, New IZBG
Testament Studies, New CPI, ETL, IRPL, IZBG, NTA, RE, RPI
Testamente, Grande Lessico del Neue B
Testamento, Commenti Spirituali dell' Antico Testamento del Nuovo B
Testamento del Nuovo Testamento, Commenti Spirituali dell' Antico B
Testaments, Abhandlungen Zur Theologie des Alten und Neuen B, IZBG
Testaments, Forschungen Zur Religion und Literatur des Alten und Neuen B, IZBG
Testaments, Studien Zur Umwelt des Neuen IZBG
Testamentum, Novum ETL, IRPL, IZBG, NTA, RE, RTA
Testamentum, Vetus ETL, IRPL, IZBG, NTA, RTA

Testimonianze NTA

Texte und Untersuchungen B, IZBG
Textes, Bulletin de l' Institut de Recherche et D' Histoire des RE

Textes, Revue D' Histoire des B
Textforschung, Arbeiten Zur Neutestamentlichen IZBG
Texts of the Desert of Judah, Studies on the ETL
Textus B, IZBG
Themelios SISPL
Theokratia B
Theologen in Nederland, Jaarboek Werkgenootschap van Kathclieke B
Theologen in Nederland, Werkgenootschap voor Katholieke ETL, IOB
Theologia IOB
Theologia Evangelica IZBG
Theologia Practica B, IOB
Theologia Viatcrum IZBG
Theologiai Azemla IOB
Theologica B
Theologica, Collectanea ETL, IZBG
Theologica, Melita ETL, IZBG, NTA
Theologica, Scripta B
Theologica, Studia ETL, IRPL, IZBG, NTA, RE
Theologica Varsaviensia, Studia RE
Theologicae Lovanienses, Ephemerides ETL, IZBG, NTA, RE
Theological Abstracts, Religious and IZBG
Theological Cassettes, Thesis UMPI
Theological Dictionary of the New Testament B
Theological Education IRPL, RPI
Theological Educator GSSRPL, SBPI
Theological Institute, Annual of the Swedish B IBHR, IZBG, NTA
Theological Journal, Africa SISPL
Theological Journal, Calvin CPI, ETL, IRPL, IZBG, RE, RPI
Theological Journal, Weslyan SISPL
Theological Journal, Westminister CPI, ETL, IRPL, IZBG, NTA, RPI, RTA
Theological Monthly, Concordia CPI, ETL, IRPL, IZBG, NTA, RPI, RTA
Theological Quarterly, Irish CPLI, ETL, IZBG, RE
Theological Quarterly, Lexington ETL, IRPL, NTA, RPI

Theological Quarterly, St. Vladimir's ETL, IRPL, IZBG, NTA, RPI

Theological Review, Anglican B, ETL, IBHR, IRPL, IZBG, NTA, SISPL
Theological Review, Church RPI
Theological Review, Greek Orthodox IRPL, RPI
Theological Review, Harvard B, ETL, IRPL, IZBG, NTA, RE, RPI, RTA
Theological Review, Reformed ETL, IRPL, IZBG, NTA
Theological Seminary Register, Chicago B, SISPL
Theological Seminary Review, Lutheran SISPL
Theological Society, Journal of the Evangelical B
Theological Society of America Proceedings, Catholic CPLI
Theological Studies CPLI, ETL, IRPL, IZBG, NTA, RE, RPI, RTA
Theological Studies, Harvard IZBG
Theological Studies, Journal of ETL, IRPL, IZBG, RE, RTA
Theologicka Priloha Krestanske Revue IZBG
Theologie, Annuaire de l' Academie B
Theologie, Arbeiten Zur IZBG
Theologie, Beitraege Zur Evangelischen B, IZBG
Theologie, Beitraege Zur Forderung Christlicher IZBG
Theologie, Bijdragen. Tijdschrift voor Filosofie en RE
Theologie, Eglise et IZBG
Theologie, Evangelische ETL, IZBG, NTA, RE, RTA
Theologie, Freiburger Zeitschrift fur Philosophie und ETL, NTA, RE
Theologie, Jahrbuch fur Mystiche ETL
Theologie, Kerk en B, IOB
Theologie, Revue D' Histoire de Philosophie et de ETL
Theologie, Tijdschrift voor ETL, IZBG, NTA, RE
Theologie, Zeitschrift fur Katholische ETL, IZBG, NTA
Theologie, Zeitschrift fur Systemantische IZBG
Theologie Ancienne et Medievale, Bulletin de IZBG, RE
Theologie Ancienne et Medievale, Recherches de ETL, IZBG, NTA, RE
Theologie Biblique, Bulletin de B
Theologie Catholique, Dictionnaire de B
Theologie des Alten und Neuen Testaments, Abhandlungen Zur B, IZBG

Theologie en Pastoral, Collationes Vlaoms Tijdschaft voor B

Theologie en Zielzorg IOB
Theologie et de Philosophie, Revue de ETL, IZBG, NTA, RE

Theologie in Praktijk IOB
Theologie Pastorale au Rwanda et Burundi B
Theologie. Pastorale et Spiritualite ETL
Theologie und Glaube ETL, IZBG, NTA, RE
Theologie und Kirche, Zeitschrift fur ETL, IRPL, IZBG, RE, RTA
Theologie und Philosophie ETL, IZBG, NTA, RE
Theologie und Religionsphilosophie, Neue Zeitschrift fur Systematische ETL, IRPL, RE, RTA
Theologique, Nouvelle Revue CPLI, ETL, IZBG, NTA, RE
Theologique de Louvain, Revue RE
Theologique et Philosophique, Laval ETL, NTA
Theologiques, Cahiers ETL
Theologiques, Revue des Sciences Philosophiques et B, ETL, IBHR, IZBG, NTA, RE
Theologiques de l' Actualite Protestante, Cahiers IZBG
Theologiques et Religieuses, Etudes ETL, IRPL, IZBG, NTA, RE
Theologisch Praktische Quartalschrift IZBG, RE
Theologisch Tijdschrift, Gereformeerd ETL, IZBG, NTA, RE, RTA
Theologisch Tijdschrift, Nederlands ETL, IRPL, IZBG, NTA, RE
Theologische Literaturzeitung IZBG
Theologische Akademie IBHR
Theologische Bericht B
Theologische Bucherei IZBG
Theologische Existenz Heute B, IZBG
Theologische Forschung IZBG
Theologische Literaturzeitung ETL, IRPL, NTA, RE
Theologische Quartalschrift ETL, IBHR, NTA, RE
Theologische Quartalschrift, Tubinger ETL, IZBG
Theologische Revue ETL, IZBG, NTA, RE
Theologische Rundschau ETL, IRPL, IZBG, RE, RTA
Theologische Studien ETL, IZBG
Theologische Studien, Erfurter IZBG
Theologische Studien, Marburger IZBG
Theologische Studien, Trierer IZBG
Theologische Umschau, Schweizerische IOB

Theologische Zeitschrift ETL, IRPL, IZBG, NTA, RE, RTA
Theologische Zeitschrift, Munchener ETL, IZBG, NTA, RE
Theologische Zeitschrift, Trierer ETL, IZBG, NTA, RE
Theologisches Handworter zum Alten Testament B
Theologisches Jahrbuch IZBG
Theologisches Worterbuch zum Alten Testament B
Theologisches Worterbuch zum Neue Testament B
Theologisch-Praktische Quartelschrift B
Theology ETL, IRPL, IZBG, NTA
Theology, Biblical NTA
Theology, Canadian Journal of ETL, IRPL, IZBG, RTA
Theology, Indian Journal of IZBG, NTA, RTA
Theology, Scottish Journal of ETL, IRPL, IZBG, RTA
Theology, South East Asia Journal of IRPL, NTA
Theology, Southwestern Journal of CPI, ETL, IRPL, IZBG, NTA, RPI, RTA, SBPI
Theology, Studies in Biblical IZBG
Theology and Life RTA
Theology and the Church, Journal for IRPL, RPI
Theology Bulletin, Biblical B, IZBG
Theology Digest CPLI, ETL, IZBG, RPI
Theology Journal, Perkins School of NTA
Theology of the World Presbyterian Alliance and the World Alliance of Reformed Churches, Bulletin of the Department of IOB
Theology Society, Proceedings of the College CPLI
Theology Today ETL, IRPL, IZBG, NTA, RPI, RTA
Theomas More, Moreana. Bulletin RE
Theory, History and RE
These Times GSSRPI
Thesis Theological Cassettes UMPI
Thijmgenootschap, Annalen van het B, IOB, RE
Thomas, Divus ETL, ICB, IZBG, NTA, RE
Thomist CPLI, ETL, RE
Thomiste, Revue ETL, IZBG, NTA, RE
Thomisticae, Aquinas Ephemerides ETL
Thought CPLI, RE, RPI
Thought, Brethern Life and ETL, IRPL, RPI, RTA
Thought, Faith and SISPL
Thought, Journal of Religious IRPL, RPI
Three/Four UMPI
Thuringen, Amtsblatt der Evangelisch-Lutherischen Kirche in IOB
Tidsckrift, Norsk Teologisk ETL
Tidsskrift, Dansk Teologisk ETL, IRPL, IZBG, NTA

Tidsskrift, Findsh Teologisk IOB
Tidsskrift, Historisk (Oslo) RE
Tidsskrift, Norsk Teologisk ETL, IRPL, IZBG, NTA
Tidsskrift, Ny Kyrklig ETL, IZBG
Tidsskrift for Bok och Biblioteksvasen, Nordisk RE
Tidsskrift for Misjon, Norsk IOB
Tidsskrift for Teologi og Kirche ETL, IZBG
Tiempos, Signos de los B
Tijdschaft voor Theologie en Pastoral,
Collationes Vlaoms B
Tijdschrift, Gereformeerd Theologisch ETL,
IZBG, NTA, RE, RTA
Tijdschrift, Nederlands Theologisch ETL, IRPL,
IZBG, NTA, RE
Tijdschrift Gewijd Aan de Geschiedenis der
Kruisheren, Clairlieu. RE
Tijdschrift Hasselt, Diocesaan ETL
Tijdschrift voor Filosofie en Theologie,
Bijdragen. RE
Tijdschrift voor Geschiedenis RE
Tijdschrift voor Liturgie IZBG
Tijdschrift voor Nederlandse Tall en Letterkunde RE
Tijdschrift voor Philosophie RE
Tijdschrift voor Rechtsgeschiedenis B, RE
Tijdschrift voor Theologie ETL, IZBG, NTA, RE
Tijdschrift voor Wijsbegeerte en Psychologie,
Algemeen Nederlands ETL
Times, Church ICB
Times, Expository ETL, IRPL, IZBG, RTA
Times, Hi UMPI
Times, Junior Hi UMPI
Times, These GSSRPL
Times Literary Supplement B
Tische des Wortes, am B
Today CPLI
Today, Christianity CPI, GSSRPL, IRPL, IZBG, RPI
Today, Encounter B
Today, History RE
Today, Migration ICB
Today, Philosophy CPLI
Today, Psychology GSSRPL
Today, Sisters CPLI, RPI
Today, Theology ETL, IRPL, IZBG, NTA, RPI, RTA
Today's Education GSSRPL
Today's Family Digest CPLI
Together RPI
Toledo Archdiocesan Messenger RPI
Tomista, Ciencia ETL, ICB, IZBG, NTA, RE

Tomistica, Rassegna di Letteratura RE
Tomorrow's World SISPI
Toscana, Rassegna Storica RE
Touraine, Bulletin Trimestriel de la Societe Archeologique de RE
Tournai, Confrontations. Revue Diocesaine de B, ETL
Tournai, Revue Diocesaine de ETL
Traditio CPLI, ETI, NTA, RE, RPI
Tradition IJP, NTA
Tradition und Erneuerung IBHR, IOB
Traditions Populaires, Arts et RE
Training, Church SBPI
Transaction Proceeding, American Philological Association B
Transactions, Glasgow University Oriental Society B
Transactions and Proceedings of the American Philological Association Re
Transactions of the Royal Historical Society RE
Translation, Notes on SISPL
Translator, Bible IZBG
Travaux, Etudes et B
Travaux et Jours IOB
Travaux et Memoires du Centre de Recherche D' Histoire et Civilisation Byzantines RE
Travaux Historiques et scientifiques, Bulletin Philologique et Historique du Comite des RE
Trends, Faith and Order IOB
Trierer Landes und Seiner Nachbargebiete, Trierer Zeitschrift fur Geschichte und Kunst des RE
Trierer Theologische Studien IZBG
Trierer Theologische Zeitschrift ETL, IZBG, NTA, RE
Trierer Zeitschrift fur Geschichte und Kunst des Trierer Landes und Seiner Nachbargebiete RE
Trieste, Annali della Facalta di Letare e Filosafia dell' Universita degli Studi di IBHR
Trimestriel de la Societe Academique des Antiquaires de la Marinie, Bulletin RE
Trimestriel de la Societe Archeologique de Touraine, Bulletin RE
Trimestriel de la Societe des Antiquaires de Picardie, Bulletin RE
Trinitario, Secretariado ETL
Trinitarios, Estudios B
Triumph CPLI, RPI
Tro, for Biblisk IOB
Tro och Liv IOB

True Light RPI

Truth, Plain SISPL
Tschechoslowakei, Protestantischen Kirchen der IZBG
Tubinger Theologische Quartalschrift ETL, IZBG
Turkish Review of Archaeology IBHR
Tuuk Arkeologi Dergisi IBHR
Twelve/Fifteen UMPI
Tydskrif, Nederduitse Gereformeerde Teologiese E, IBHR, IZBG
Tyndale Bulletin IZBG
Ubersee, Afrika und IBHR
Ugarit Forschungen B
Uitgaff der Bronnen van het Oud Vaderlandsche Recht, Verslagen en Mededeelingen der Vereeniging tot RE
Uitger Door de Vereniging Gelre, Bijdragen en Mededelingen RE
Ukrainian Orthodox Work RPI
Umanistica, Italaia Medioevale e RE
Umanita Classica e Cristiana, Orpheus. Rivista di RE
Umeni RE
Umschau, Schweizerische Theologische IOB
Umschau in Wissenschaft und Technik B
Umwelt des Neuen Testaments, Studien Zur IZBG
Una Sancta ETL, IRPL, IZBG, NTA, RPI
Unam Sanctam IZBG
Unio, Catholica IOB
Union College Annual, Hebrew ETL, NTA
Union Seminary Quarterly Review ETL, IRPL, RPI, RTA
Union Xollege Annual, Hevrew IZBG
Unitarian Universalist World RPI
Unitas ETL, NTA
Unite Chretienne, Vers l' ETL, IOB
United Bible Societies Bulletin B
United Biblical Societies, Bulletin of the IZBG
United Church Review IOB
United Evangelical Action CPI, GSSRPL, RPI
United Methodist Student (Series) UMPI
United Methodist Teacher (Series) UMPI
United Synagogue Review CPLI, RPI
Unity Information Service, Secretariat for Promoting Christian IOB
Universalist World, Unitarian RPI
Universita degli Studi di Trieste, Annoli della Facalta di Letare e Filosafia dell' IBHR

Universitat, Wissenschaftliche Zeitschrift der Karl Marx
Re IZBG

Universitat Graz, Jahrbuch des Kunsthistorischen Instiutes der RE
Universitat Greifswald, Wissenschaftliche Zeitschrift der IZBG

Universitat Halle Wittenberg, Wissenschaftliche Zeitschrift der Martin Luther IBHR, IZBG
Universitat Halte Wittenberg, Wissenschaftliche Zeitschrift der Martin Luther RERE
Universitat Jena, Wissenschaftliche Zeitschrift der IZBG
Universitat Jena, Wissenschaftliche Zeitschrift der Friedrich Schiller RE
Universitat Rostock, Wissenschaftliche Zeitschrift der RE
Universitat zu Berlin, Wissenschaftliche Zeitschrift der Humbolt RE
Universitatis Gotoburgensis, Acta IZBG
Universitatis Gregorianae, Pontificiae B
Universitatis Upsaliensis, Acta IZBG
Universite D' Ottawa, Revue de l' CPLI, ETL, IZBG, RE
Universite de Paris, Annales de l' RE
Universite de Strasbourg, Revue des Sciences Religieuses de l' RE
Universite St. Joseph, Melanges de l' B, IBHR, IZBG, RE
Universitets Arsskrift, Lunds IZBG
University Journal, Durham IZBG
University of Birmingham Historical Journal RE
University of Bombay, Journal of the IBHR
University of California Publications in Classical Archaelogy and Semitic Philology IZBG
University Oriental Society Transactions, Glasgow B
University Quarterly, Free RTA
University Seminary Studies, Andrews B, ETL, IBHR, IRPL, IZBG, NTA, SISPL
Uniwersytetu Lubelskiego, Zeszyty Naukowe Katolickiego B, RE
Untersuchungen, Biblische B
Untersuchungen, Texte und B, IZBG
Untersuchungen zum Neue Testament, Wissenschafliche B

Untersuchungen zum Neuen Testament, Wissenschaftliche IZBG

Unum Sint", Revista Ecumenica "Ut ETL
Unum Sint, Ut ICB
UN-Versita Statale de Milano, Annali del Facolta di Filosofia e Letter di RE
Upsaliensis, Acta Seminarii Neotestamentici ETL, IZBG
Upsaliensis, Acta Universitatis IZBG
Upsaliensis, Nuntius Sodalicii Neotestamentici IZBG
Urbinati di Storia, Filosofia e Letteratura Studi RE
Urchristentums, Arbeiten Zur Geschichte des Antiken Judentums und des B
Ure, Te Elfder ICB
Ut Unum Sint ICB
Utgitt Av Det Norsk Videnskaps Akademi i Oslo, Avhandlinger IZBG
Utgitt Av Det Norske Videnskaps Akademie i Oslo, Skrifter IZBG
Vaderlandsche Recht, Verslagen en Mededeelingen der Vereeniging tot Uitgaff der Bronnen van het Oud RE
Val (Ecclesia) ICB
Var Losen IOB
Varsaviensia, Studia Theologica RE
Vedat, Escritos del B
Velazquez, Melanges de la Casa de RE
Veneto, Archivio RE
Veneto, Arhivio RE
Veneto di Scienze, Lettere di Arte Atti dell' Istituto RE
Verbum Caro ETL, IRPL, IZBG
Verbum Caro, Communio B
Verbum Domini ETL, IZBG, NTA
Verdad y Vida RE
Vereeniging tot Uitgaff der Bronnen van het Oud Vaderlandsche Recht, Verslagen en Mededeelingen der RE
Vereinigung, Jahrbuch der Hessischen Kirchengeschichtlichen IOB
Vereins, Zeitschrift des Deutschen Palastina ETL, NTA, RE
Vereins Bamberg, Bericht des Historischin RE
Vereins fur der Niererrhein, Annalen der Historischen RE

Vereins fur Kunstwisswenschaft, Zeitschrift des Deutschen RE
Vereniging Gelre, Bijdragen en Mededelingen Uitger Door de RE
Vergangenheit und Gegenwart, Heilige Land in IZBG
Vergleichende Sprachforschung auf dem Gebiet der Indogermanischen Sprachen, Zeitschrift fur B
Vergleichinde Rechtsgeschichte, Einschliesslich der Ethnologischen Rechtsforshung Zeitschrift fur B, IBHR
Verhandelingen der Amsterdam Akademie van Wetenschappen B
Verhandelingen van het Vooraziatisch-Egytisch Genootschap "ex Oriente Lux", Mededlingen en ETL
Verhandlugn der Sachsischen Akademie der Wissenschaften zu Leipzig, Berichte uber die RE
Verhandlungen der Akademie van Wetenschappen B
Verhandlungen der Naturforschenden Gesleischaft in Basel IBHR
Verkuendigung, Concept G. Arbeiten aus dem Referat fur Fragen der Iob
Verkundigung und Forschung ETL, IOB, IZBG, NTA
Vers l' Unite Chretienne ETL, IOB
Verslagen en Mededeelingen der Vereeniging tot Uitgaff der Bronnen van het Oud Vaderlandsche Recht RE
Verslagen en Mededelingen van de Leiegouw RE
Vestnik, Bogoslovni B
Vestnik, Bratskij IOB
Vestnik, Carkoven IOB
Vetera, Nova et ETL, IZBG, NTA
Vetera, Nova et (Suisse) B, ETL
Vetera Christianorum RE
Vetus Testamentum ETL, IRPL, IZBG, NTA, RTA
Viatorum, Communic ETL, IRPL, IZBG, NTA, RE
Viatorum, Theologia IZBG
Victoriense, Scriptorium RE
Vida, Verdad y RE
Vida Cristia, Questions de B
Videnskaps Akademi i Oslo, Avhandlinger Utgitt Av Det Norsk IZBG
Videnskaps Akademie i Oslo, Skrifter Utgitt Av Det Norske IZBG
Vie, Collection Lumiere et IZBG
Vie, Esprit et ETL, NTA
Vie, Foi et ETL, IRPL
Vie, Lumiere et CPLI, ETL, IZBG, RE
Vie Chretienne, Bible et ETL, IZBG, NTA

Vie Consacree ETL
Vie Spirituelle IZBG
Vierteljahresschrift fur Kirchen und Geistesgeschichte Osterucpas, Kyrios. RE
Vierteljahrhefte fur Zeitgeschichte RE
Vierteljahrsblatter, Rheinische RE
Vierteljahrsschrift fur Literaturwissenschaft und Geistegeschechte, Deutsche B, RE
Vierteljahrsschrift fur Social und Wirtschaftsgeschishte RE
View, World GSSRPL, RPI
Viewpoint, Biblical SISPL
Vigilae Christianae ETL, IRPL, IZBG, NTA, RE
Vigilia IOB
Vilaine, Bulletin et Memoirs de la Societe Archeologique du Department D' Ille et RE
Vision SBPI
Vision, World SISPL
Vita, Citta di ETL
Vita, Parcle di B
Vita Religiosa ETL
Vitae, Lumen CPLI, ETL, IZBG
Vital Christianity GSSRPL, RPI
Viva, Iglesia B
Vivante, Archeologie B
Vivante, Foi (Suisse) ETL
Vivante Afrique ICB
Vivarais, Revue du RE
Vivarium RE
Vladimir's Theclogical Quarterly, St. ETL, IRPL, IZBG, NTA, RPI
Vlaoms Tijdschaft voor Theologie en Pastoral, Cellaticnes B
Volgari, Studi Mediolatini e RE
Volkenbunder zu Leipzig, Jahrbuch des Museums fur IBHR
Volkenkunde, Bijdragen tot de Taal-Land en IBHR
Volkskunde, Osterreichische Zeitschrift fur IBHR
Volkskunde, Schweizerisches Archiv fur IBHR, RE
Volkskunde. Beitrage Zur Heimantkunde, Carinthia I. Geschichliche und KARNTENS RE
Volkskunde Westfalen. Hefte fur Geschichte, Kunst und RE
Volkunde in Dresden, Abhandlungen und Berichte des Staatlichen Museum fur IBHR
Vollversammlung des Lutherischen Weltbundes, Offizieller Bericht der Iob
Voltaire and the XVIIIth Century, Studies on RE

Vom Alten und Neuen Testament, Beitraege Zur Wissenschaft IZBG

Vooraziatisch Egyptisch Genootschap ex Oriente Lux, Jaarbericht van het IBHR
Vooraziatisch Egyptisch Genootschap ex Oriente Lux, Jarrbericht van het B
Vooraziatisch Egyptisch Genotschap ex Oriente Lux, Jaarbericht van het IZBG
Vooraziatisch-Egytisch Genootschap "ex Oriente Lux", Mededlingen en Verhandelingen van het ETL
Voprosy Filosofu IOB
Vorderasiatische Archaeologie, Zeitschrift fur Assyriclogie und ETL, IZBG
Vorgare IOB
Vox Evangelica ETL, IZBG, NTA
Vox Reformata NTA
Vozes IOB
Vrije Fries RE
Wahrheit, Wort und ICB, IZBG
Wales, Journal of the Historical Society of the Church in RE
Wallraf Richartz Jahrbuch RE
Wappenkunde Archiv fur Diplomatik Schriftgeschichte, Siegel und RE
War Cry GSSRPL
Warande en Belfort, Dietsche RE
Warburg and Courtauld Institutes, Journal of the RE
Warminkie, Studia B
Way CPLI, NTA, RPI
Week, North American Liturgical CPLI
Weekly, Classical B
Wege zum Menschen ETL, IOB
Weisheit, Wissenschaft und ETL, IZBG, NTA
Welt, Antike B
Welt, Bibel in der B, IOB
Welt, Evangelische ICB
Welt der Slaven IOB
Welt des Islams ICB
Welt des Orients IZBG
Weltbild, Wissenschaft und IZBG
Weltbundes, Offizieller Bericht der Vollversammlung des Lutherischen IOB
Wencling IOB
Wereldwijd IOB
Werkgemeenskap van Suid-Afrika, Ou-Testamentiese IZBG

Werkgenootschap van Katholieke Theologen in Nederland, Jaarboek B
Werkgenootschap voor Katholieke Theologen in Nederland ETL, ICB
Werkshefte ICB
Wesley Quarterly UMPI
Wesleyan Studies in Religion IZBG, SISPL
Weslyan Theolcgical Journal SISPL
West, East and B
West Africian Archaeolcgical Newsletter IBHR
Western Pacific, Folk Religion and the Worldview in the South IBHR
Westfalen. Hefte fur Geschichte, Kunst und Vclkskunde RE
Westfalen. Hefte fur Geschichte, Kunst und Vclkskunde RE
Westfalische Forschungen RE
Westfalische Zeitschrift RE
Westminister Theological Journal CPI, ETL, IRPL, IZBG, NTA, RPI, RTA
Wetenschappen, Verhandelingen der Amsterdam Akademie van B
Wetenschappen, Verhandlungen der Akademie van B
Wichmann Jahrbuch fur Kirchengeschichte Im Bistum Berlin RE
Wien, Jahrbuch der Kunsthistorischen Sammlungen RE
Wiener Zeitschrift fur Kunde des Morgenlandes B, ETL, IZBG
Wiener Zeitschrift fur Philosophie ETL
Wiesbaden, Klio. Beitrage Zur Alten Geschichte Berlin et RE
Wijsbegeerte en Psychologie, Algemeen Nederlands Tijdschrift vcor ETL
Wirtschaftsgeschichte, Jahrbuch fur RE
Wirtschaftsgeschishte, Vierteljahrsschrift fur Social und RE
Wissenschafliche Untersuchungen zum Neue Testament B
Wissenschaft, Beihefte Zur Zeitschrift fur die Altestamentliche B, IZBG
Wissenschaft, Bibliothek und RE
Wissenschaft, Bild der B
Wissenschaft, Zeitschrift fur die Alttestamentliche ETL, IRPL, IZBG, RTA
Wissenschaft, Zeitschrift fur die Neutestamentliche ETL, IRPL, IZBG, NTA, RE, RTA
Wissenschaft UN Prozis in Kirche und Gesellschaft B
Wissenschaft und Technik, Umschau in B

Wissenschaft und Weisheit ETL, IZBG, NTA

Wissenschaft und Weltbild IZBG
Wissenschaft Vom Alten und Neuen Testament, Beitraege Zur IZBG
Wissenschaft von Alten und Neuen Testament, Butraege Zur B
Wissenschaften, Anzeiger der Oestereichischen Akademie der RE
Wissenschaften, Sitzungsberichte der Bayerischen Akademie der RE
Wissenschaften, Sitzungsberichte der Deutschen Akademie der IZBG, RE
Wissenschaften, Sitzungsberichte der Heidelberger Akademie der IZBG, RE
Wissenschaften, Sitzungsberichte der Cesterreicheschen Akademie der Izbg
Wissenschaften, Sitzungsberichte der Oesterreichischen Akademie der Re
Wissenschaften in Gottingen, Nachrichten der Akademie der RE
Wissenschaften zu Gottingen, Nachrichter der Akademie der B
Wissenschaften zu Leipzig, Berichte uber die Verhandlugn der Sachsischen Akademie der RE
Wissenschaften zu Leipzig, Sitzungsberichte der Sachsischen Adademie der RE
Wissenschaftliche Monographien zum Alten und Neuen Testament ETL, IZBG
Wissenschaftliche Untersuchungen zum Neuen Testament IZBG
Wissenschaftliche Zeitschrift der Friedrich Schiller Universitat Jena Re
Wissenschaftliche Zeitschrift der Humbolt Universitat zu Berlin RE
Wissenschaftliche Zeitschrift der Karl Marx Universitat
Re IZBG
Wissenschaftliche Zeitschrift der Martin Luther Universitat Halle Wittenberg IBHR, IZBG
Wissenschaftliche Zeitschrift der Martin Luther Universitat Halte Wittenberg RERE
Wissenschaftliche Zeitschrift der Universitat Greifswald IZBG
Wissenschaftliche Zeitschrift der Universitat Jena IZBG
Wissenschaftliche Zeitschrift der Universitat Rostock RE

Wissenschaftlishe Padogogik, Schriften des Deutschen Instituts fur Etl
Witness RPI
Witness, Advent Christian RPI
Witness, Lutheran GSSRPL, RPI
Wittenberg, Wissenschaftliche Zeitschrift der Martin Luther Universitat
Wittenberg, Wissenschaftliche Zeitschrift der Martin Luther Universitat Halle IBHR
Wittenberg, Wissenschaftliche Zeitschrift der Martin Luther Universitat Halte RERE
Wochenblatt, Israelitisches IZBG
Woman, Church RPI
Woman, Methodist UMPI
Word RPI
Word, Living CPLI
Word, Orthodox RPI
Work, Faith at RPI
Work, Good CPLI
Work, Ukrainian Orthodox RPI
Worker, Catholic RPI
Workers with Youth UMPI
World, Baptist IOB, SBPL
World, Catholic Library CPLI, RPI
World, Christ to the CPLI, IOB
World, Church in the IOB
World, Lutheran IRPI, IRPL
World, Muslim IRPL, RPI
World, Reformed and Presbyterian IRPL, RPI
World, the Catholic CPLI, GSSRPL, RPI
World, Tomorrow's SISPL
World, Unitarian Universalist RPI
World Alliance of Reformed Churches, Bulletin of the Department of Theology of the World Presbyterian Alliance and the IOB
World Archaeology SISPL
World Call IOB
World Congress of Jewish Studies, Proceedings of the B
World Justice CPLI, IOB
World Mission CPLI, IOB
World Order RPI
World Outlook IOB
World Outlook, New RPI
World Presbyterian Alliance and the World Alliance of Reformed Churches, Bulletin of the Department of Theology of the IOB
World View GSSRPL, RPI

World Vision SISPL

Worldview in the South Western Pacific, Folk Religion and the IBHR
Worship CPLI, IRPL, IZBG, RPI

Worship Music the Acts, Response in IOB
Wort, Dienst am B
Wort und Dienst IZBG
Wort und Wahrheit ICB, IZBG
Worterbuch zum Alten Testament, Theologisches B
Worterbuch zum Neue Testament, Theologisches B
Wortes, am Tische des B
Wurzburger Diozesangeschichtsblatter RE
Wydawniczej i Posiedzen Naukoeych Oraz Kronika, Sprawozdania Z Czynnosci RE
Xaveriana, Ecclesiastica B
Xollege Annual, Hevrew Union IZBG
Yearbook of Liturgical Studies B
Yearbook of the History of Music, Musica Disciplina. a RE
Years, Mature UMPI
Years Ahead SBPI
Yediot IZBG
York, New (Dialog) ETL
York Public Library, Bulletin of the New RE
Young Judaean IJP
Your Church RPI
Youth, Accent on UMPI
Youth, Bible Lessons for UMPI
Youth, Workers with UMPI
Youth Leader UMPI
Youth Leadership SBPI
Youth Teacher and Counselor UMPI
Yu Cjiaohui, Shenhsueh B
Zapas, Cesky IOB
Zapiski Historyczne RE
Zeichen der Zeit B, ICB
Zeit, Stimmen der CPLI, ETL, IZBG, NTA, RE
Zeit, Zeichen der B, IOB
Zeiten, Zwischen Den IOB
Zeitgeschichte, Vierteljahrhefte fur RE
Zeitschrift, Archivalische RE
Zeitschrift, Biblische ETL, IRPL, IZBG, NTA, RE
Zeitschrift, Byzantinische RE
Zeitschrift, Ethnographisch-Archaeologische IBHT
Zeitschrift, Geographische B
Zeitschrift, Historische B, IOB, RE

Zeitschrift, Internationale Kirchliche ETL, IZBG, NTA, RE
Zeitschrift, Mainzer RE
Zeitschrift, Munchener Theologische ETL, IZBG, NTA, RE
Zeitschrift, Theologische ETL, IRPL, IZBG, NTA, RE, RTA
Zeitschrift, Trierer Theologische ETL, IZBG, NTA, RE
Zeitschrift, Westfalische RE
Zeitschrift der Deutschen Morgenlandischen Gesellschaft ETL, IZBG, NTA, RE
Zeitschrift der Friedrich Schiller Universitat Jena, Wissenschaftliche RE
Zeitschrift der Gavigny Stiftung fur Rechtsgeschichte Romanische Abteilung RE
Zeitschrift der Gesellschaft fur Schleswig Holsteinische Geschichte RE
Zeitschrift der Humbolt Universitat zu Berlin, Wissenschaftliche RE
Zeitschrift der Karl Marx Universitat, Wissenschaftliche
Re IZBG
Zeitschrift der Martin Luther Universitat Halle Wittenberg, Wissenschaftliche IBHR, IZBG
Zeitschrift der Martin Luther Universitat Halte Wittenberg, Wisserschaftliche RERE
Zeitschrift der Universitat Greifswald, Wissenschaftliche IZBG
Zeitschrift der Universitat Jena, Wissenschaftliche IZBG
Zeitschrift der Universitat Rostock, Wissenschaftliche RE
Zeitschrift des Aachener Geschichtsvereins RE
Zeitschrift des Bergischen Geschichtsvereins RE
Zeitschrift des Deutschen Palastina Vereins ETL, NTA, RE
Zeitschrift des Deutschen Vereins fur Kunstwisswenschaft RE
Zeitschrift Deutschen Palastinavereins IZBG
Zeitschrift fur Agypitsche Sprache und Alterumskunde IZBG
Zeitschrift fur Agyptische Sprache und Alterumskunde B
Zeitschrift fur Alte Geschichte, Historia. RE
Zeitschrift fur Assyriologie und Vorderasiatische Archaeologie ETL, IZBG
Zeitschrift fur Bayerische Kircheneschichte RE

Zeitschrift fur Bayerische Landergerchichte RE

Zeitschrift fur Biblicthekswissen und Bibliographie RE
Zeitschrift fur Celtische Philologie RE
Zeitschrift fur das Klassische Altertum, Philologus. RE
Zeitschrift fur Deutsche Philclogie RE
Zeitschrift fur Deutsches Altertum und Deutsche Literatur RE
Zeitschrift fur die Altestamentliche Wissenschaft, Beihefte Zur B, IZBG
Zeitschrift fur die Alttestamentliche Wissenschaft ETL, IRPL, IZBG, RTA
Zeitschrift fur die Geschichte des Oberrheins RE
Zeitschrift fur die Geschichte und Altertumskunde Ermlands RE
Zeitschrift fur die Neutestamentliche Wissenschaft ETL, IRPL, IZBG, NTA, RE, RTA
Zeitschrift fur Englische Philologie, Anglia. RE
Zeitschrift fur Erzahlforschung, Fabula. RE
Zeitschrift fur Ethnolcgie B, IBHR
Zeitschrift fur Evangelische Ethik ETL, IRPL, RTA
Zeitschrift fur Franzosische Sprache und Literatur RE
Zeitschrift fur Geschichte, Schweizerische RE
Zeitschrift fur Geschichte des Judentums B
Zeitschrift fur Geschichte und Altertumskunde, Basler RE
Zeitschrift fur Geschichte und Kunst des Trierer Landes und Seiner Nachbargebiete, Trierer RE
Zeitschrift fur Geschichtswissenschaft RE
Zeitschrift fur Internationale Zusammenarbeit, Dckumente. Iob
Zeitschrift fur Jagdwissenshaft IBHR
Zeitschrift fur Katholische Theologie ETL, IZBG, NTA
Zeitschrift fur Kirchengeschichte RE
Zeitschrift fur Klassische Philolcgie, Hermes. RE
Zeitschrift fur Kunde des Morgenlandes, Wiener B, ETL, IZBG
Zeitschrift fur Kunst, Pantheon. Internationale RE
Zeitschrift fur Kunst und Denkmalpflege, Oesterreichische RE
Zeitschrift fur Literaturgeschichte, Euphorion. RE
Zeitschrift fur Luxemburger Geschichte, Hemecht. RE

Zeitschrift fur Missionswissenschaft, Neue
IZBG, RE
Zeitschrift fur Missionwissenschaft und
Religionswissenschaft ETL, IRPL, RE
Zeitschrift fur Ostforschung RE
Zeitschrift fur Papyrologie und Epigraphik B
Zeitschrift fur Philosophie, Deutsche RE
Zeitschrift fur Philosophie, Wiener ETL
Zeitschrift fur Philosophie und Theologie,
Freiburger ETL, NTA, RE
Zeitschrift fur Philosophische Forschung ETL, RE
Zeitschrift fur Religions und Geistesgeschichte
ETL, IRPL, IZBG, NTA, RE, RTA
Zeitschrift fur Schweizerische Archaologie und
Kunstgeschichte RE
Zeitschrift fur Schweizerische Kirchengeschichte
ICB, RE
Zeitschrift fur Slavische Philologie RE
Zeitschrift fur Systemantische Theologie IZBG
Zeitschrift fur Systematische Theologie und
Religionsphilosophie, Neue ETL, IRPL, RE, RTA
Zeitschrift fur Theologie und Kirche ETL, IRPL,
IZBG, RE, RTA
Zeitschrift fur Vergleichende Sprachforschung
auf dem Gebiet der Indogermanischen Sprachen B
Zeitschrift fur Vergleichinde Rechtsgeschichte,
Einschliesslich der Ethnologischen Rechtsforshung
E, IBHR
Zeitschrift fur Vergleichinde Rechtsgeschichte,
Einschliesslich der Ethnologischen Rechtsforshung
E, IBHR
Zeitschrift fur Volkskunde, Osterreichische IBHR
Zeszyty Naukowe Katolickiego Uniwersytetu
Lubelskiego E, RE
Zeugnis, Lebendiges IOB
Zielzorg, Theologie en IOB
Zintralblatt fur Bubliothekswesen RE
Zion IZBG
Zionist, American IJP
Zrodloznawcze, Studia RE
Zukunft, Perspektive der B
Zurnal Moskovskoj Patriarchii B, IBHR
Zusammenarbeit, Dokumente. Zeitschrift fur
Internationale ICB
Zweige, Studien und Mitteilungen Zur Geschichte
des Benediktiner Ordens und Seiner RE
Zwingliana IZBG
Zwischen Den Zeiten ICB

Zygon GSSRPL, IRPL, RPI

LISTING BY SERVICE

B BIBLICA

Abhandlungen Zur Theolcgie des Alten und Neuen Testaments B

Academie Royale de Belgique B
Accademie e Biblicteche D' Italia B

Actes du Congres International de Numismatique B
Actes du Congres International de Papyrologie B
Actes du Congres International des Etudes Byzantines B
Actes du Congres International des Orientalistes B
Aevum. Rassegna di Scienze Storiche, Linguistiche e Filologiche B
Akkadusches Handworterbuch B
Akten des Internationale Kongresses B
Al-Machriq B
Alter Orient und Altes Testament B
Am Tische des Wortes B
American Journal of Archaeology B
American Journal of Philology B
American Philclogical Association Transaction Proceeding B
American Studies in Papyrology B
Analecta Cracovina B
Analecta Lovaniensia Biblica et Orientalia B
Anatclian Studies Journal cf the British Institute of Archaeology at Anakara B
Ancient Society B
Andover Newton Quarterly B
Andrews University Seminary Studies B
Anglican Theological Review B
Annalen van het Thijmgenootschap B
Annales Archeologiques Arabe Syriennes B
Annales de Ethiopie B
Annales du Centre D' Etude des Religiones B
Annales du Service des Antiquites de l' Egypte B
Annales. Economies, Societes, Civilisations B
Annali del' Istituto Orientale di Napoli B
Annali della Scuola Normale Superiore di Pisa B
Annee Philclogique B
Annuaire de l' Academie Theologie B

Annuaire de l' Institut de Philologie et D' Historie Orientales et Slaves B
Annual Egyptological Bibliography B
Annual of the Department of Antiquities of Jordan B
Annual of the Swedish Theological Institute B
Annuario di Studi Ebraici B
Antike Welt B
Antiquaries Journal B
Antiquite Classique B
Antiquites Africaines B
Antiquity B
Anzeiger fur die Altertumswissenschaft B
Arbeiten Zur Geschichte des Antiken Judentums und des Urchristentums B
Archaeologische Bibliographie B
Archaeologische Mitteilungen aus Iran B
Archaeologischer Anzeiger B
Archaeology B
Archeologia Classica B
Archeologie Vivante B
Archiv fur Begriffsgeschichte B
Archiv fur Geschichte der Philosophie B
Archiv fur Kulturgeschichte B
Archiv fur Liturgiewissenschaft B
Archiv fur Orientforschung B
Archiv fur Papyrusforschung B
Archiv Orientalni B
Archives D' Historie Doctrinale et Litteraire du Moyen Age B
Archives de l' Historie des Sciences B
Archives de Sociologie de Religions B
Archivio Glottologico Italiano B
Archivo Espanol de Arqueologia B
Argentina (Revista Biblica) B
Assemblees die Seigneur B
Atti della Pontificia Accademia Romana di Archeologia B
Atti della Settimana Biblica B
Augustinianum B
Augustinus (Madrid) B
Baghader Mitteilungen B
Bazmaveb B
Beihefte Zur Zeitschrift fur die Altestamentliche Wissenschaft B
Beitraege Zur Evangelischen Theologie B
Beitraege Zur Namenforschung B
Beth Mikra B

Bibel in der Welt B

Biblica B
Biblica et Orientalias B
Biblical Archeologist B
Biblical Theology Bulletin B
Biblische Untersuchungen B
Bild der Wissenschaft B
Boeken van het Oude Tectament B
Bogoslovni Vestnik B
Bogoslovska Smotra B
Boletin del Instituto de Estudios Helenicos B
Bollettino Bibliografiro Internazionale B
Bollettino dell' Amiciza Ebraico-Cristiana di Firanze B
Bollettino della Societa Geografica Italiano B
Bonner Biblische Beitrage B
Buletin of the Catholic Research Institute China Academy B
Bulletin D' Archeologie Algevienne B
Bulletin de Correspondance Hellenique B
Bulletin de l' Association Guillaume Bude B
Bulletin de la Societe de Linguietique de Paris B
Bulletin de la Societe de'Archeologie Copte B
Bulletin de la Societe Francaise D' Egyptologie B
Bulletin de la Societe Francaise D' Etudes Marianles B
Bulletin de Theologic Biblique D
Bulletin del' Institut Francais D' Archeologie Orientale B
Bulletin du Musee de Beyrouth B
Bulletin of the American Schools of Oriental Research B
Bulletin of the Institute of Archaeology B
Bulletin Secretariatus pro Non Christianis B
Bulletin Signaletique B
Butraege Zur Wissenschaft von Alten und Neuen Testament B
Cahiers D' Historie Mondiale B
Cahiers de Civilisation Medievale B
Central Conference of American Rabbis Journal B
Chicago Assyrian Dictionary B
Chicago Theological Seminary Register B
Christelijk Oosten B
Christus B
Classical Quarterly B
Classical Review B
Classical Weekly B

Collaticnes Vlaoms Tijdschaft voor Theclogie en Pastoral B
Collectanea Franciscana B
Commentaar op het Cude Testament B
Commenti Spirituali dell' Antico Testamento del Nuovc Testamertc B
Communio Verbum Caro B
Ccmptes Rendus B
Comptes Rendus du Groupe Linguistique D' Etudes Chamito-Semitiques B
Computers in the Humanities B
Concilium B
Confrontaticns. Revue Diocesaine de Tournai B
Coniectanea Biblica Lurd B
Corpus Scriptcrum Christianorum Orientalium B
Cultura e Scucla B
De Homine Deo B
Deutsche Literaturzeitung B
Deutsche Vierteljahrsschrift fur Literaturwissenschaft und Geistegeschechte B
Deutsches Archiv fur der Erforschung des Mittelalters B
Deutsches Pfarrerblatt B
Dicticnnaire D' Historie et de Geographie Ecclesiastiques B
Dictionnaire de Theologie Catholique B
Didaskalia B
Dienst am Wort B
Discoveries in the Judaean Desert B
Dumbartcn Oaks Papers B
Dusseldorf (Kommentare und Beitrage zum Alten und Neuen Testament) B
East and West B
Ecclesiastica Xaveriana B
Ecole Pratique des Hautes Etudes B
Elenchus Suppletorius ad Elerchum Bibliographe Biblicum B
Encounter Today B
Encyclopedia Judaica B
Escritos del Vedat B
Estudio Augustiniano B
Estudios de Filosofia y Religion Orientales B
Estudics Josefircs B
Estudios Marianos B
Estudics Trinitarics B
Etudes de Papyrologie B
Etudes et Travaux B
Etudes Moriales B

Evangelisch Katholischer Kommentar B

Evangelische Kommentare B
Expedition B

Forschungen Zur Religion und Literatur des Alten und Neuen Testaments B
Franciscanum B
Geographical Journal B
Geographical Review B
Geographische Zeitschrift B
Getuigenis B
Giornali Italiano di Filologia B
Glasgow University Oriental Society Transactions B
Gottingische Gelehrte Anzeigen B
Grande Lessico del Neue Testamente B
Gregorianae, Pontificiae Universitatis B
Gymnasium B
Handbuch der Orientalistik B
Handes Amsorya B
Harvard Semitic Series B
Harvard Studies in Classical Philology B
Harvard Theological Review B
Heilig Land B
Hervormde Teologiese Studies B
Histerisenes Jahrbuch der Gorresgeuschaft B
Historia B
Historische Zeitschrift B
Historisches Jahrbuch der Gorresgesellschaft B
Holland (Ministerium) B
Hsientai Hsuehyuan B
Iglesia Viva B
Illustrated London News B
Index Quaderri Camerti di Studi Romanistici B
Indian Ecclesiastical Studies B
Indogermanische Forschungen B
Indo-Iranian Journal B
International Journal for the Philosophy of Religion B
International Review of Missions B
Ipse hic Elerchus Bibliographicus Biblicus B
Iranica Antiqua B
Islamic Quarterly B
Jaarboek Werkgenootschap van Katholieke Theologen in Nederland B
Jahrbuch des Deutschen Archaelogischen Instituts B
Jahrbuch fur Liturgik und Hymnologie B
Jahrbuch fur Numismatik und Geldgeschichte B

Jarrbericht van het Vooraziatisch Egyptisch Genootschap ex Oriente Lux B

Jewish Journal of Sociology B
Journal des Savants B
Journal for the Study of Judaism in the Persian Helenistic and Roman Periods B
Journal of American Research Center in Egypt B
Journal of Ancient Near Eastern Society of Columbia B
Journal of Christian Education B
Journal of Classical Studies B
Journal of Economic and Social History of the Orient B
Journal of Ethiopian Studies B
Journal of Glass Studies B
Journal of Hebraic Studies, the B
Journal of Jewish Lore and Philosophy B
Journal of Juristic Papyrology B
Journal of Roman Studies B
Journal of the Evangelical Theological Society B
Journal of the History of Ideas B
Journal of the Northwest Semitic Languages B
Katallagete B
Katholische Erzieher B
Kerk en Theologie B
Kirchenblatt fur die Reformierte Schweiz B
Kliene Pauly B
Kommentare und Beitrage zum Alten und Neuen Testament (Dusseldorf) B
Lexikon der Christichen Ikonographie B
Libri e Riviste D' Italia B
Lingusitica Biblica B
Liturgisches Jahrbuch B
Madrid (Augustinus) B
Marian Studies ·B
Mariologische Studien B
Materialdienst des Konfessionskundlichen Instituts B
Medieval Studies B
Melanges de l' Institut Dominicain D' Etudes Orientales B
Melanges de l' Universite St. Joseph B
Ministerium (Holland) B
Miscelanea de Estudios Arabes y Hebreos B
Mision Avierta al Servicio de al Fe B
Mitteilungen des Instituts fur Orientforschung B
Mitteilunger der Deutschen Orient Gesellschaft B

Mitteilunger des Deutschen Archaeologischen
 Instituts B
Modern Churchman B
Munchener Studien Zur Sprachwissenschaft B
Museum Helveticum B
Nachrichter der Akademie der Wissenschaften
 zu Gottingen B
National Geographic B
Naturaleza y Gracia B
Nederduitse Gereformeerde Teologiese Tydskrif B
Nouvelles Chretiennes D' Israel B
Nova et Vetera (Suisse) B
Numismatic Chronicle and Journal B
Oecumenica B
Oekumenische Rundschau B
One Geestelijk Leven B
Ordens Korrespondenz B
Oriental Institute Communications B
Orientalia et Biblica Lovaniensia B
Orientalia Lovaniensia Periodica B
Orientalia Suecana B
Oudtestamentische Studien B
Parola del Passato B
Parola per l' Assemblea Festiva, la B
Parole de l' Orient B
Parole di Vita B
Parole et Mission B
Patrologia Latina B
Pensee Catholique, la B
Perspectiva Teologica B
Perspektive der Zukunft B
Philippiana Sacra B
Philippine Studies B
Philosophischer Literaturanzeiger B
Philosophisches Jahrbuch B
Positions Lutheriennes B
Presence Orthodoxe B
Proceedings of the American Academy for Jewish
 Research B
Proceedings of the American Philosophical Society B
Proceedings of the Israel Academy of Sciences
 and Humanities B
Proceedings of the World Congress of Jewish
 Studies B
Przeglad Orientalistyczny B
Quadermi di Semiliatica B
Questions de Vida Cristia B
Rassegna di Ascetica e Mistica B

Rassegna di Studi Etiopici B
Rassegna Mensile di Israel B
Reallexikon fur Antike und Christentum B
Recherches Augustiniennes B
Recherches Bibliques B
Rechtsforshung Zeitschrift fur Vergleichinde Rechtsgeschichte, Einschliesslich der Ethnolcgischen B
Recontre Assyriologique Internationale B
Religion y Cultura B
Revista Agustiniana de Espiritualidad B
Revista Biblica (Argentina) B
Revista di Pastorale Liturgica B
Revista di Teclogia Morale B
Revue D' Archeologique B
Revue D' Egyptclogie B
Revue D' Histoire des Textes B
Revue de l' Institut des Belles Letters Arabes B
Revue des Etudes Anciennes B
Revue des Etudes Armeniennes B
Revue des Etudes Byzartines B
Revue des Etudes Islamiques B
Revue des Etudes Juives B
Revue des Sciences Philosophiques et Theologiques B
Revue du Lcuvre et des Museede Frcme B
Revue Histcrique B
Revue Hittite et Asianique B
Revue Numismatique B
Rivista degli Studi Crientali B
Rivista di Liturgia B
Rivista di Pedagogia e Scienze Religiose B
Rivista di Studi Fenici B
Scripta Theolcgica B
Sein und Sendung B
Selecciones de Libros B
Semana Biblica Espancla B
Semana Espanola de Teologia B
Shenhsueh Yu Cjiaohui B
Siculorum Gymnasium B
Signos de los Tiempos B
Speculum B
Sprachforschung auf dem Gebiet der Indogermanischen Sprachen, Zeitschrift fur Vergleichende B
Stimme der Orthodoxie B
Streeven B
Studi Classici e Orientali B
Studi e Materiali di Storia della Religioni B

Studi Francescani B
Studi Romani B
Studia et Documenta Historiae et Iuris B
Studia Islamica B
Studia Moralia B
Studia Orientalia B
Studia Orientalia Christiana B
Studia Papyrologica B
Studia Patristica B
Studia Warminkie B
Studies in Comparative Religion B
Studies in the History of Religions B
Studies Journal of the British Institute of Archaeology at Anakara, Anatolian B
Studii Teologice B
Studium Legionense B
Stuttgarter Bibelstudien B
Suisse (Nova et Vetera) B
Sumer B
Symbolae Osloenses B
Teologia del Presente B
Teologia Espiritual B
Teologinen Aikakauskirja B
Terra Santa B
Texte und Untersuchungen B
Textus B
Theokratia B
Theologia Practica B
Theologica B
Theological Dictionary of the New Testament B
Theologie Pastorale au Rwanda et Burundi B
Theologische Bericht B
Theologische Existenz Heute B
Theologisches Handworter zum Alten Testament B
Theologisches Worterbuch zum Alten Testament B
Theologisches Worterbuch zum Neue Testament B
Theologisch-Praktische Quartelschrift B
Tijdschrift voor Rechtsgeschiedenis B
Times Literary Supplement B
Ugarit Forschungen B
Umschau in Wissenschaft und Technik B
United Bible Societies Bulletin B
Verhandelingen der Amsterdam Akademie van Wetenschappen B
Verhandlungen der Akademie van Wetenschappen B
Vierteljahrsschrift fur Literaturwissenschaft und Geistegeschechte, Deutsche B
Wiener Zeitschrift fur Kunde des Morgenlandes B

Wissenschafliche Untersuchungen zum Neue Testament
B
Wissenschaft UN Prczis in Kirche und Gesellschaft B
Yearbook cf Liturgical Studies B
Zeichen der Zeit B
Zeitschrift fur Agyptische Sprache und
Alterumskunde B
Zeitschrift fur Ethnclogie B
Zeitschrift fur Geschichte des Judentums B
Zeitschrift fur Papyrologie und Epigraphik B
Zeitschrift fur Vergleichende Sprachforschung
auf dem Gebiet der Indogermanischen Sprachen B
Zeitschrift fur Vergleichinde Rechtsgeschichte,
Einschliesslich der Ethnologischen Rechtsforshung
B
Zeszyty Naukowe Katolickiego Uniwersytetu
Lubelskiego B
Zurnal Mcskovskoj Patriarchii B

CPI CHRISTIAN PERIODICAL INDEX

Biblical Archeologist CPI
Bibliotheca Sacra CPI
Calvin Theological Journal CPI
Christian CPI
Christian Librarian CPI
Christian Life CPI
Christianity Today CPI
Church History CPI
Concordia Theological Monthly CPI
Eternity Magazine CPI
Evangelical Quarterly CPI
Frontier CPI
His CPI
International Review of Missions CPI
Moody Monthly CPI
New Testament Studies CPI
Pastoral Psychology CPI
Practical Anthropology CPI
Southwestern Journal of Theology CPI
United Evangelical Action CPI
Westminister Theological Journal CPI

CPLI CATHOLIC PERIODICAL LITERATURE INDEX

Acta Apostalicae Sedis CPLI
America CPLI
American Catholic Historical Records CPLI
American Catholic Philosophical Association Proceedings CPLI
American Journal of Jurisprudence CPLI
Anthropological Quarterly CPLI
Ave Maria CPLI
Biblical Archeologist CPLI
Catholic Business Education Review CPLI
Catholic Charities Review CPLI
Catholic Digest CPLI
Catholic Educator CPLI
Catholic Historical Review CPLI
Catholic Lawyer CPLI
Catholic Library World CPLI
Catholic School Journal CPLI
Catholic Theological Society of America Proceedings CPLI
Catholic World, the CPLI
Chicago Studies CPLI
Christ to the World CPLI
Cithera CPLI
Clergy Review CPLI
Columbia CPLI
Commonweal CPLI
Continuum CPLI
Critic CPLI
Cross and Crown CPLI
Cross Currents CPLI
Diakonia CPLI
Dominicana CPLI
Dublin Review CPLI
Ecumenist CPLI
Envoy CPLI
Etudes CPLI
Extension Magazine CPLI
Franciscan Studies CPLI
Furrow CPLI
Good Work CPLI
Herder Correspondence CPLI

Heythrop Journal CPLI
Homiletic and Pastoral Review CPLI
Hospital Progress CPLI
Insight CPLI
Irish Ecclesiastical Record CPLI
Irish Theological Quarterly CPLI
Journal of Ecumenical Studies CPLI
L' Osservatore CPLI
Liguorian CPLI
Liturgical Arts CPLI
Living Light CPLI
Living Word CPLI
London (Tablet) CPLI
Louvain Studies CPLI
Lumen Vitae CPLI
Lumiere et Vie CPLI
Manuscripta CPLI
Marian Studies CPLI
Marriage CPLI
Mid America CPLI
Modern Schoolman CPLI
Modern Society CPLI
Momentum CPLI
Monastic Studies CPLI
Month CPLI
Musart CPLI
National Catholic Education Association Bulletin
CPLI
National Catholic Guidance Conference Journal CPLI
National Catholic Reporter CPLI
National Guild of Catholic Psychiatrists Bulletin
CPLI
Natural Law Forum CPLI
New Blackfriars CPLI
New City CPLI
New Scholasticism CPLI
North American Liturgical Week CPLI
Notre Dame Journal of Education CPLI
Nouvelle Revue Theologique CPLI
Philosophical Studies CPLI
Philosophy Today CPLI
Pope Speaks CPLI
Preaching CPLI
Priest CPLI
Proceedings of the College Theology Society CPLI
Religion Teacher's Journal CPLI
Renaiscence CPLI
Resonance CPLI

Review for Religious CPLI
Review of Politics CPLI
Review of Social Economy CPLI
Revue de l' Universite D' Ottawa CPLI
Revue Philosophique de Louvain CPLI
Sacred Music CPLI
Schema XIII CPLI
Scripture CPLI
Scripture Bulletin CPLI
Sign CPLI
Sister Formation Bulletin CPLI
Sisters Today CPLI
Social Justice Review CPLI
Spirit CPLI
Spiritual Life CPLI
St. Anthony Messenger CPLI
Stimmen der Zeit CPLI
Studies CPLI
Tablet (London) CPLI
Teilhard Review CPLI
Theological Studies CPLI
Theology Digest CPLI
Thomist CPLI
Thought CPLI
Today CPLI
Today's Family Digest CPLI
Traditio CPLI
Triumph CPLI
United Synagogue Review CPLI
Way CPLI
World Justice CPLI
World Mission CPLI
Worship CPLI

ETL EPHEMERIDES THEOLOGICAE LOVANIENSES

Abr-Nahrain ETL
Academia Internazionale dei Lincei ETL
Acta Apostalicae Sedis ETL
Acta Seminarii Neotestamentici Upsaliensis ETL
Actualidad Biblica ETL
Algemeen Nederlands Tijdschrift voor Wijsbegeerte en Psychologie ETL
Altertum ETL
American Journal of Archaeology ETL
Amico del Clerc ETL
Analecta Gregoriana ETL
Analecta Ordinis Fratrum Minorum ETL
Analecta Praemonstratensia ETL
Analecta Sacri Ordinis Cistercienis ETL
Analecta Sacri Ordinis Fratrum Praedicatorum ETL
Andover Newton Quarterly ETL
Andrews University Seminary Studies ETL
Anglican Theological Review ETL
Annali del' Istituto Orientale di Napoli ETL
Annee Canonique ETL
Annuarium Historiae Conciliorum ETL
Anthropos ETL
Antiquite Classique ETL
Antonianum ETL
Apollinaris ETL
Aquinas Ephemerides Thomisticae ETL
Archief voor de Geschiedenis van de Katholieke Kerk in Nederland ETL
Archiv fur Katholisches Kirchenrecht ETL
Archiv fur Liturgiewissenschaft ETL
Archiv fur Orientforschung ETL
Archiv fur Rechts und Sozialphilosophie ETL
Archiv fur Reformationsgeschichte ETL
Archiv Orientalni ETL
Archiva Ecclesiae ETL
Archives de Philosophie ETL
Archives de Sociologie de Religions ETL
Archivio Giuridico "Filippo Serafini" ETL
Archivo Teologico Agustiniano ETL
Archivum Franciscanum Historicum ETL
Archivum Fratrum Praedicatorum ETL

Archivum Historicum Societatis Iesu ETL
Asiatische Studien ETL
Asprenas ETL
Associazione Biblica Italiana, Esegesi Biblica ETL
Attempto ETL
Augustinianum ETL
Australasian Catholic Record ETL
Australian Biblical Review ETL
Benedictina ETL
Berytus ETL
Bibbia e Oriente ETL
Bibel und Kirche ETL
Bibel und Leben ETL
Bibel und Liturgie ETL
Bible et Vie Chretienne ETL
Biblical Archeologist ETL
Bibliotheca Orientalis ETL
Bibliotheca Sacra ETL
Biblische Zeitschrift ETL
Bijdragen ETL
Bonner Biblische Beitrage ETL
Brethern Life and Thought ETL
Bulletin de l' Association Guillaume Bude ETL
Bulletin de la Societe de l' Historie du Protestantisme Francais ETL
Bulletin de Litterature Ecclesiastique ETL
Bulletin of the American Schools of Oriental Research ETL
Bulletin of the John Rylands Library ETL
Byzantion ETL
Cahiers Laennec ETL
Cahiers Theologiques ETL
Calvin Theological Journal ETL
Canadian Journal of Theology ETL
Carmelus ETL
Catholic Biblical Quarterly ETL
Catholic Historical Review ETL
Catholica (Copenhagen) ETL
Catholica (Munster) ETL
Chicago Studies ETL
Christus ETL
Church History ETL
Church Quarterly ETL
Ciencia Tomista ETL
Citaux ETL
Citeaux ETL
Citta di Vita ETL
Ciudad de Dios ETL

Civilta Cattolica ETL
Civitas ETL
Clergy Review ETL
Collationes Brugenses et Gandavenses ETL
Collectanea Franciscana ETL
Collectanea Mechliniensia ETL
Collectanea Oridinis Cistericciensium Reformatorum ETL
Collectanea Theologica ETL
Communio ETL
Communio Viatorum ETL
Concilium ETL
Concordia Historical Institute Quarterly ETL
Concordia Theological Monthly ETL
Confrontations. Revue Diocesaine de Tournai ETL
Continuum ETL
Copenhagen (Catholica) ETL
Cultura Biblica ETL
Dansk Teologisk Tidsskrift ETL
Diakonia ETL
Dialog (New York) ETL
Diocesaan Tijdschrift Hasselt ETL
Diritto e Giurisprudenza ETL
Divinitas ETL
Divus Thomas ETL
Doctor Communis ETL
Doctrine and Life ETL
Downside Review ETL
Dublin Review ETL
Eglise et Mission ETL
Ephemerides Carmelitica ETL
Ephemerides Iuris Canonici ETL
Ephemerides Liturgicae ETL
Ephemerides Mariologicae ETL
Ephemerides Theologicae Lovanienses ETL
Erbe und Auftrag ETL
Esprit et Vie ETL
Estudios ETL
Estudios Biblicos ETL
Etudes ETL
Etudes Classiques ETL
Etudes Franciscaines ETL
Etudes Philosophiques ETL
Etudes Teilhardiennes ETL
Etudes Theologiques et Religieuses ETL
Euntes Docete ETL
Evangelische Theologie ETL
Evangeliser ETL

Expository Times ETL
Foi et Vie ETL
Foi Vivante (Suisse) ETL
Forschungen und Fortschritte ETL
Franciscan Studies ETL
Franciscana ETL
Franciskaans Leven ETL
Franziskanische Studien ETL
Freiburger Zeitschrift fur Philosophie und Theologie ETL
Geist und Leben ETL
Gereformeerd Theologisch Tijdschrift ETL
Geschiedenis en Oudheidkundige Kring voor Leuven en Omgeving, Mededlingen van de ETL
Giornale Critico della Filosofia Italiana ETL
Giurisprudenza Italiana ETL
Gnomon ETL
Gregorianium ETL
Harvard Theological Review ETL
Hebrew Union College Annual ETL
Herder Correspondence ETL
Heythrop Journal ETL
Hibbert Journal ETL
Hispania Sacra ETL
History of Religions ETL
Homelitica en Biblica ETL
Informations Catholiques Internationales ETL
International Review of Missions ETL
Internationale Kirchliche Zeitschrift ETL
Interpretation ETL
Irenikon ETL
Irish Ecclesiastical Record ETL
Irish Theological Quarterly ETL
Israel Exploration Journal ETL
Iustitia ETL
Jahrbuch fur Mystiche Theologie ETL
Jewish Quarterly Review ETL
Jordan Lectures in Comparative Religions ETL
Journal of Biblical Literature ETL
Journal of Ecclesiastical History ETL
Journal of Ecumenical Studies ETL
Journal of Historical Studies ETL
Journal of Jewish Studies ETL
Journal of Near Eastern Studies ETL
Journal of Religious History ETL
Journal of Semitic Studies ETL
Journal of the American Academy of Religion ETL
Journal of Theological Studies ETL

Judaism ETL
Jus ETL
Justice dans de Monde ETL
Kairos ETL
Kant Studien ETL
Katholiek Archief ETL
Kerk en Missie ETL
Kerygma und Dogma ETL
Latomus ETL
Laval Theologique et Philosophique ETL
Lexington Theological Quarterly ETL
Liturgie und Monchtum ETL
Lumen ETL
Lumen Vitae ETL
Lumiere et Vie ETL
Lutheran Quarterly ETL
Lutherische Monatshefte ETL
Lutherische Rundschau ETL
Maison Dieu ETL
Marianum ETL
Mededlingen en Verhandelingen van het Vooraziatisch-Egytisch Genootschap "ex Oriente Lux" ETL
Mededlingen van de Geschiedenis en Oudheidkundige Kring voor Leuven en Omgeving ETL
Melanges de Science Religieuse ETL
Melita Theologica ETL
Miscelanea Comillas ETL
Modern Churchman ETL
Monitor Ecclesiasticus ETL
Month ETL
Munchener Theologische Zeitschrift ETL
Munster (Catholica) ETL
Museon ETL
Mysterium ETL
Nederlands Katholische Stemmen ETL
Nederlands Theologisch Tijdschrift ETL
Neue Ordnung ETL
Neue Zeitschrift fur Systematische Theologie und Religionsphilosophie ETL
Neukirchener Studienbucher ETL
New Blackfriars ETL
New Scholasticism ETL
New Testament Studies ETL
New York (Dialog) ETL
Norsk Teologisk Tidsckrift ETL
Norsk Teologisk Tidsskrift ETL
Nouvelle Revue Theologique ETL

Nova et Vetera ETL
Nova et Vetera (Suisse) ETL
Novum Testamentum ETL
Numen, International Review for the History of Religions ETL
Ny Kyrklig Tidsskrift ETL
Oesterreichisches Archiv fur Kirchenrecht ETL
Oesterreichisches Klerusblatt ETL
Orient Syrien ETL
Orientalia ETL
Orientalia Christiana Periodica ETL
Orientalistische Literaturzeitung ETL
Orientierung ETL
Ostkirchliche Studien ETL
Palabra de Clero ETL
Palabra Inspirada ETL
Palestine Exploration Quarterly ETL
Parole et Pain ETL
Pastor Bonus ETL
Pastoral Blatter ETL
Perfice Munus ETL
Phoenix ETL
Phoibos ETL
Pretoria Oriental Studies ETL
Princeton Seminary Bulletin ETL
Quaestiones Disputatae ETL
Razon y Fe ETL
Recherches de Science Religieuse ETL
Recherches de Theologie Ancienne et Medievale ETL
Recueil Dalloz ETL
Reformed Theological Review ETL
Regnum Dei ETL
Religion in Geschichte und Gegenwart ETL
Renovation ETL
Review and Expositor ETL
Review for Religious ETL
Revista Agustiniana de Espiritualidad ETL
Revista de Cultura Biblica ETL
Revista de Cultura Teologica ETL
Revista Eclesiastica Brasileria ETL
Revista Ecumenica "Ut Unum Sint" ETL
Revista Espanola de Teologia ETL
Revue Benedictine ETL
Revue Biblique ETL
Revue D' Ascetique et de Mystique ETL
Revue D' Histoire de Philosophie et de Theologie ETL
Revue D' Histoire Ecclesiastique ETL

Revue D' Histoire et de Philosophie Religieuses ETL
Revue de Etudes Augustiniennes ETL
Revue de l' Histoire des Religions ETL
Revue de l' Universite D' Ottawa ETL
Revue de Qumran ETL
Revue de Theologie et de Philosophie ETL
Revue des Communautes Religieuses ETL
Revue des Sciences Philosophiques et Theologiques
ETL
Revue des Sciences Religieuses ETL
Revue Diocesaine de Namur ETL
Revue Diocesaine de Tournai ETL
Revue du Droit Canonique ETL
Revue Philosophique de Louvain ETL
Revue Thomiste ETL
Ricerche Bibliche e Religiose ETL
Rivista Biblica ETL
Rivista degli Studi Orientali ETL
Rivista del Diritto Matrimoniale e Dello Stato
Delle Persone ETL
Rivista di Ascetica e Mistica ETL
Rivista di Diritto Civile ETL
Rivista di Filologia ETL
Rivista di Studi Classici ETL
Rivista Internazionale de Filosofia de Diritto ETL
Roczniki Reologiczno Kanoniczne ETL
Romische Quartalschrift ETL
Ruch Biblijny i Liturgiczny ETL
Sacerdos ETL
Sacra Doctrina ETL
Sacris Erudiri ETL
Salmanticensis ETL
Sapienza ETL
Schriften des Deutschen Instituts fur
Wissenschaftlishe Padogogik ETL
Science et Esprit ETL
Sciences Ecclesiastiques ETL
Scottish Journal of Theology ETL
Scripture ETL
Scripture Bulletin ETL
Scuola Cattolica ETL
Secretariado Trinitario ETL
Sefarad ETL
Seminarios ETL
Seminarium ETL
Social Compass ETL
Southwestern Journal of Theology ETL
St. Vladimir's Theological Quarterly ETL

Stimmen der Zeit ETL

Studi e Materiali di Storia della Religioni ETL
Studia Montis Reglii ETL

Studia Patavina ETL
Studia Theologica ETL
Studies on the Texts of the Desert of Judah ETL
Studii Biblici Franciscani Liber Annuus ETL
Studium ETL
Suisse (Foi Vivante) ETL
Suisse (Nova et Vetera) ETL
Sumer ETL
Svensk Exegetisk Arsbok ETL
Svensk Teologisk Kvartalskrift ETL
Tarbiz ETL
Theological Studies ETL
Theologie. Pastorale et Spiritualite ETL
Theologie und Glaube ETL
Theologie und Philosophie ETL
Theologische Literaturzeitung ETL
Theologische Quartalschrift ETL
Theologische Revue ETL
Theologische Rundschau ETL
Theologische Studien ETL
Theologische Zeitschrift ETL
Theology ETL
Theology Digest ETL
Theology Today ETL
Thomist ETL
Tidsskrift for Teologi og Kirche ETL
Tijdschrift voor Theologie ETL
Traditio ETL
Trierer Theologische Zeitschrift ETL
Tubinger Theologische Quartalschrift ETL
Una Sancta ETL
Union Seminary Quarterly Review ETL
Unitas ETL
Verbum Caro ETL
Verbum Domini ETL
Verkundigung und Forschung ETL
Vers l' Unite Chretienne ETL
Vetus Testamentum ETL
Vie Consacree ETL
Vigilae Christianae ETL
Vita Religiosa ETL
Vox Evangelica ETL
Wege zum Menschen ETL

Werkgenootschap voor Katholieke Theologen in Nederland ETL
Westminister Theological Journal ETL
Wiener Zeitschrift fur Kunde des Morgenlandes ETL
Wiener Zeitschrift fur Philosophie ETL
Wissenschaft und Weisheit ETL
Wissenschaftliche Monographien zum Alten und Neuen Testament ETL
Zeitschrift der Deutschen Morgenlandischen Gesellschaft ETL
Zeitschrift des Deutschen Palastina Vereins ETL
Zeitschrift fur Assyriologie und Vorderasiatische Archaeologie ETL
Zeitschrift fur die Alttestamentliche Wissenschaft ETL
Zeitschrift fur die Neutestamentliche Wissenschaft ETL
Zeitschrift fur Evangelische Ethik ETL
Zeitschrift fur Katholische Theologie ETL
Zeitschrift fur Missionwissenschaft und Religionswissenschaft ETL
Zeitschrift fur Philosophische Forschung ETL
Zeitschrift fur Religions und Geistesgeschichte ETL
Zeitschrift fur Theologie und Kirche ETL

GSSRPL GUIDE TO THE SOCIAL SCIENCE ...

American Journal of Sociology GSSRPL
American Opinion GSSRPL
American Scholar GSSRPL
American Sciolcgical Review GSSRPL
Annals GSSRPL
Banner GSSRPL
Baptist Bulletin GSSRPL
Catholic Historical Review GSSRPL
Catholic World, the GSSRPL
Center Magazine GSSRPL
Ceres GSSRPL
Change GSSRPL
Christian Advocate GSSRPL
Christian Century GSSRPL
Christian Herald GSSRPL
Christian Life GSSRPL
Christian Ministry GSSRPL
Christian Reader GSSRPL
Christian Standard GSSRPL
Christianity and Crisis GSSRPL
Christianity Today GSSRPL
Church Herald GSSRPL
Commonweal GSSRPL
Critic GSSRPL
Cross Currents GSSRPL
Ecumenical Review GSSRPL
Education GSSRPL
Encounter GSSRPL
Environment GSSRPL
Episcopalian GSSRPL
Eternity Magazine GSSRPL
Herald of Holiness GSSRPL
His GSSRPL
History of Religions GSSRPL
Jewish Frontier GSSRPL
Jewish Spectator GSSRPL
Journal of Biblical Literature GSSRPL
Journal of Ecclesiastical History GSSRPL
Journal of Marriage and the Family GSSRPL
Journal of Modern African Studies GSSRPL
Journal of Religion GSSRPL

Journal of the American Academy of Religion GSSRPL
Link GSSRPL
Lutheran GSSRPL
Lutheran Standard GSSRPL
Lutheran Witness GSSRPL
Mennonite GSSRPL
Messenger GSSRPL
Metonoia GSSRPL
Middle East Journal GSSRPL
Moody Monthly GSSRPL
Pastoral Psychology GSSRPL
Pentecostal Evangel GSSRPL
Phylon GSSRPL
Presbyterian Life GSSRPL
Psychology Today GSSRPL
Religious Education GSSRPL
Religious Humanism GSSRPL
Sighted Pathways GSSRPL
Theological Educator GSSRPL
These Times GSSRPL
Today's Education GSSRPL
United Evangelical Action GSSRPL
Vital Christianity GSSRPL
War Cry GSSRPL
World View GSSRPL
Zygon GSSRPL

IBHR INTERNATIONAL BIBLIOGRAPHY ...

Abhandlungen und Berichte des Staatlichen Museum
 fur Volkunde in Dresden IBHR
Acta Antiqua Academiae Scientiarum Hungaricae IBHR
Acta Ethnographica Academiae Scientiarum
 Hungaricae IBHR
Acta Iranica IBHR
African Studies IBHR
African Studies (Johannesburg) IBHR
Afrika und Ubersee IBHR
America Indigena IBHR
American Anthropologist IBHR
American Journal of Archaeology IBHR
American Journal of Philology IBHR
Anadolu Sanatu Arastermalan IBHR
Anatolian Studies Journal of the British Institute
 of Archaeology at Anakara IBHR
Andover Newton Quarterly IBHR
Andrews University Seminary Studies IBHR
Anglican Theological Review IBHR
Annales Archeologiques Arabe Syriennes IBHR
Annales de Sociologie IBHR
Annales Islamclogiques IBHR
Annali del' Istituto Orientale di Napoli IBHR
Annali di Sociologia IBHR
Annoli della Facalta di Letare e Filosafia dell'
 Universita degli Studi di Trieste IBHR
Annuaire de l' Institut de Philologie et D'
 Historie Orientales et Slaves IBHR
Annual of the Swedish Theological Institute IBHR
Anthropological Quarterly IBHR
Antik Tanulmanyok IBHR
Antiquite Classique IBHR
Antiquites Africaines IBHR
Antropologica IBHR
Anzeiger fur die Altertumswissenschaft IBHR
Archiv fur Katholisches Kirchenrecht IBHR
Archiv fur Liturgiewissenschaft IBHR
Archiv Orientalni IBHR
Archives de Sociologie de Religions IBHR
Arctic Anthropology IBHR
Armenian Church IBHR

Ars Orientalis IBHR
Arts Asiatiques IBHR
Asian Folklore Studies IBHR
Augustiniana IBHR
Augustinianum IBHR
Baghader Mitteilungen IBHR
Bible und Quran IBHR
Biblical Archeologist IBHR
Bijdragen tot de Taal-Land en Volkenkunde IBHR
British Journal of Sociology IBHR
Bulletin D' Etudes Orientalis de Institut Francais IBHR
Bulletin de l' Institut Fondamentale D' Afrique Noire IBHR
Bulletin de la Scciete de Etudes Indochinoses IBHR
Bulletin de la Societe Prehistorique Francaise IBHR
Bulletin del' Institut Francais D' Archeologie Orientale IBHR
Bulletin of the American Schools of Oriental Research IBHR
Bulletin of the Faculty of Arts, University of Libya IBHR
Bulletin Saint Jean-Baptist IBHR
Byzantino Sloavica IBHR
Cahiers D' Historie Mondiale IBHR
Cahiers des Religiones Africaines IBHR
Cahiers Internationaux de Sociologie IBHR
Cambridge History of Iran IBHR
Central Asiatic Journal IBHR
Comptes Rendus IBHR
Cultura e Scuola IBHR
Current Anthropology IBHR
Deutsche Literaturzeitung IBHR
Deutsches Pfarrerblatt IBHR
Ecole Pratique des Hautes Etudes IBHR
Ethnomusicology IBHR
Ethologcia IBHR
Evangelische Erziekar IBHR
Evangelische Kommentare IBHR
Facalta di Letare e Filosafia dell' Universita degli Studi di Trieste, Annoli della IBHR
Foliu Orientalia IBHR
Folk Religion and the Worldview in the South Western Pacific IBHR
Forschungen und Berichte IBHR
Harvard Studies in Classical Philology IBHR
History of Religions IBHR
Indo-Iranian Journal IBHR

Innsbrucker Beitraege Zur Kulturwissenschaft IBHR
International Review of Missions IBHR
Iranistische Mittelungen IBHR
Jaarbericht van het Vooraziatisch Egyptisch
Genootschap ex Oriente Lux IBHR
Jahrbuch der Stallichen Kunstsammulugen in
Baden-Wurttemberg IBHR
Jahrbuch des Museums fur Volkenbunder zu Leipzig
IBHR
Jewish Journal of Sociology IBHR
Johannesburg (African Studies) IBHR
Journal de la Societe des Americanistes IBHR
Journal of African History IBHR
Journal of Historical Studies IBHR
Journal of Social Psychology IBHR
Journal of the Polynesian Society IBHR
Journal of the University of Bombay IBHR
Judaism IBHR
Language. Journal of the Linguistic Society
of America IBHR
Man, the Journal of the Royal Anthropologist
Institute IBHR
Medieval Studies IBHR
Melanges D' Archeologie et D' Historier de l'
Ecole Francaise de Rome IBHR
Melanges de l' Universite St. Joseph IBHR
Middle East Studies Association Bulletin IBHR
Mitteilungen des Instituts fur Orientforschung IBHR
Mitteilunger der Deutschen Orient Gesellschaft IBHR
Mitteilunger des Deutschen Archaeologischen
Instituts IBHR
Munchener Studien Zur Sprachwissenschaft IBHR
Musees de Geneve IBHR
Museum of Far Eastern Antiquities, the IBHR
Nederduitse Gereformeerde Teologiese Tydskrif IBHR
Neutestamentliche Abhandlungen IBHR
Notes Africaines IBHR
Opuscula Atheniensia IBHR
Orientalia Suecana IBHR
Oriente Moderno IBHR
Osterreichische Zeitschrift fur Volkskunde IBHR
Parola del Passato IBHR
Parole et Mission IBHR
Paul and Qumran IBHR
Philippine Studies IBHR
Philosophische Rundschau IBHR
Pravoslavna Misao IBHR
Quarterly Review of Historical Studies, the IBHR

Rassegna Mensile di Israel IBHR

Rendiconti della Academia Nazionale dei Lincei IBHR
Rendiconti della Pontifica Accademia Romana de Archaeologia IBHR
Revue D' Egyptologie IBHR
Revue de l' Histoire de la Medicine Hebraique IBHR
Revue de l' Institut des Belles Letters Arabes IBHR
Revue de l' Occident Musulman et de la Mediterranee IBHR
Revue des Etudes Anciennes IBHR
Revue des Etudes Armeniennes IBHR
Revue des Etudes Byzantines IBHR
Revue des Etudes Islamiques IBHR
Revue des Etudes Juives IBHR
Revue des Etudes Sud-Est Europeenes IBHR
Revue des Sciences Philosophiques et Theologiques IBHR
Revue du Louvre et des Museede Frome IBHR
Revue Hittite et Asianique IBHR
Rivista degli Studi Orientali IBHR
Schweizerisches Archiv fur Volkskunde IBHR
Scuola Pasitiva Serie Iv IBHR
Sicilia Archeologica IBHR
Sociologia Religiosa IBHR
Sociological Analysis IBHR
Studi Classici e Orientali IBHR
Studi di Saciologia IBHR
Studi e Materiali di Storia della Religioni IBHR
Studi Mahrebini IBHR
Studi Micenci Ed Egeo-Anatolici IBHR
Studia Evangelica IBHR
Studia Islamica IBHR
Studia Orientalia IBHR
Studia Papyrologica IBHR
Studies in Comparative Religion IBHR
Studies in Islam IBHR
Studies Journal of the British Institute of Archaeolcgy at Anakara, Anatolian IBHR
Sudost-Forschungen IBHR
Symbolae Oslcenses IBHR
Synthronon Art et Archeologie de la Fin de l' Antiquite IBHR
Theologische Akademie IBHR
Theologische Quartalschrift IBHR
Tradition und Erneuerung IBHR
Turkish Review of Archaeology IBHR
Tuuk Arkeologi Dergisi IBHR

Verhandlungen der Naturforschenden Gesleischaft in Basel IBHR
West Africian Archaeological Newsletter IBHR
Wissenschaftliche Zeitschrift der Martin Luther Universitat Halle Wittenberg IBHR
Zeitschrift der Martin Luther Universitat Halle Wittenberg, Wissenschaftliche IBHR
Zeitschrift fur Ethnologie IBHR
Zeitschrift fur Jagdwissenshaft IBHR
Zeitschrift fur Vergleichinde Rechtsgeschichte, Einschliesslich der Ethnologischen Rechtsforshung IBHR
Zurnal Moskovskoj Patriarchii IBHR

IJP INDEX TO JEWISH PERIODICALS

American Jewish Archives IJP
American Jewish Historical Quarterly IJP
American Zionist IJP
Anti-Defamation League Bulletin IJP
Ariel IJP
Central Conference of American Rabbis Journal IJP
Congress Bi-Weekly IJP
Conservative Judaism IJP
European Judaism IJP
Hadassah Magazine IJP
Israel Digest IJP
Israel Magazine IJP
Jewish Digest IJP
Jewish Educator IJP
Jewish Frontier IJP
Jewish Heritage IJP
Jewish Life IJP
Jewish Observer and Middle East Review IJP
Jewish Quarterly Review IJP
Jewish Spectator IJP
Journal of Biblical Literature IJP
Journal of Jewish Communal Service IJP
Judaism IJP
Keeping Posted IJP
National Jewish Monthly IJP
Near East Reporter IJP
Patterns of Prejudice IJP
Pedagogic Reporter IJP
Reconstructionist IJP
Religious Education IJP
Studies in Bibliography and Booklore IJP
Synagogue School Quarterly IJP
Tradition IJP
Young Judaean IJP

IOB INTERNATIONALE OEKUMENISCHE ...

Africa (London) IOB
African Studies (Johannesburg) IOB
Amtsblatt der Evangelischen Kirche in Deutschland IOB
Amtsblatt der Evangelisch-Lutherischen Kirche in Thuringen IOB
Amtsblatt des Evangelischen Konsistoriums in Greifswald IOB
Anima IOB
Annalen van het Thijmgenootschap IOB
Anthropos IOB
Archief voor de Geschiedenis van de Katholieke Kerk in Nederland IOB
Archiv fur Kulturgeschichte IOB
Archiv fur Mittelrheinische Kirchengeschichte IOB
Arsbok for Kristen Humanism IOB
Artz und Christ IOB
Augustinus (Madrid) IOB
Background Information IOB
Baptist World IOB
Bekehirnoek IOB
Bern-Tubengen (Ehe.) IOB
Bibel in der Welt IOB
Biserica Ortodoxa Romana IOB
Bogoskovje IOB
Bratskij Vestnik IOB
Buletin du Centre Protestant D' Etudes IOB
Bulletin of the Church History Association of India IOB
Bulletin of the Department of Theology of the World Presbyterian Alliance and the World Alliance of Reformed Churches IOB
Bulletin of the Society for African Church History IOB
Bulletin Saint Jean-Baptist IOB
Bulletin Secretariatus pro Non Christianis IOB
Cahiers D' Action Religieuse et Sociale IOB
Carkoven Vestnik IOB
Catholica Unio IOB
Centre Protestant D' Etudes et de Documentation IOB
Cesky Zapas IOB

Chcisir IOB
Christ tc the Wcrld IOB
Christelijk Oosten IOB
Christian Council Quarterly IOB
Christian News from Israel IOB
Christian Peace Conference IOB
Christian Schclar IOB
Christianisme au 20e Siecle IOB
Christianisme Social IOB
Christlich-Judisches Forum IOB
Chrysostom IOB
Church in Metropolis IOB
Church in the Wcrld IOB
Church Times IOB
Ciencia Tomista IOB
Civitas IOB
Collationes Brugenses et Gandavenses IOB
Collectanea Mechliniensia IOB
Communaute des Dissemines IOB
Concept E. Papers from the Department on Studies in Evangelism IOB
Concept G. Arbeiten aus dem Referat fur Fragen der Verkuendigung IOB
Concilium IOB
Contacts IOB
Criterio IOB
Cuadernos Teolcgicos IOB
Current Developments in the Eastern European Churches IOB
Deutscher Evangelischer Kirchentag IOB
Dialog (Freiburg) IOB
Dialog (New York) IOB
Dialogo IOB
Dialogue IOB
Divus Thomas IOB
Documents from the Department for the Laity IOB
Dokumente. Zeitschrift fur Internationale Zusammenarbeit IOB
Duchovna Kultura IOB
Ecanos-Jahrbuch IOB
Ecclesia (Val) IOB
Ecumenical Notes IOB
Ehe. (Bern-Tubengen) IOB
Ekklesia IOB
Emuna IOB
Episcopal Overseas Mission Review IOB
Erbe und Auftrag IOB
Esprit IOB

Estudios Biblicos IOB

Ethiopia Observer IOB
Evangelijus Flet IOB

Evangelische Welt IOB
Evangelisches Pfarrerblatt IOB
Evangelishas Missionamagazin IOB
Faith and Order Trends IOB
Fede e Civilta IOB
Findsh Teologisk Tidsskrift IOB
Fomenta Social IOB
For Biblisk Tro IOB
Forum IOB
Frankfurter Hefte IOB
Franziskanische Studien IOB
Freiburg (Dialog) IOB
Freiburger Rundbrief IOB
Freide uber Israel IOB
Gemeenschap der Kerken IOB
Geneve-Afrique IOB
Getuigenis IOB
Gidoggyosasang IOB
Gregorios o Palamas IOB
Grosse Entschluss, der IOB
Guardian IOB
Hechos y Dichos IOB
Heerbaan IOB
Heiliger Dienst IOB
Historische Zeitschrift IOB
Hochland IOB
Igreja e Missao IOB
In Lichte der Reformation IOB
Information Evangelisation IOB
Information Service (New York) IOB
Information Service, Secretariat for Promoting Christian Unity IOB
Informations Catholiques Internationales IOB
International Reformed Bulletin IOB
Internationales Jahrbuch fur Religions-Sociologie IOB
Internationales Katholiche Informatie IOB
Irish Ecclesiastical Record IOB
Jaarbock voor de Eredienst IOB
Jahrbuch der Hessischen Kirchengeschichtlichen Vereinigung IOB
Jahrbuch der Osterreichischen Byzantinistichen Gesellschaft IOB

Jahrbuch des Instituts fur Christliche Sozialwissenschaften IOB
Jahrbuch des Martin Luther-Bundes IOB
Jahrbuch Evangelischer Mission IOB
Jahrbuch fur Geschichte Osteuropas IOB
Jahrbuch fur Liturgik und Hymnologie IOB
Japan Missionary Bulletin IOB
Japanese Religions IOB
Johannesburg (African Studies) IOB
Journal of Marriage and the Family IOB
Judaism IOB
Junge Kirche IOB
Katholischen Missionen IOB
Katholisches Missionejahrbuch der Schweiz IOB
Kerk en Theologie IOB
Kerkelijk Leven IOB
Kirchlichen Dienst IOB
Kirchliches Jahrbuch fur die Evangelische Kirche in Deutschland IOB
Kirke og Luther IOB
Kommunist IOB
Kosmos en Oecumene IOB
Kostnicke Jiskry IOB
Krestanska Revue IOB
Kristel Forum IOB
Kristen Gemenskap IOB
Kulturarbeit IOB
Kultuurleven IOB
Kunst und Kirche IOB
Language. Journal of the Linguistic Society of America IOB
Lebendige Seelsorge IOB
Lebendiges Zeugnis IOB
Lelkopasztor IOB
London (Africa) IOB
London (Sobornost) IOB
Lumen IOB
Lumen (Madrid) IOB
Madrid (Augustinus) IOB
Madrid (Lumen) IOB
Masses Ouvrieres IOB
Materialdienst des Konfessionskundlichen Instituts IOB
Mennonite IOB
Messager de l' Exauchat de Patriarche Russe en Europe Occidentale IOB
Messager Orthodoxe IOB
Migration Today IOB

Migrations IOB
Milarbeit IOB
Ministry IOB
Misiones Extranjeras IOB
Missie Integraal IOB
Missiewerk IOB
Missionary Research Library IOB
Missioni Catholiche IOB
Mitropolia Ardealului IOB
Mitropolia Banatului IOB
Mitropolia Moldavei si Sucevei IOB
Mitropolia Oltenici IOB
Monthly Letter About Evangelism IOB
Munster, Zeitschrift fur Christliche Kunst und Kunstwissenschaft IOB
Musik und Altar IOB
Musik und Kirche IOB
Nabozenska Revue IOB
National Christian Council Review IOB
Near East Council of Churches IOB
Nederlands Archief voor Kerkgeschiedenis IOB
Neue Ordnung IOB
Neue Rundschau IOB
Neues Forum IOB
New Christian IOB
New York (Dialog) IOB
New York (Information Service) IOB
Newman-Studien IOB
Newsletter, National Council of Churches Committee on the Church and Jewish People IOB
Nieuwe Mens IOB
Norsk Tidsskrift for Misjon IOB
Nunc et Senyser IOB
Oecumene IOB
Oekumenische Diskussion IOB
Oekumenische Rundschau IOB
Oesterreichisches Archiv fur Kirchenrecht IOB
Oikoumenikon IOB
Ons Geestelijk IOB
Oriente Christiano IOB
Orthodoxia IOB
Osteuropa IOB
Oud-Katholiek IOB
Pages Documentaires IOB
Pastoraltheologie, Wissenschaft und Praxis IOB
Perspectives de Catholicite IOB
Philosophia Reformata IOB
Polish Ecumenical Review IOB

Porefthendes IOB
Positions Lutheriennes IOB
Pravoslavna Misao IOB
Predicador Evangelicio IOB
Presbyterian Alliance and the World Alliance
 of Reformed Churches, Bulletin of the Department
 of Theology of the World IOB
Prism IOB
Project IOB
Quatember IOB
Recherches et Debats du Centre Catholiques des
 Intellectuals Francais IOB
Reconciliation IOB
Recontre Oecumenique IOB
Reformatasok Lajsja IOB
Reformation Review IOB
Reformatus Egykaz IOB
Reforme IOB
Reformierte Kirchenzeitung IOB
Regelrecht IOB
Religion and Society IOB
Religion y Cultura IOB
Response in Worship Music the Acts IOB
Revue del' Evangelisation IOB
Revue du Droit Canonique IOB
Risk IOB
Romische Quartalschrift IOB
Santissima Eucharistia IOB
Schweizer Rundschau IOB
Schweizerische Theologische Umschau IOB
Search IOB
Semeur IOB
Signes du Temps IOB
Sinhagbondan IOB
Sinhagyeicgu IOB
Sjaloom IOB
Sobornost (London) IOB
Sociologisch Bulletin IOB
South Indian Churchman IOB
Spiritus IOB
Stimme der Generde IOB
Stimme der Orthodoxie IOB
Streeven IOB
Stromata IOB
Studium Generale IOB
Te Elfder Ure IOB
Teologia Espiritual IOB
Theologia IOB

Theologia Practica IOB
Theologiai Azemla IOB
Theologie en Zielzorg IOB
Theologie in Praktijk IOB
Tradition und Erneuerung IOB
Travaux et Jours IOB
Tro och Liv IOB
United Church Review IOB
Ut Unum Sint IOB
Val (Ecclesia) IOB
Var Losen IOB
Verkundigung und Forschung IOB
Vers l' Unite Chretienne IOB
Vigilia IOB
Vivante Afrique IOB
Voprosy Filosofu IOB
Vorgare IOB
Vozes IOB
Wege zum Menschen IOB
Welt der Slaven IOB
Welt des Islams IOB
Wencling IOB
Wereldwijd IOB
Werkgenootschap voor Katholieke Theologen in
 Nederland IOB
Werkshefte IOB
World Call IOB
World Justice IOB
World Mission IOB
World Outlook IOB
Wort und Wahrheit IOB
Zeichen der Zeit IOB
Zeitschrift fur Schweizerische Kirchengeschichte
 IOB
Zwischen Den Zeiten IOB

IRPL INDEX TO RELIGIOUS PERIODICAL ...

American Quarterly IRPL
Andover Newton Quarterly IRPL
Andrews University Seminary Studies IRPL
Anglican Theological Review IRPL
Archiv fur Reformationsgeschichte IRPL
Baptist Quarterly IRPL
Biblica IRPL
Biblical Archeologist IRPL
Bibliotheca Sacra IRPL
Biblische Zeitschrift IRPL
Brethern Life and Thought IRPL
Calvin Theological Journal IRPL
Canadian Journal of Theology IRPL
Catholic Biblical Quarterly IRPL
Christianity and Crisis IRPL
Christianity Today IRPL
Church and Society IRPL
Church History IRPL
Church Man IRPL
Church Quarterly IRPL
Communio Viatorum IRPL
Concordia Theological Monthly IRPL
Continuum IRPL
Criterion IRPL
Dansk Teologisk Tidsskrift IRPL
Dialog (New York) IRPL
Downside Review IRPL
Drew Gateway IRPL
Duke Divinity School Review IRPL
Encounter IRPL
Etudes Theologiques et Religieuses IRPL
Evangelical Quarterly IRPL
Expository Times IRPL
Foi et Vie IRPL
Foundations IRPL
Frontier IRPL
Greek Orthodox Theological Review IRPL
Hartford Quarterly IRPL
Harvard Theological Review IRPL
History of Religions IRPL
International Review of Missions IRPL

Interpretation IRPL
Irenikon IRPL
Istina IRPL
Jewish Quarterly Review IRPL
Journal for the Scientific Study of Religion IRPL
Journal for Theology and the Church IRPL
Journal of Biblical Literature IRPL
Journal of Church and State IRPL
Journal of Ecclesiastical History IRPL
Journal of Ecumenical Studies IRPL
Journal of Pastoral Care IRPL
Journal of Presbyterian History IRPL
Journal of Religion IRPL
Journal of Religion and Health IRPL
Journal of Religious History IRPL
Journal of Religious Thought IRPL
Journal of Semitic Studies IRPL
Journal of the American Academy of Religion IRPL
Journal of Theological Studies IRPL
Judaism IRPL
Katallagete IRPL
Kerygma und Dogma IRPL
Lexington Theological Quarterly IRPL
Lutheran Quarterly IRPL
Lutheran World IRPL
McCormick Quarterly IRPL
Mennonite Quarterly Review IRPL
Methodist History IRPL
Modern Churchman IRPL
Muslim World IRPL
Nederlands Theologisch Tijdschrift IRPL
Neue Zeitschrift fur Systematische Theologie und Religionsphilosophie IRPL
New Testament Studies IRPL
New York (Dialog) IRPL
Norsk Teologisk Tidsskrift IRPL
Novum Testamentum IRPL
Numen, International Review for the History of Religions IRPL
Palestine Exploration Quarterly IRPL
Pastoral Psychology IRPL
Perspective IRPL
Practical Anthropology IRPL
Princeton Seminary Bulletin IRPL
Quaker History IRPL
Recherches de Science Religieuse IRPL
Reformed and Presbyterian World IRPL
Reformed Review IRPL

Reformed Theolcgical Review IRPL
Religious Studies IRPL
Renewal IRPL
Review and Expositor IRPL
Review of Religicus Research IRPL
Revue Biblique IRPL
Revue D' Histcire Ecclesiastique IRPL
Revue D' Histcire et de Philosophie Religieuses IRPL
Revue de l' Histoire des Religions IRPL
Revue de Qumran IRPL
Revue des Sciences Religieuses IRPL
Scottish Jcurnal of Theolcgy IRPL
Social Action IRPL
Soundings IRPL
South East Asia Journal of Theology IRPL
Southwestern Jcurnal of Theology IRPL
Springfielder IRPL
St. Vladimir's Theological Quarterly IRPL
Studia Liturgica IRPL
Studia Theologica IRPL
Study Enccunter IRPL
Svensk Teologisk Kvartalskrift IRPL
Theological Education IRPL
Theological Studies IRPL
Theologische Literaturzeitung IRPL
Theologische Rundschau IRPL
Theologische Zeitschrift IRPL
Theology IRPL
Theology Tcday IRPL
Una Sancta IRPL
Union Seminary Quarterly Review IRPL
Verbum Caro IRPL
Vetus Testamentum IRPL
Vigilae Christianae IRPL
Westminister Theolcgical Journal IRPL
Worship IRPL
Zeitschrift fur die Alttestamentliche Wissenschaft IRPL
Zeitschrift fur die Neutestamentliche Wissenschaft IRPL
Zeitschrift fur Evangelische Ethik IRPL
Zeitschrift fur Missionwissenschaft und Religionswissenschaft IRPL
Zeitschrift fur Religions und Geistesgeschichte IRPL
Zeitschrift fur Theclogie und Kirche IRPL
Zygon IRPL

IZBG INTERNATIONALE ZEITSCHRIFTENSHAU ...

Abhandlungen Zur Theologie des Alten und Neuen Testaments IZBG
Abr-Nahrain IZBG
Acta Antiqua IZBG
Acta Archaeolcgica Ljubliana IZBG
Acta Orientalia Budapest IZBG
Acta Seminarii Neotestamentici Upsaliensis IZBG
Acta Universitatis Gotoburgensis IZBG
Acta Universitatis Upsaliensis IZBG
Aegyptus IZBG
Aevum. Rassegna di Scienze Storiche, Linguistiche e Filologiche IZBG
Alter Orient und Altes Testament IZBG
Altertum IZBG
American Journal of Archaeology IZBG
Ami du Clerge IZBG
Analecta Biblica IZBG
Analecta Lovaniensia Biblica et Orientalia IZBG
Analecta Orientalia IZBG
Andover Newton Quarterly IZBG
Andrews University Seminary Studies IZBG
Angelicum IZBG
Anglican Theological Review IZBG
Annales Academiae Scientiarum Fennicae IZBG
Annali del' Istituto Orientale di Napoli IZBG
Annual of the American School of Oriental Research IZBG
Annual of the Swedish Theological Institute IZBG
Anthropos IZBG
Antonianum IZBG
Apostolado Sacerdotal IZBG
Arbeiten Zur Neutestamentlichen Textforschung IZBG
Arbeiten Zur Theologie IZBG
Archaeologischer Anzeiger IZBG
Archaeolcgy IZBG
Archiv fur Liturgiewissenschaft IZBG
Archiv fur Orientforschung IZBG
Archiv Orientalni IZBG
Archivo Hispalense IZBG
Archivo Teologico Granadino IZBG
Archivum Linguisticum IZBG

Asiatische Studien IZBG
Asprenas IZBG
Augustinianum IZBG
Australian Biblical Review IZBG
Australian Journal of Biblical Archaeology IZBG
Avhandlinger Utgitt Av Det Norsk Videnskaps Akademi i Oslo IZBG
Baptist Quarterly IZBG
Beihefte Zur Zeitschrift fur die Altestamentliche Wissenschaft IZBG
Beitraege Zur der Biblischen Hermeneutik IZBG
Beitraege Zur Evangelischen Theologie IZBG
Beitraege Zur Forderung Christlicher Theologie IZBG
Beitraege Zur Geschichte der Biblischen Exegese IZBG
Beitraege Zur Wissenschaft Vom Alten und Neuen Testament IZBG
Bibbia e Oriente IZBG
Bibel und Kirche IZBG
Bible et Terre Sainte IZBG
Bible et Vie Chretienne IZBG
Bible Society Record IZBG
Bible Translator IZBG
Biblia Revuo IZBG
Biblical Archeologist IZBG
Biblical Research IZBG
Biblical Theology Bulletin IZBG
Bibliotheca Orientalis IZBG
Bibliotheca Sacra IZBG
Biblische Beitraege IZBG
Biblische Studien IZBG
Biblische Zeitschrift IZBG
Bijdragen IZBG
Boek der Boeken IZBG
Boletin del Instituto Caro y Cuervo IZBG
Bollettino del Centro Camuno di Studi Preistorici IZBG
Bollettino della Societa Internazionale Scottista IZBG
Bonner Biblische Beitrage IZBG
Buenos Aires (Revista Biblica) IZBG
Bulletin Archeologique IZBG
Bulletin de l' Institut Francais D' Archeologie Orientale IZBG
Bulletin de la Classe des Lettres IZBG
Bulletin de la Societe D' Archeologie Copte IZBG
Bulletin de Litterature Ecclesiastique IZBG
Bulletin de Theologie Ancienne et Medievale IZBG

Bulletin E. Renan IZBG
Bulletin of the American Academy of Religion IZBG
Bulletin of the American Schools of Oriental Research IZBG
Bulletin of the John Rylands Library IZBG
Bulletin of the United Biblical Societies IZBG
Burgense. Collectanea Scientifica de la Real Academia IZBG
Cahiers de la Revue Biblique IZBG
Cahiers Renan IZBG
Cahiers Theologiques de l' Actualite Protestante IZBG
California Publications in Classical Archaelogy and Semitic Philology, University of IZBG
Calvin Theological Journal IZBG
Calwer Hefte IZBG
Canadian Journal of Theology IZBG
Catechese IZBG
Catechistes IZBG
Catholic Biblical Quarterly IZBG
Christian News from Israel IZBG
Christianity Today IZBG
Christus IZBG
Chronique D' Egypte IZBG
Ciencia Tomista IZBG
Ciudad de Dios IZBG
Civilta Cattolica IZBG
Collationes Brugenses et Gandavenses IZBG
Collectanea Franciscana IZBG
Collectanea Mechliniensia IZBG
Collectanea Theologica IZBG
Collection Lumiere et Vie IZBG
Commentary IZBG
Communio Viatorum IZBG
Compostellanum IZBG
Comptes Rendus de l' Academie des Inscriptions et Belles Lettres IZBG
Concilium IZBG
Concordia Theological Monthly IZBG
Coniectanea Biblica, New Testament Series Lund IZBG
Coniectanea Neotestamentica IZBG
Cultura Biblica IZBG
Dansk Teologisk Tidsskrift IZBG
Deutsche Literaturzeitung IZBG
Dissertation Abstracts IZBG
Divinitas IZBG
Divus Thomas IZBG
Documenta IZBG

Downside Review IZBG
Dunwoodie Review IZBG
Durham University Journal IZBG
Eglise et Theologie IZBG
Encounter IZBG
Ephemerides Carmelitica IZBG
Ephemerides Liturgicae IZBG
Ephemerides Theologicae Lovanienses IZBG
Eranos Jahrbuch IZBG
Erbe und Auftrag IZBG
Eretz Israel IZBG
Erfurter Theologische Studien IZBG
Estudios Eclesiasticos IZBG
Eternity IZBG
Etudes IZBG
Etudes Carmelitaines IZBG
Etudes Classiques IZBG
Etudes Theologiques et Religieuses IZBG
Evangelical Quarterly IZBG
Evangelische Kommentare IZBG
Evangelische Theologie IZBG
Evangile IZBG
Expedition IZBG
Expository Times IZBG
Folklore IZBG
Franciscan Studies IZBG
Franziskanische Studien IZBG
Freiburger Rundbrief IZBG
Geist und Leben IZBG
Gereformeerd Theologisch Tijdschrift IZBG
Gregorianium IZBG
Harvard Theological Review IZBG
Harvard Theological Studies IZBG
Heilig Land IZBG
Heilige Land in Vergangenheit und Gegenwart IZBG
Herder Korrespondenz IZBG
Hervormde Teologiese Studies IZBG
Hevrew Union Xollege Annual IZBG
Heythrop Journal IZBG
History of Religions IZBG
Homelitica en Biblica IZBG
Indian Journal of Theology IZBG
Internationale Kirchliche Zeitschrift IZBG
Interpretation IZBG
Iraq IZBG
Irenikon IZBG
Irish Theological Quarterly IZBG
Israel Exploration Journal IZBG

Israel Forum IZBG

Israelitisches Wochenblatt IZBG
Italiana (Revista Biblica) IZBG

Jaarbericht van het Vooraziatisch Egyptisch
Genotschap ex Oriente Lux IZBG
Jahrbuch fur Antike und Christentum IZBG
Jewish Quarterly Review IZBG
Jewish Social Studies IZBG
Journal Asiatique IZBG
Journal des Moskauer Patriarchats IZBG
Journal for the Study of Judaism IZBG
Journal of American Oriental Society IZBG
Journal of Biblical Literature IZBG
Journal of Cuneiform Studies IZBG
Journal of Ecclesiastical History IZBG
Journal of Ecumenical Studies IZBG
Journal of Historical Studies IZBG
Journal of Jewish Studies IZBG
Journal of Near Eastern Studies IZBG
Journal of Religion IZBG
Journal of Religious History IZBG
Journal of Semitic Studies IZBG
Journal of the American Academy of Religion IZBG
Journal of Theological Studies IZBG
Judaica IZBG
Judaism IZBG
Kairos IZBG
Katechetische Blatter IZBG
Kerygma und Dogma IZBG
Kirjath Sepher IZBG
Kratkie Soobscenija Institute Narodov Azii IZBG
Krestanska Revue IZBG
Language. Journal of the Linguistic Society
of America IZBG
Leshonenu IZBG
Letopis IZBG
Linguistica Biblica IZBG
Linguistische Berichte IZBG
Liturgie und Monchtum IZBG
Lown Institute for Judaiistic Studies IZBG
Lumen Vitae IZBG
Lumiere et Vie IZBG
Lunds Universitets Arsskrift IZBG
Lutheran Quarterly IZBG
Lutherische Monatshefte IZBG
Marburger Theologische Studien IZBG

Melanges de l' Institut Dominicain D' Etudes Orientales IZBG
Melanges de l' Universite St. Joseph IZBG
Melanges de Science Religieuse IZBG
Melita Theologica IZBG
Miscelanea Comillas IZBG
Mitteilungen der Deutschen Orient-Gesellschaft IZBG
Mitteilungen des Instituts fur Orientforschung IZBG
Modern Language Notes IZBG
Molad IZBG
Monde Juie. la Revue du Centre de Documentation Juife Contemporaine IZBG
Munchener Theologische Zeitschrift IZBG
Museon IZBG
Mysterium IZBG
Nederduitse Gereformeerde Teologiese Tydskrif IZBG
Nederlands Theologisch Tijdschrift IZBG
Neue Zeitschrift fur Missionswissenschaft IZBG
Neutestamentliche Abhandlungen IZBG
New Testament Abstracts IZBG
New Testament Studies IZBG
Norsk Teologisk Tidsskrift IZBG
Noticias Cristianas de Israel IZBG
Notre Catechese IZBG
Nouvelle Revue Theologique IZBG
Nova et Vetera IZBG
Novum Testamentum IZBG
Numen IZBG
Nuntius Scdalicii Neotestamentici Upsaliensis IZBG
Ny Kyrklig Tidsskritt IZBG
Orbis Catholicus IZBG
Oriens IZBG
Oriens Antiquus IZBG
Oriens Christianus IZBG
Orient Syrien IZBG
Orientalia IZBG
Orientalia et Biblica Lovaniensia IZBG
Orientalistische Literaturzeitung IZBG
Oudtestamentische Studien IZBG
Ou-Testamentiese Werkgemeenskap van Suid-Afrika IZBG
Palestine Exploration Quarterly IZBG
Palestinskii Sbaornik IZBG
Palestra del Clero IZBG
Paroisse et Liturgie IZBG
Parole de l' Orient IZBG
Pazmaveb IZBG
Positions Lutheriennes IZBG

Princeton Seminary Bulletin IZBG
Protestantesimo IZBG
Protestantischen Kirchen der Tschechoslowakei IZBG
Prozdor IZBG
Przeglad Orientalistyczny IZBG
Quaestiones Disputatae IZBG
Rassegna Mensile di Israel IZBG
Recherches de Science Religieuse IZBG
Recherches de Theologie Ancienne et Medievale IZBG
Reformed Review IZBG
Reformed Theological Review IZBG
Religion, Wissenschaft, Kultur IZBG
Religious and Theological Abstracts IZBG
Rendiconti de Scienze Morali IZBG
Review and Expositor IZBG
Revista Biblica (Buenos Aires) IZBG
Revista Biblica (Italiana) IZBG
Revista de Cultura Biblica IZBG
Revista degli Studi Orientali IZBG
Revista di Cultura Tehologica IZBG
Revista Eclesiastica Brasileria IZBG
Revista Espanola de Teologia IZBG
Revue Biblique IZBG
Revue D' Ascetique et de Mystique IZBG
Revue D' Histoire Ecclesiastique IZBG
Revue D' Histoire et de Philosophie Religieuses IZBG
Revue de l' Histoire de la Medicine Hebraique IZBG
Revue de l' Histoire des Religions IZBG
Revue de l' Universite D' Ottawa IZBG
Revue de Qumran IZBG
Revue de Theologie et de Philosophie IZBG
Revue des Etudes Juives IZBG
Revue des Sciences Philosophiques et Theologiques IZBG
Revue des Sciences Religieuses IZBG
Revue Historique IZBG
Revue Internationale des Droits de l' Antiquite IZBG
Revue Roumaine D' Histoire IZBG
Revue Thomiste IZBG
Rheinisches Museum fur Philologie IZBG
Roczniki Orientalistyczny IZBG
Roczniki Teologiczne Chrzescijanskiej Akademii Teologicznej IZBG
Roczniki Teologiczno Kanoniczne IZBG
Ruch Biblijny i Liturgiczny IZBG
Sacris Erudiri IZBG

Saeculum IZBG
Salesianum IZBG
Salmanticensis IZBG
Science et Esprit IZBG
Scottish Journal of Theology IZBG
Scripture Bulletin IZBG
Scuola Cattolica IZBG
Sefarad IZBG
Seminario Conciliar IZBG
Semitica IZBG
Sitzungsberichte der Deutschen Akademie der Wissenschaften IZBG
Sitzungsberichte der Heidelberger Akademie der Wissenschaften IZBG
Skrifter Utgitt Av Det Norske Videnskaps Akademie i Oslo IZBG
Sluzba Slova IZBG
Southwestern Journal of Theology IZBG
St. Vladimir's Theological Quarterly IZBG
Stimmen der Zeit IZBG
Streeven IZBG
Stromata IZBG
Studi Biblici IZBG
Studi e Materiali di Storia della Religioni IZBG
Studi Semitici IZBG
Studia Liturgica IZBG
Studia Orientalia IZBG
Studia Theologica IZBG
Studien zum Alten und Neuen Testament IZBG
Studien Zur Umwelt des Neuen Testaments IZBG
Studies in Biblical Theology IZBG
Studies in Religion IZBG
Studies in the Geography of Israel IZBG
Studii Biblici Franciscani Liber Annuus IZBG
Stuttgarter Bibelstudien IZBG
Stuttgarter Biblische Monographien IZBG
Sumer IZBG
Svensk Exegetisk Arsbok IZBG
Svensk Teologisk Kvartalskrift IZBG
Symbolae Osloenses IZBG
Syria IZBG
Tarbiz IZBG
Teologinen Aikakauskirja IZBG
Terre Sainte IZBG
Texte und Untersuchungen IZBG
Textus IZBG
Theologia Evangelica IZBG
Theologia Viatorum IZBG

Theological Studies IZBG

Theologicka Priloha Krestanske Revue IZBG
Theologie und Glaube IZBG
Theologie und Philosophie IZBG
Theologisch Praktische Quartalschrift IZBG
Theologische Literaturzeitung IZBG
Theologische Bucherei IZBG
Theologische Existenz Heute IZBG
Theologische Forschung IZBG
Theologische Revue IZBG
Theologische Rundschau IZBG
Theologische Studien IZBG
Theologische Zeitschrift IZBG
Theologisches Jahrbuch IZBG
Theology IZBG
Theology Digest IZBG
Theology Today IZBG
Tidsskrift for Teologi og Kirche IZBG
Tijdschrift voor Liturgie IZBG
Tijdschrift voor Theologie IZBG
Trierer Theologische Studien IZBG
Trierer Theologische Zeitschrift IZBG
Tubinger Theologische Quartalschrift IZBG
Tyndale Bulletin IZBG
Una Sancta IZBG
Unam Sanctam IZBG
University of California Publications in Classical Archaelogy and Semitic Philology IZBG
Verbum Caro IZBG
Verbum Domini IZBG
Verkundigung und Forschung IZBG
Vetus Testamentum IZBG
Vie Spirituelle IZBG
Vigilae Christianae IZBG
Vox Evangelica IZBG
Welt des Orients IZBG
Wesleyan Studies in Religion IZBG
Westminister Theological Journal IZBG
Wiener Zeitschrift fur Kunde des Morgenlandes IZBG
Wissenschaft und Weisheit IZBG
Wissenschaft und Weltbild IZBG
Wissenschaftliche Monographien zum Alten und Neuen Testament IZBG
Wissenschaftliche Untersuchungen zum Neuen Testament IZBG
Wissenschaftliche Zeitschrift der Karl Marx Universitat IZBG

Wissenschaftliche Zeitschrift der Martin Luther
Universitat Halle Wittenberg IZBG
Wissenschaftliche Zeitschrift der Universitat
Greifswald IZBG
Wissenschaftliche Zeitschrift der Universitat
Jena IZBG
Worship IZBG
Wort und Dienst IZBG
Wort und Wahrheit IZBG
Yediot IZBG
Zeitschrift der Deutschen Morgenlandischen
Gesellschaft IZBG
Zeitschrift der Martin Luther Universitat Halle
Wittenberg, Wissenschaftliche IZBG
Zeitschrift Deutschen Palastinavereins IZBG
Zeitschrift fur Agypitsche Sprache und
Alterumskunde IZBG
Zeitschrift fur Assyriclogie und Vorderasiatische
Archaeologie IZBG
Zeitschrift fur die Alttestamentliche Wissenschaft
IZBG
Zeitschrift fur die Neutestamentliche Wissenschaft
IZBG
Zeitschrift fur Katholische Theologie IZBG
Zeitschrift fur Religions und Geistesgeschichte
IZBG
Zeitschrift fur Systemantische Theologie IZBG
Zeitschrift fur Theologie und Kirche IZBG
Zion IZBG
Zwingliana IZBG

NTA NEW TESTAMENT ABSTRACTS

American Benedictine Review NTA
American Church Quarterly NTA
Andover Newton Quarterly NTA
Andrews University Seminary Studies NTA
Angelicum NTA
Anglican Theological Review NTA
Annual of the Swedish Theological Institute NTA
Antonianum NTA
Auchland (Colloquium) NTA
Augustinianum NTA
Australasian Catholic Record NTA
Australian Biblical Review NTA
Bausteine NTA
Bibbas (Manresa) NTA
Bibbia e Oriente NTA
Bibel und Kirche NTA
Bibel und Leben NTA
Bibel und Liturgie NTA
Bible et Vie Chretienne NTA
Biblica NTA
Biblical Archeologist NTA
Biblical Theology NTA
Bibliotheca Orientalis NTA
Bibliotheca Sacra NTA
Biblische Zeitschrift NTA
Bijdragen NTA
Bulletin de Litterature Ecclesiastique NTA
Bulletin of the American Schools of Oriental Research NTA
Bulletin of the John Rylands Library NTA
Burgense. Collectanea Scientifica de la Real Academia NTA
Cahiers de Josephologie NTA
Carmelus NTA
Catholic Biblical Quarterly NTA
Catholica (Copenhagen) NTA
Catholica (Munster) NTA
Chicago Studies NTA
Christian Scholar's Review NTA
Christus NTA
Church Quarterly NTA

Ciencia Tomista NTA
Ciudad de Dios NTA
Civilta Cattolica NTA
Clergy Monthly NTA
Collationes Brugenses et Gandavenses NTA
Collectanea Mechliniensia NTA
Colloquium (Auchland) NTA
Communio NTA
Communio Viatorum NTA
Concilium NTA
Concordia Theological Monthly NTA
Copenhagen (Catholica) NTA
Cross and Crown NTA
Cultura Biblica NTA
Dansk Teologisk Tidsskrift NTA
Diakonia NTA
Divinitas NTA
Divus Thomas NTA
Doctor Communis NTA
Doctrine and Life NTA
Ecumenical Review NTA
Ecumenist NTA
Ephemerides Carmelitica NTA
Ephemerides Liturgicae NTA
Ephemerides Mariologicae NTA
Ephemerides Theologicae Lovanienses NTA
Erbe und Auftrag NTA
Esprit et Vie NTA
Estudios Biblicos NTA
Etudes NTA
Etudes Franciscaines NTA
Etudes Theologiques et Religieuses NTA
Euntes Docete NTA
Evangelische Theologie NTA
Franciscan Studies NTA
Franziskanische Studien NTA
Freiburger Zeitschrift fur Philosophie und
 Theologie NTA
Furrow NTA
Geist und Leben NTA
Gereformeerd Theologisch Tijdschrift NTA
Gnomon NTA
Gregorianium NTA
Harvard Theological Review NTA
Hebrew Union College Annual NTA
Homiletic and Pastoral Review NTA
Indian Ecclesiastical Studies NTA
Indian Journal of Theology NTA

Internationale Kirchliche Zeitschrift NTA
Interpretation NTA
Irenikon NTA
Israel Exploration Journal NTA
Istina NTA
Journal of Biblical Literature NTA
Journal of Historical Studies NTA
Journal of Jewish Studies NTA
Journal of Near Eastern Studies NTA
Journal of Semitic Studies NTA
Journal of the American Academy of Religion NTA
Kairos NTA
Laval Theologique et Philosophique NTA
Lexington Theological Quarterly NTA
London (Sobornost) NTA
Louvain Studies NTA
Lutherische Monatshefte NTA
Lutherische Rundschau NTA
Maison Dieu NTA
Manresa (Bibbas) NTA
Marianum NTA
Melanges de Science Religieuse NTA
Melita Theologica NTA
Miscelanea Comillas NTA
Modern Churchman NTA
Month NTA
Munchener Theologische Zeitschrift NTA
Munster (Catholica) NTA
Museon NTA
Mysterium NTA
Nederlands Theologisch Tijdschrift NTA
New Testament Studies NTA
Norsk Teologisk Tidsskrift NTA
Nouvelle Revue Theologique NTA
Nova et Vetera NTA
Novum Testamentum NTA
Numen, International Review for the History of Religions NTA
Orient Syrien NTA
Orientalia NTA
Orientalia Christiana Periodica NTA
Orientalistische Literaturzeitung NTA
Orientierung NTA
Ostkirchliche Studien NTA
Palabra de Clero NTA
Palestine Exploration Quarterly NTA
Pastoral Blatter NTA
Perkins School of Theology Journal NTA

Razon y Fe NTA
Recherches de Science Religieuse NTA
Recherches de Theclogie Ancienne et Medievale NTA
Reformed Theolcgical Review NTA
Review and Expcsitor NTA
Review for Religious NTA
Revista Agustiniana de Espiritualidad NTA
Revista de Cultura Biblica NTA
Revista de Cultura Teologica NTA
Revista Eclesiastica Brasileria NTA
Revista Espancla de Teologia NTA
Revue Benedictine NTA
Revue Biblique NTA
Revue D' Ascetique et de Mystique NTA
Revue D' Histcire Ecclesiastique NTA
Revue D' Histoire et de Philosophie Religieuses NTA
Revue de Etudes Augustiniennes NTA
Revue de l' Histoire des Religions NTA
Revue de Theolcgie et de Philosophie NTA
Revue des Sciences Philosophiques et Theologiques NTA
Revue des Sciences Religieuses NTA
Revue Thomiste NTA
Rivista Biblica NTA
Rivista di Ascetica e Mistica NTA
Roczniki Reolcgiczno Kanoniczne NTA
Romische Quartalschrift NTA
Ruch Biblijny i Liturgiczny NTA
Sacra Doctrina NTA
Sacris Erudiri NTA
Salmanticensis NTA
Sapienza NTA
Science et Esprit NTA
Scripture Bulletin NTA
Scuola Cattolica NTA
Sefarad NTA
Sobornost (London) NTA
South East Asia Journal of Theology NTA
Southwestern Journal of Theology NTA
St. Ncmata NTA
St. Vladimir's Theclcgical Quarterly NTA
Stimmen der Zeit NTA
Studia Liturgica NTA
Studia Patavina NTA
Studia Theologica NTA
Studii Biblici Franciscani Liber Annuus NTA
Studium NTA
Svensk Exegetisk Arsbok NTA

Svensk Teologisk Kvartalskrift NTA
Testimcnianze NTA
Theological Studies NTA
Theologie und Glaube NTA
Theologie und Philcsophie NTA
Theolcgische Literaturzeitung NTA
Theologische Quartalschrift NTA
Theologische Revue NTA
Theologische Zeitschrift NTA
Theology NTA
Theology Today NTA
Tijdschrift vccr Theclogie NTA
Traditio NTA
Tradition NTA
Trierer Theolcgische Zeitschrift NTA
Una Sancta NTA
Unitas NTA
Verbum Dcmini NTA
Verkundigung und Forschung NTA
Vetus Testamentum NTA
Vigilae Christianae NTA
Vox Evangelica NTA
Vox Reformata NTA
Way NTA
Westminister Theolcgical Journal NTA
Wissenschaft und Weisheit NTA
Zeitschrift der Deutschen Morgenlandischen Gesellschaft NTA
Zeitschrift des Deutschen Palastina Vereins NTA
Zeitschrift fur die Neutestamentliche Wissenschaft NTA
Zeitschrift fur Katholische Theologie NTA
Zeitschrift fur Religions und Geistesgeschichte NTA

RE REVUE D' HISTOIRE ECCLESIASTIQUE

Aachener Kunstblatter RE

Academie Revue de Belgique. Bulletin de la Classe des Beaux Arts RE
Academie Revue de Belgique. Bulletin de la Classe des Lettres et des Sciences Morales et Politiques RE

Acta Historiae Neerlandica RE
Acta Historica RE
Acta Poloniae Historica RE
Aevum. Rassegna di Scienze Storiche, Linguistiche e Filologiche RE
Al Andalus. Revista de las Escuelas de Estudios Arabes RE
American Ecclesiastical Review RE
American Historical Review RE
American Journal of Legal History RE
Analecta Augustiniana RE
Analecta Bollandiana RE
Analecta Cisterciensia RE
Analecta Praemonstratensia RE
Analecta Sacra Tarraconensia RE
Anciens Pays et Assemblees D' Etats RE
Angelicum RE
Anglia. Zeitschrift fur Englische Philologie RE
Annalen der Historischen Vereins fur der Niererrhein RE
Annalen van het Thijmgenootschap RE
Annales de Bourgogne RE
Annales de Bretagne RE
Annales de Demographie Historique RE
Annales de l' Est RE
Annales de l' Institut Archeologique du Luxembourg RE
Annales de l' Ordre Souverain Militaire de Malte RE
Annales de l' Universite de Paris RE
Annales de la Societe Archeologique de Namur RE
Annales du Midi RE
Annales. Economies, Societes, Civilisations RE
Annales Historiques de la Revolution Francaise RE

Annali del Facclta di Filosofia e Letter di
UN-Versita Statale de Milano RE

Annali della Fondazione Italiana per la Storia
Amministrativa RE
Annali della Scuola Normale Superiore di Pisa RE

Annali di Storia del Diritto RE
Annali di Storia Economica e Sociale RE
Annee Canonique RE
Annuaire D' Histoire Liegeoise RE
Annuaire de la Societe D' Histoire et D'
Archeologie de la Lorraine RE
Annuale Mediaevale RE
Annuarium Historiae Conciliorum RE
Antemurale RE
Anthologica Annua RE
Antiquaries Journal RE
Antiquite Classique RE
Antonianum RE
Anuario de Estudios Medievales RE
Anuario de Historia del Derecho Espanol RE
Anzeiger der Oestereichischen Akademie der
Wissenschaften RE
Apollinaris RE
Aquinas RE
Arbor RE
Archaeologia Cantiana RE
Archaeological Journal RE
Archeologia RE
Archief voor de Geschiedenis van de Katholieke
Kerk in Nederland RE
Archiv fur das Studium der Neueren Sprachen
und Literaturen RE
Archiv fur Diplomatik Schriftgeschichte, Siegel
und Wappenkunde RE
Archiv fur Geschichte der Philosophie RE
Archiv fur Katholisches Kirchenrecht RE
Archiv fur Kulturgeschichte RE
Archiv fur Liturgiewissenschaft RE
Archiv fur Mittelrheinische Kirchengeschichte RE
Archiv fur Osterreichische Geschichte RE
Archiv fur Reformationsgeschichte RE
Archiv fur Schlesische Kirchengeschichte RE
Archiv Orientalni RE
Archiva Ecclesiae RE
Archivalische Zeitschrift RE
Archivar RE

Archives D' Histoire Doctrinale et Litteraire du Paris RE

Archives de l' Eglise D' Alsace RE
Archives de Philosophie RE
Archives de Philosophie du Droit RE
Archives de Sociologie de Religions RE
Archives et Bibliotheques de Belgique RE
Archives Internationales D' Histoire des Sciences RE
Archivio di Societa Romana di Storia Patria RE
Archivio Giuridico "Filippo Serafini" RE
Archivio Italiano per la Storia della Pieta RE
Archivio Storico Italiano RE
Archivio Storico Lombardo RE
Archivio Storico per la Sicilia Orientale RE
Archivio Storico per Le Province Napoletane RE
Archivio Storico per Le Province Parmensi RE
Archivio Veneto RE
Archivium Hibernicum RE
Archivo Espanol de Arte RE
Archivo Ibero Americano RE
Archivo Teologico Granadino RE
Archivos Leoneses RE
Archivum Franciscanum Historicum RE
Archivum Fratrum Praedicatorum RE
Archivum Historicum Societatis Iesu RE
Archivum Latinitatis Medii Aevi. Bulletin du Cange RE
Archivum. Revue Internationale des Archives RE
Archiwa, Biblioteki Muzea Koscielne RE
Arhivio Veneto RE
Art Bulletin RE
Art Journal RE
Arte Antica e Moderna RE
Arte Lombarda RE
Artistiques du Lot Bulletin de la Societe des Etudes Litteraires, Scientifiques et RE
Arts, du Departement de la Marne Memoires de la Societe D' Agriculture, Commerce, Sciences et RE
Arts et Traditions Populaires RE
Asprenas RE
Atti dell' Istituto Veneto di Scienze, Lettere di Arte RE
Atti di Societa Ligure di Storia Patria RE
Atti e Memorie de Deputazione di Storia Patria per Le Antiche Provincie Modenesi RE

Atti e Memorie de Deputazione di Storia Patria
per Le Province di Romagna RE
Atti e Memorie de Societa Istriana di Archeologia
e Storia Patria RE
Augustinian Studies RE
Augustiniana RE
Basler Zeitschrift fur Geschichte und
Altertumskunde RE
Beitraege Zur Altbayerischen Kirchengeschichte RE
Beitraege Zur Geschichte der Deutschen Sprache
und Literatur RE
Benedictina RE
Bericht des Historischin Vereins Bamberg RE
Berichte uber die Verhandlugn der Sachsischen
Akademie der Wissenschaften zu Leipzig RE
Bibel und Leben RE
Biblica RE
Bibliofilia RE
Bibliografia Nazionale Italiana RE
Bibliographie de Belgique RE
Bibliographie de la France RE
Bibliotheca Sacra RE
Bibliothek und Wissenschaft RE
Bibliotheque D' Humanisme et Renaissance RE
Bibliotheque de l' Ecole des Chartes RE
Biblische Zeitschrift RE
Biekorf RE
Bijdragen en Mededelingen Uitger Door de
Vereniging Gelre RE
Bijdragen. Tijdschrift voor Filosofie en Theologie
RE
Bijdragen tot de Geschiedenis RE
Biuletyn Historii Sztuki RE
Blatter fur Deutsche Landesgeschichte RE
Bodleian Library Record RE
Boletin de Historia y Antiguedades RE
Boletin de la Real Academia de la Historia RE
Boletin de la Real Academia Espanola RE
Boletin del Seminario de Estudios de Arte y
Arqueologia RE
Bollettino D' Arte RE
Bollettino di Badia Greca di Grottaferrata RE
Bollettino Ligustico per la Storia e la Cultura
Regionale RE
Bollettino Storico Bibliografico Subalpino RE
Bollettino Storico Piacentino RE
Bonner Geschichtsblatter RE
Bossche Bijdragen RE

Bracara Augusta RE
Bulletin de l' Association Guillaume Bude RE
Bulletin de l' Institut de Recherche et D' Histoire des Textes RE
Bulletin de l' Institut Historique Belge de Rome RE
Bulletin de l' Institut Royal du Patrimoine Artistique RE
Bulletin de la Commission Royale D' Histoire RE
Bulletin de la Commission Royale de Anciennes Lois et Ordonnances de Belgique RE
Bulletin de la Section D' Historie Moderne et Contemperaine RE
Bulletin de la Societe Archeologie et Historique de Nantes et de Loire Atlantique RE
Bulletin de la Societe Archeologique D' Eure et Loir RE
Bulletin de la Societe Archeologique et Historique du Limousin RE
Bulletin de la Societe D' Archeologie Copte RE
Bulletin de la Societe D' Archeologie et de Statistique de la Drome RE
Bulletin de la Societe D' Art et D' Historie du Diocese de Liege RE
Bulletin de la Societe de l' Historie de l' Art Francais RE
Bulletin de la Societe de l' Historie du Protestantisme Francais RE
Bulletin de la Societe des Antiquaires de l' Ouest et des Musees de Poitiers RE
Bulletin de la Societe des Antiquaires de Normandie RE
Bulletin de la Societe Historique et Archeologique du Perigord RE
Bulletin de la Societe Nationale des Antiquaires de France RE
Bulletin de Litterature Ecclesiastique RE
Bulletin de Theologie Ancienne et Medievale RE
Bulletin des Etudes Portugaises, Publie Par l' Institut Francais au Portugal RE
Bulletin des Musees Royaux D' Art et D' Histoire RE
Bulletin des Musees Royaux des Beaus Arts de Belgique RE
Bulletin et Memoirs de la Societe Archeologique du Department D' Ille et Vilaine RE
Bulletin Hispanique RE
Bulletin Monumental RE
Bulletin of the Institute of Historical Research RE
Bulletin of the John Rylands Library RE

Bulletin of the New York Public Library RE
Bulletin of the School of Oriental and African Studies RE
Bulletin Philologique et Historique du Comite des Travaux Historiques et scientifiques RE
Bulletin Trimestriel de la Societe Academique des Antiquaires de la Marinie RE
Bulletin Trimestriel de la Societe Archeologique de Touraine RE
Bulletin Trimestriel de la Societe des Antiquaires de Picardie RE
Bullettino dell' Istituto Storico Italiano per Il Medio Evo e Archivio Muratoriano RE
Burlington Magizine RE
Byzantina RE
Byzantinische Forschungen RE
Byzantinische Zeitschrift RE
Byzantino Sloavica RE
Byzantion RE
Cahiers Archeologiques, Fin de l' Antiquite et Moyen Age RE
Cahiers Bruxellois RE
Cahiers D' Etudes Cathares RE
Cahiers D' Histoire RE
Cahiers D' Historie Mondiale RE
Cahiers de Civilisation Medievale RE
Cahiers Leopold Delisle RE
Calvin Theological Journal RE
Canadian Historical Review RE
Carinthia I. Geschichliche und Volkskunde. Beitrage Zur Heimantkunde Karntens RE
Carmelus RE
Catholic Biblical Quarterly RE
Catholic Historical Review RE
Ceskoslovensky Casopis Historicky RE
Christelijk Oosten RE
Church History RE
Ciencia Tomista RE
Cistercienser Chronik RE
Citaux RE
Citeaux RE
Ciudad de Dios RE
Civilta Cattolica RE
Clairlieu. Tijdschrift Gewijd Aan de Geschiedenis der Kruisheren RE
Classica et Mediaevalia RE
Classical Folia RE
Classical Quarterly RE

Classical Review RE
Clergy Review RE
Collationes RE
Collectanea Cisterciensia RE
Collectanea Franciscana RE
Commentari RE
Commission Royale de Anciennes Lois et Ordonnances de Belgique, Bulletin de la RE
Communio RE
Communio Viatorum RE
Comparative Studies in Society and History RE
Comptes Rendus des Seances de l' Academie des Inscriptions et Belles Lettres RE
Concilium RE
Corsi di Cultura Sull' Arte Ravennate e Bizantina RE
Cuadernos de Estudios Gallegos RE
Cuadernos de Historia de Espana RE
Cultura Neolatina RE
Departement de la Marne Memoires de la Societe D' Agriculture, Commerce, Sciences et Arts, du RE
Deutsche Bibliographie RE
Deutsche Kunst und Denkmalpflete RE
Deutsche Literaturzeitung RE
Deutsche Vierteljahrsschrift fur Literaturwissenschaft und Geistegeschechte RE
Deutsche Zeitschrift fur Philosophie RE
Deutsches Archiv tur der Erforschung des Mittelalters RE
Dietsche Warande en Belfort RE
Diogene RE
Divinitas RE
Divus Thomas RE
Doctor Communis RE
Ecomomia e Storia RE
Economic History Review RE
Economisch Historisch Jaarboek RE
Ecumenical Review RE
Eigen Schoon en de Brabander RE
English Historical Review RE
English Studies RE
Ephemerides Carmelitica RE
Ephemerides Iuris Canonici RE
Ephemerides Liturgicae RE
Ephemerides Mariologicae RE
Ephemerides Theologicae Lovanienses RE
Epigraphica RE
Eranos RE

Erasmus. Speculum Scientiarum RE
Estudios Biblicos RE
Estudios Eclesiasticos RE
Estudios Franciscanos RE
Estudios Lulianos RE
Etudes RE
Etudes Celtiques RE
Etudes Classiques RE
Etudes Franciscaines RE
Etudes Gregoriennes RE
Etudes Philosophiques RE
Etudes Theologiques et Religieuses RE
Euntes Docete RE
Euphorion. Zeitschrift fur Literaturgeschichte RE
Evangelische Theologie RE
Fabula. Zeitschrift fur Erzahlforschung RE
Federation der Societes D' Histoire et D' Archeologie de l' Aisne, Memoires de la RE
Fivista Italiana di Numismatica e Scienze Affini RE
Foi et Le Temps RE
Folklore RE
Forschungen Zur Osteuropaischen Geschichte RE
Franciscan Studies RE
Freiburger Diozesan Archiv RE
Freiburger Zeitschrift fur Philosophie und Theologie RE
French Review RE
French Studies RE
Fruhmittelalrerliche Studien RE
Gazette des Beaus Arts RE
Geist und Leben RE
Geneva RE
Gentse Bijdragen tot de Kunstgeschiedenis en de Oudheidkunde RE
Gereformeerd Theologisch Tijdschrift RE
Germanisch Romanische Monatsschrift RE
Geschichte und Kunst des Trierer Landes und Seiner Nachbargebiete, Trierer Zeitschrift fur RE
Geschichtliche Landeskunde RE
Geschiedenis en Oudheidkundige Kring voor Leuven en Omgeving, Mededlingen van de RE
Gesta RE
Giornale Critico della Filosofia Italiana RE
Giornale Storico della Letteratura Italiana RE
Gnomon RE
Gottingische Gelehrte Anzeigen RE
Goya. Revista de Arte RE
Greek, Roman, and Byzantine Studies RE

Gregorianium RE

Gulden Passer RE
Handeling van het Genootschap voor Geschiedenis Gesticht Onder de Benaming Societe D' Emulation de Bruges RE

Hansische Geschichtsblatter RE
Harvard Theological Review RE
Heidelberger Jahrbucher RE
Helmantica RE
Hemecht. Zeitschrift fur Luxemburger Geschichte RE
Hermes. Zeitschrift fur Klassische Philologie RE
Hesperis Tamuda RE
Heythrop Journal RE
Hispania. Revista Espanola de Historia RE
Hispania Sacra RE
Hispanic Review RE
Histoire du Droit et des Institutions des Anciens Pays Bourguignons, Comtois et Romands Memoires de la Societe Pour l' RE
Historia RE
Historia. Zeitschrift fur Alte Geschichte RE
Historica RE
Historical Journal RE
Historique du Comite des Travaux Historiques et scientifiques, Bulletin Philologique et RE
Historische Zeitschrift RE
Historisches Jahrbuch der Gorresgesellschaft RE
Historisk Tidsskrift (Oslo) RE
History RE
History and Theory RE
History of Religions RE
History Today RE
Hochland RE
Imago Mundi RE
Indice Historico Espanol RE
Information Historique RE
International Review of Social History RE
Internationale Kirchliche Zeitschrift RE
Interpretation RE
Irenikon RE
Irish Ecclesiastical Record RE
Irish Historical Studies RE
Irish Theological Quarterly RE
Isis RE
Islam RE
Istina RE

Istituto Storico Italiano per Il Medio Evo e
Archivio Muratoriano, Bullettino dell' RE

Italaia Medioevale e Umanistica RE
Ius Canonicum RE
Ius Commune RE
Jahrbuch der Berliner Museen RE
Jahrbuch der Gesellschaft fur Niedersachsische
Kirchengeschichte RE
Jahrbuch der Kunsthistorischen Sammlungen Wien RE
Jahrbuch der Osterreichischin Byzantinistik RE
Jahrbuch des Kolnischen Geschichtsvereins RE
Jahrbuch des Kunsthistorischen Instiutes der
Universitat Graz RE
Jahrbuch fur Antike und Christentum RE
Jahrbuch fur die Geschichte Mittelingen und
Ostdeutschlands RE
Jahrbuch fur Frankische Landesforschung RE
Jahrbuch fur Landeskunde voor Niederosterreich RE
Jahrbuch fur Liturgik und Hymnologie RE
Jahrbuch fur Numismatik und Geldgeschichte RE
Jahrbuch fur Wirtschaftsgeschichte RE
Jahrbucher fur Geschichte Osteuropas RE
Jewish Quarterly Review RE
Journal Asiatique RE
Journal des Savants RE
Journal for the Scientific Study of Religion RE
Journal of African History RE
Journal of Biblical Literature RE
Journal of Contemporary History RE
Journal of Ecclesiastical History RE
Journal of Eccmonic History RE
Journal of Ecumenical Studies RE
Journal of English and Germanic Philology RE
Journal of Modern History RE
Journal of Religion RE
Journal of Religion in Africa RE
Journal of Religious History RE
Journal of Roman Studies RE
Journal of the American Academy of Religion RE
Journal of the British Archaeological Association
RE
Journal of the Economic and Social History of
the Orient RE
Journal of the Historical Society of the Church
in Wales RE
Journal of the History of Ideas RE
Journal of the History of Philosophy RE

Journal of the Royal Asiatic Society of Great Britain and Ireland RE
Journal of the Royal Society of Antiquaries of Ireland RE
Journal of the Warburg and Courtauld Institutes RE
Journal of Theological Studies RE
Jurist RE
Kairos RE
Kant Studien RE
Kerygma und Dogma RE
Kirche Im Osten RE
Kirkehistorike Samlinger RE
Klio. Beitrage Zur Alten Geschichte Berlin et Wiesbaden RE
Kwartalnik Historyczny RE
Kyrios. Vierteljahresschrift fur Kirchen und Geistesgeschichte Osteruopas RE
Kyrkohistorisk Arsskrift RE
Lateinamerika Jahrbuch RE
Latomus RE
Leodium RE
Lettres Romanis RE
Leuvense Bijdragen RE
Limburg RE
Literaturwissenschaftliches Jahrbuch RE
Liturgisches Jahrbuch RE
Lumiere et Vie RE
Lusitania Sacra RE
Luther Jahrbuch RE
Maasgouw RE
Mainzer Zeitschrift RE
Maison Dieu RE
Manuscripta RE
Marianum RE
Mededlingen van de Geschiedenis en Oudheidkundige Kring voor Leuven en Omgeving RE
Mededlingen van het Nederlands Historie Instituut Te Rome RE
Mediaeval and Renaissance RE
Mediaeval Scandinavia RE
Mediaeval Studies RE
Medieval Archaeology RE
Medievalia et Humanistica RE
Medium Aevum RE
Melanges D' Archeologie et D' Histoire RE
Melanges de l' Instiut Domincain D' Etudes Orientales de Caire RE
Melanges de l' Universite St. Joseph RE

Melanges de la Casa de Velazquez RE
Melanges de Science Religieuse RE
Memoires de la Federation der Societes D' Histoire et D' Archeologie de l' Aisne RE
Memoires de la Federation des Societes Historie et Archeclogie de Paris et de l' Ile de France RE
Memoires de la Scciete Archeolcgie et Historique de la Charente RE
Memoires de la Scciete D' Agriculture, Commerce, Sciences et Arts, du Departement de la Marne RE
Memoires de la Scciete Pour l' Histoire du Droit et des Institutions des Anciens Pays Bourguignons, Comtois et Romands RE
Memoirs de la Scciete Archeologique du Department D' Ille et Vilaine, Bulletin et RE
Memorie de Deputazione di Storia Patria per Le Province di Romagna, Atti e RE
Memorie Storiche Forogiuliesi RE
Metropclitan Museum of Art Bulletin RE
Mid America RE
Miscelanea Comillas RE
Miscellanea Franciscana RE
Missionalia Hispanica RE
Missionary Research Library RE
Mitropclia Moldavei si Sucevei RE
Mitropolia Oltenici RE
Mitteilungen des Instituts fur Osterreichesche Geschichtsforschung RE
Mitteilungen des Oesterreichischen Staatsarchivs RE
Mitteilungen und Forschungsbeitrage der Cusanus Gesellschaft RE
Mitteilungen Zur Geschichte des Benediktiner Ordens und Seiner Zweige, Studien und RE
Mittellanteinisches Jahrbuch RE
Mnemosyne RE
Modern Language Notes RE
Modern Language Quarterly RE
Modern Language Review RE
Modern Philolcgy RE
Modern Schoolman RE
Month RE
Monuments Historuques de la France RE
Moreana. Bulletin Thecmas More RE
Moyen Age RE
Munchener Theclogische Zeitschrift RE
Munster, Zeitschrift fur Christliche Kunst und Kunstwissenschaft RE
Museon RE

Musica Disciplina. a Yearbook of the History
of Music RE

Nachrichten der Akademie der Wissenschaften
in Gottingen RE
Namurcum RE

Nasza Przeszlosc RE
Nederlands Archief voor Kerkgeschiedenis RE
Nederlands Archievenblad RE
Nederlands Kunsthistorisch Jaarboek RE
Nederlands Theologisch Tijdschrift RE
Neophilologus RE
Neue Zeitschrift fur Missionswissenschaft RE
Neuphilologische Mitteilungen RE
New Scholasticism RE
New Testament Studies RE
Niederdeutsche Beitrage Zur Kunstgeschichte RE
Niedersachsisches Jahrbuch fur Landesgeschichte RE
Nordisk Tidsskrift for Bok och Biblioteksvasen RE
Nottingham Mediaeval Studies RE
Nouva Rivista Storica RE
Nouvelle Revue Theologique RE
Novare RE
Novum Testamentum RE
Numen RE
Numismatic Chronicle RE
Oberbayerisches Archiv RE
Odrodzenie i Reformacja W Polsce RE
Oesterreichische Bibliographie RE
Oesterreichische Zeitschrift fur Kunst und
Denkmalpflege RE
Oesterreichisches Archiv fur Kirchenrecht RE
Oratorium RE
Oriens RE
Oriens Christianus RE
Orientalia RE
Orientalia Christiana Periodica RE
Orientalistische Literaturzeitung RE
Orpheus. Rivista di Umanita Classica e Cristiana RE
Oslo (Historisk Tidsskrift) RE
Ostkirchliche Studien RE
Oud Holland RE
Oude Land van Loon RE
Oxoniensia RE
Paedagogica Historica RE
Palladia. Rivista di Storia dell' Architettura RE
Pantheon. Internationale Zeitschrift fur Kunst RE

Par l' Institut Francais au Portugal Bulletin
 des Etudes Portugaises, Publie RE

Parole de l' Orient RE
Past and Present RE

Pays Lorrain RE
Pensamiento RE
Periodica de Re Morali, Canonica, Liturgica RE
Philological Quarterly RE
Philologus. Zeitschrift fur das Klassische
 Altertum RE
Philosophical Review RE
Philosophischer Literaturanzeiger RE
Prawo Kanoniczne RE
Proceedings of the British Academy RE
Proche Orient Chretien RE
Province du Maine RE
Przeglad Historyczny RE
Publications de la Section Historique de l'
 Institut Ducal de Luxembourg RE
Publications de la Societe Historique et
 Archologique dans Le Limbourg a Maestricht RE
Publications of the Modern Language Association RE
Quaderni Storici RE
Quadrivium RE
Quaerendo RE
Quartalschrift fur Christliche Alterumskunde
 und Kirchengeschichte, Romanische RE
Quellen und Forschungen aus Italienischen Archiven
 und Bibliotheken RE
Questions Liturgiques RE
Rassegna di Letteratura Tomistica RE
Rassegna Storica del Risorgimento RE
Rassegna Storica Toscana RE
Razon y Fe RE
Recherches Augustiniennes RE
Recherches de Science Religieuse RE
Recherches de Theologie Ancienne et Medievale RE
Records of the American Catholic Historical
 Society of Philadelphia RE
Recusant History RE
Regnum Dei RE
Renaissance and Modern Studies RE
Rendiconti dell' Istituto Lombardo di Scienze
 e Lettere RE
Rendus des Seances de l' Academie des Inscriptions
 et Belles Lettres, Comptes RE

Reniconti della Pontifica Accademia Romana di Archeolcgia RE
Review of English Studies RE
Review of Politics RE
Review of Religious Research RE
Revista de Archivos, Bibliotecas y Museos RE
Revista de Espiritualidad RE
Revista de Filologia Espanola RE
Revista de Indias RE
Revista Eclesiastica Brasileria RE
Revista Espancla de Derecho Canonico RE
Revista Espancla de Teologia RE
Revue Archeolcgique RE
Revue Belge D' Archeolcgie et D' Historie de l' Art RE
Revue Belge D' Historie Contemporaine RE
Revue Belge de Musicclcgie RE
Revue Belge de Numismatique et de Sigillcgraphie RE
Revue Belge de Philclogie et D' Histoire RE
Revue Benedictine RE
Revue Biblique RE
Revue D' Ascetique et de Mystique RE
Revue D' Auvergne RE
Revue D' Histcire de l' Amerique Francaise RE
Revue D' Histoire de l' Eglise de France RF
Revue D' Histcire des Religions RE
Revue D' Histoire des Sciences et de Leurs Applications RE
Revue D' Histcire Diplcmatique RE
Revue D' Histcire Ecclesiastique RE
Revue D' Histcire Econcmique Sociale RE
Revue D' Histoire et de Philosophie Religieuses RE
Revue D' Histcire Litteraire de la France RE
Revue D' Histoire Mitteilungen RE
Revue D' Histcire Moderne et Contemporaine RE
Revue de Drcit Cancnique RE
Revue de l' Anranchin et du Pays de Granville RE
Revue de l' Art RE
Revue de l' Universite D' Ottawa RE
Revue de Litteratur Comparee RE
Revue de Metaphysiqye et de Morale RE
Revue de Philclogie, de Litterature et D' Histoire Anciennes RE
Revue de Qumran RE
Revue de Synthese RE
Revue de Theolcgie et de Philosophie RE
Revue des Etudes Armeniennes RE
Revue des Etudes Augustiniennes RE

Revue des Etudes Byzantines RE
Revue des Etudes Italiennes RE
Revue des Etudes Juives RE
Revue des Etudes Latines RE
Revue des Etudes Slaves RE
Revue des Etudes Sud-Est Europeenes RE
Revue des Sciences Humaines RE
Revue des Sciences Philosophiques et Theologiques RE
Revue des Sciences Religieuses de l' Universite de Strasbourg RE
Revue du Louvre et des Musees de France RE
Revue du Moyen Age Latina RE
Revue du Nord RE
Revue du Vivarais RE
Revue Generale RE
Revue Historique RE
Revue Historique du Droit Francais et Etranger RE
Revue Internationale de Philosophie RE
Revue Internationale des Droits de l' Antiquite RE
Revue Mabillon RE
Revue Numismatique RE
Revue Philosophique de la France et de l' Etranger RE
Revue Philosophique de Louvain RE
Revue Theologique de Louvain RE
Revue Thomiste RE
Rheinische Vierteljahrsblatter RE
Ribista Rosminiana di Filosofia e di Cultura RE
Rinascimento RE
Risorgimento RE
Rivista Biblica RE
Rivista degli Studi Orientali RE
Rivista di Archeologia Cristiana RE
Rivista di Cultura Classica e Medioevale RE
Rivista di Filologia e di Istruzione Classica RE
Rivista di Filosofia Neoscolastica RE
Rivista di Storia del Diritto Italiano RE
Rivista di Storia della Chiesa in Italia RE
Rivista di Storia e Letteratura Religiosa RE
Rivista Storica Italiana RE
Roczniki Historyczne RE
Roczniki Humanistyczne RE
Roczniki Teologiczno Kanoniczne RE
Romance Philology RE
Romania RE
Romanic Review RE
Romanische Forschungen RE

Romanische Quartalschrift fur Christliche
Alterumskunde und Kirchengeschichte RE

Romanistisches Jahrbuch RE
Romische Historische Mitteilungen RE
Romisches Jahrbuch fur Kunstgeschichte RE
Sacra Doctrina RE
Sacris Erudiri RE
Saeculum RE
Salesianum RE
Salmanticensis RE
Sapienza RE
Scandinavian Economic History Review RE
Schweizer Buchhandel RE
Schweizerische Zeitschrift fur Geschichte RE
Schweizerisches Archiv fur Volkskunde RE
Science et Esprit RE
Scottish Historical Review RE
Scriptorium RE
Scriptorium Victoriense RE
Scuola Cattolica RE
Seanchas Ard Mhacha RE
Siculorum Gymnasium RE
Sitzungsberichte der Bayerischen Akademie der
Wissenschaften RE
Sitzungsberichte der Deutschen Akademie der
Wissenschaften RE
Sitzungsberichte der Heidelberger Akademie der
Wissenschaften RE
Sitzungsberichte der Oesterreichischen Akademie
der Wissenschaften RE
Sitzungsberichte der Sachsischen Adademie der
Wissenschaften zu Leipzig RE
Slavia RE
Slavia Antiqua RE
Slavia Occidentalis RE
Social Compass RE
Societe Archeologie et Historique de Nantes
et de Loire Atlantique, Bulletin de la RE
Societe Historique et Archologique dans Le
Limbourg a Maestricht, Publications de la RE
Societes Historie et Archeologie de Paris et
de l' Ile de France, Memoires de la Federation
des RE
Sophia. Rassegna Critica di Filosofia e Storia
della Filosofia RE
Soviet Studies in History RE
Speculum RE

Spicilegium Historicum Congregationis Ssmi Redemptoris RE
Spiegel Historiael RE
Sprawozdania Z Czynnosci Wydawniczej i Posiedzen Naukoeych Oraz Kronika RE
Starinar RE
Stimmen der Zeit RE
Storia Contemporanea RE
Streeven RE
Strenna Storica Bolognese RE
Stromata RE
Studi e Materiali di Storia della Religioni RE
Studi Francescani RE
Studi Medievali RE
Studi Mediolatini e Volgari RE
Studi Romani RE
Studi Senesi RE
Studi Storici RE
Studi Storici dell' Ordine dei Servi di Maria RE
Studi Urbinati di Storia, Filosofia e Letteratura RE
Studia et Documenta Historiae et Iuris RE
Studia Hibernica RE
Studia Historica Slovaca RE
Studia Liturgica RE
Studia Missionalia RE
Studia Monastica RE
Studia Neophilologica RE
Studia Orientalia Christiana RE
Studia Picena RE
Studia Theologica RE
Studia Theologica Varsaviensia RE
Studia Zrodloznawcze RE
Studien und Mitteilungen Zur Geschichte des Benediktiner Ordens und Seiner Zweige RE
Studies in English Literature RE
Studies in Medieval and Renaissance History RE
Studies in Philology RE
Studies in the Renaissance RE
Studies on Voltaire and the XVIIIth Century RE
Studii Teologice RE
Supplement RE
Svensk Exegetisk Arsbok RE
Svensk Teologisk Kvartalskrift RE
Taxandria RE
Temenos. Studies in Comparative Religion RE
Theological Studies RE
Theologie und Glaube RE

Theologie und Philosophie RE

Theologisch Praktische Quartalschrift RE
Theologische Literaturzeitung RE
Theologische Quartalschrift RE
Theologische Revue RE
Theologische Rundschau RE
Theologische Zeitschrift RE
Thomist RE
Thought RE
Tijdschrift voor Geschiedenis RE
Tijdschrift voor Nederlandse Tall en Letterkunde RE
Tijdschrift voor Philosophie RE
Tijdschrift voor Rechtsgeschiedenis RE
Tijdschrift voor Theologie RE
Traditio RE
Transactions of the Royal Historical Society RE
Travaux et Memoires du Centre de Recherche D' Histoire et Civilisation Byzantines RE
Trierer Theologische Zeitschrift RE
Trierer Zeitschrift fur Geschichte und Kunst des Trierer Landes und Seiner Nachbargebiete RE
Trimestriel de la Societe Academique des Antiquaires de la Marinie, Bulletin RE
Umeni RE
University of Birmingham Historical Journal RE
Verdad y Vida RE
Vereeniging tot Uitgaff der Bronnen van het Oud Vaderlandsche Recht, Verslagen en Mededeelingen der RE
Verhandlugn der Sachsischen Akademie der Wissenschaften zu Leipzig, Berichte uber die RE
Verslagen en Mededeelingen der Vereeniging tot Uitgaff der Bronnen van het Oud Vaderlandsche Recht RE
Verslagen en Mededelingen van de Leiegouw RE
Vetera Christianorum RE
Vierteljahresschrift fur Kirchen und Geistesgeschichte Osteruopas, Kyrios. RE
Vierteljahrhefte fur Zeitgeschichte RE
Vierteljahrsschrift fur Literaturwissenschaft und Geistegeschechte, Deutsche RE
Vierteljahrsschrift fur Social und Wirtschaftsgeschishte RE
Vigilae Christianae RE
Vivarium RE
Vrije Fries RE
Wallraf Richartz Jahrbuch RE

Westfalen. Hefte fur Geschichte, Kunst und Volkskunde RE
Westfalische Forschungen RE
Westfalische Zeitschrift RE
Wichmann Jahrbuch fur Kirchengeschichte Im Bistum Berlin RE
Wissenschaftliche Zeitschrift der Humbolt Universitat zu Berlin RE
Wissenschaftliche Zeitschrift der Karl Marx Universitat
Re
Wissenschaftliche Zeitschrift der Universitat Rostock RE
Wurzburger Diozesangeschichtsblatter RE
Zapiski Historyczne RE
Zeitschrift der Deutschen Morgenlandischen Gesellschaft RE
Zeitschrift der Gavigny Stiftung fur Rechtsgeschichte Romanische Abteilung RE
Zeitschrift der Gesellschaft fur Schleswig Holsteinische Geschichte RE
Zeitschrift des Aacherer Geschichtsvereins RE
Zeitschrift des Bergischen Geschichtsvereins RE
Zeitschrift des Deutschen Palastina Vereins RE
Zeitschrift des Deutschen Vereins fur Kunstwisswenschaft RE
Zeitschrift fur Bayerische Kircheneschichte RE
Zeitschrift fur Bayerische Landergerchichte RE
Zeitschrift fur Bibliothekswissen und Bibliographie RE
Zeitschrift fur Celtische Philologie RE
Zeitschrift fur Deutsche Philologie RE
Zeitschrift fur Deutsches Altertum und Deutsche Literatur RE
Zeitschrift fur die Geschichte des Oberrheins RE
Zeitschrift fur die Geschichte und Altertumskunde Ermlands RE
Zeitschrift fur die Neutestamentliche Wissenschaft RE
Zeitschrift fur Franzosische Sprache und Literatur RE
Zeitschrift fur Geschichtswissenschaft RE
Zeitschrift fur Kirchengeschichte RE
Zeitschrift fur Missionwissenschaft und Religionswissenschaft RE
Zeitschrift fur Ostforschung RE
Zeitschrift fur Philosophische Forschung RE
Zeitschrift fur Religions und Geistesgeschichte RE

Zeitschrift fur Schweizerische Archaologie und
Kunstgeschichte RE
Zeitschrift fur Schweizerische Kirchengeschichte RE
Zeitschrift fur Slavische Philologie RE
Zeitschrift fur Theologie und Kirche RE
Zeszyty Naukowe Katolickiego Uniwersytetu
Lubelskiego RE
Zintralblatt fur Bublicthekswesen RE

RPI RELIGIOUS PERIODICAL INDEX

A.D. RPI
Advance RPI
Advent Christian Witness RPI
America RPI
American Benedictine Review RPI
Ave Maria RPI
Banner RPI
Baptist Bulletin RPI
Baptist Herald RPI
Baptist Leader RPI
Bible Society Record RPI
Biblical Archeologist RPI
Brethern Life and Thought RPI
Calvin Theological Journal RPI
Cathedral Age RPI
Catholic Biblical Quarterly RPI
Catholic Charities Review RPI
Catholic Historical Review RPI
Catholic Library World RPI
Catholic School Journal RPI
Catholic Worker RPI
Catholic World, the RPI
Chaplain RPI
Chicago Studies RPI
Christian Advocate RPI
Christian Bookseller RPI
Christian Century RPI
Christian Herald RPI
Christian Life RPI
Christian Ministry RPI
Christianity and Crisis RPI
Christianity Today RPI
Church Administration RPI
Church and Society RPI
Church Herald RPI
Church History RPI
Church Library Magazine RPI
Church Man RPI
Church Messenger RPI
Church Quarterly RPI
Church Theological Review RPI

Church Woman RPI
Columbia RPI
Commonweal RPI
Concern RPI
Concordia Theological Monthly RPI
Congregationalist, the RPI
Continuum RPI
Cord RPI
Credinta RPI
Criterion RPI
Critic RPI
Cross Currents RPI
Diakonia RPI
Dialog (New York) RPI
Dimensions in American Judaism RPI
Drew Gateway RPI
Duke Divinity School Review RPI
Ecumenical Review RPI
Encounter RPI
Engage RPI
Episcopal Recorder RPI
Episcopalian RPI
Eternity Magazine RPI
Eucharist RPI
Evangelical Quarterly RPI
Event RPI
Extension Magazine RPI
Faith and Forum RPI
Faith at Work RPI
Fellowship RPI
Foundations RPI
Franciscan Herald RPI
Franciscan Message RPI
Franciscan Studies RPI
Friar RPI
Friends Journal RPI
Greek Orthodox Theological Review RPI
Harvard Theological Review RPI
Herder Correspondence RPI
Historical Magazine of the Protestant Episcopal Church RPI
History of Religions RPI
Humanist RPI
International Review of Missions RPI
Interpretation RPI
Jewish Life RPI
Jewish Quarterly Review RPI
Jewish Spectator RPI

Journal for the Scientific Study of Religion RPI
Journal for Theology and the Church RPI
Journal of Biblical Literature RPI
Journal of Church and State RPI
Journal of Church Music RPI
Journal of Ecclesiastical History RPI
Journal of Ecumenical Studies RPI
Journal of Near Eastern Studies RPI
Journal of Pastoral Care RPI
Journal of Presbyterian History RPI
Journal of Religion RPI
Journal of Religion and Health RPI
Journal of Religious Thought RPI
Journal of the American Academy of Religion RPI
Judaism RPI
Katallagete RPI
Lexington Theological Quarterly RPI
Liguorian RPI
Link RPI
Liturgical Arts RPI
Logos RPI
Lutheran RPI
Lutheran Forum RPI
Lutheran Quarterly RPI
Lutheran Standard RPI
Lutheran Witness RPI
Marriage RPI
McCormick Quarterly RPI
Mennonite RPI
Mennonite Quarterly Review RPI
Messenger RPI
Methodist History RPI
Metanoia RPI
Motive RPI
Muslim World RPI
National Catholic Guidance Conference Journal RPI
New Book Review RPI
New Testament Studies RPI
New World Outlook RPI
New York (Dialog) RPI
Official News Digest RPI
One Church RPI
Orthodox Church RPI
Orthodox Life RPI
Orthodox Word RPI
Pastoral Life RPI
Pastoral Psychology RPI
Perspective RPI

Pope Speaks RPI
Presbyterian Life RPI
Presbyterian Outlook RPI
Presbyterian Survey RPI
Princeton Seminary Bulletin RPI
Quaker History RPI
Quaker Life RPI
Quarterly Review RPI
Reformed and Presbyterian World RPI
Reformed Review RPI
Religious Education RPI
Religious Studies RPI
Renewal RPI
Reporter for Conscience's Sake RPI
Review for Religious RPI
Review of Religious Research RPI
Sacred Music RPI
Self-Realization Magazine RPI
Serran RPI
Sign RPI
Sisters Today RPI
Social Action RPI
Social Justice Review RPI
Social Questions Bulletin RPI
Solia RPI
Soundings RPI
Southwestern Journal of Theology RPI
Spectrum RPI
Spiritual Life RPI
Springfielder RPI
St. Anthony Messenger RPI
St. Vladimir's Theological Quarterly RPI
Stained Glass RPI
Study Encounter RPI
Suchness RPI
Summit RPI
Tempo RPI
Theological Education RPI
Theological Studies RPI
Theology Digest RPI
Theology Today RPI
Thought RPI
Together RPI
Toledo Archdiocesan Messenger RPI
Traditio RPI
Triumph RPI
True Light RPI
Ukrainian Orthodox Work RPI

Una Sancta RPI
Union Seminary Quarterly Review RPI
Unitarian Universalist World RPI
United Evangelical Action RPI
United Synagogue Review RPI
Vital Christianity RPI
Way RPI
Westminister Theological Journal RPI
Witness RPI
Word RPI
World Order RPI
World View RPI
Worship RPI
Your Church RPI
Zygon RPI

RTA RELIGION AND THEOLOGY ABSTRACTS

Andover Newton Quarterly RTA
Archiv fur Reformationsgeschichte RTA
Australasian Catholic Record RTA
Baptist Quarterly RTA
Bibliotheca Sacra RTA
Brethern Life and Thought RTA
Cahiers de Josephologie RTA
Canadian Journal of Theology RTA
Christus RTA
Clergy Monthly RTA
Concordia Historical Institute Quarterly RTA
Concordia Theological Monthly RTA
Downside Review RTA
Evangelische Theologie RTA
Expository Times RTA
Free University Quarterly RTA
Gereformeerd Theologisch Tijdschrift RTA
Gregorianium RTA
Hartford Quarterly RTA
Harvard Theological Review RTA
Hibbert Journal RTA
Indian Journal of Theology RTA
International Review of Missions RTA
Interpretation RTA
Jewish Educator RTA
Journal of Biblical Literature RTA
Journal of Theological Studies RTA
Kerygma und Dogma RTA
Learning for Living RTA
Neue Zeitschrift fur Systematische Theologie
und Religionsphilosophie RTA
Novum Testamentum RTA
Orientalia Christiana Periodica RTA
Pastoral Psychology RTA
Response RTA
Revue de Qumran RTA
Sciences Ecclesiastiques RTA
Scottish Journal of Theology RTA
Social Compass RTA
Southwestern Journal of Theology RTA
Tarbiz RTA

Theological Studies RTA
Theologische Rundschau RTA
Theologische Zeitschrift RTA
Theology and Life RTA
Theology Today RTA
Union Seminary Quarterly Review RTA
Vetus Testamentum RTA
Westminister Theological Journal RTA
Zeitschrift fur die Alttestamentliche Wissenschaft RTA
Zeitschrift fur die Neutestamentliche Wissenschaft RTA
Zeitschrift fur Evangelische Ethik RTA
Zeitschrift fur Religions und Geistesgeschichte RTA
Zeitschrift fur Theologie und Kirche RTA

SBPI SOUTHERN BAPTIST PERIODICAL INDEX

Accent SBPI
Adult Leadership SBPI
Adult Student SBPI
Aware SBPI
Baptist History and Heritage SBPI
Baptist Men's Journal SBPI
Brotherhood Builder SBPI
Childrens Leadership SBPI
Church Administration SBPI
Church Recreation Magazine SBPI
Church Training SBPI
Collage SBPI
Commission SBPI
Contempo SBPI
Crusader SBPI
Crusader Counselor SBPI
Deacon SBPI
Dimension SBPI
Discovery SBPI
Gateway SBPI
Guide SBPI
Home Life SBPI
Home Missions SBPI
Newsletter, National Council of Churches Committee on the Church and Jewish People SBPI
Outlook SBPI
Outreach SBPI
Preschool Leadership SBPI
Probe SBPI
Proclaim SBPI
Report from the Capital SBPI
Response SBPI
Royal Service SBPI
Search SBPI
Southern Baptist Educator SBPI
Southwestern Journal of Theology SBPI
Southwestern News SBPI
Span SBPI
Spire SBPI
Start SBPI
Student SBPI

Theological Educator SBPI
Vision SBPI
Years Ahead SBPI
Youth Leadership SBPI

SISPL SUBJECT INDEX TO SELECT PERIODICAL ...

Accrediting Association of Bible Colleges Newsletter SISPL
Africa Theological Journal SISPL
American Journal of Archaeology SISPL
Andover Newton Quarterly SISPL
Andrews University Seminary Studies SISPL
Anglican Theological Review SISPL
Antiquity SISPL
Bible League Quarterly SISPL
Bible Science Newsletter SISPL
Biblical Archeologist SISPL
Biblical Viewpoint SISPL
Biola Broadcaster SISPL
Bulletin of the American Schools of Oriental Research SISPL
Buried History SISPL
Calvary Review SISPL
Central Bible Quarterly SISPL
Chicago Theological Seminary Register SISPL
Christian Graduate SISPL
Contemporary Religions in Japan SISPL
Context SISPL
Creation Research Society Quarterly SISPL
Crux SISPL
Discerner SISPL
Faith and Thought SISPL
Fides et Historici SISPL
Hearthstone SISPL
International Journal of Religious Education SISPL
Journal of Ancient Near Eastern Society of Columbia SISPL
Journal of Applied Behavorial Science SISPL
Journal of Christian Education SISPL
Journal of Linguistics SISPL
Journal of Religion in Africa SISPL
Lutheran Theological Seminary Review SISPL
Music Ministry SISPL
Notes on Translation SISPL
Occasional Bulletin SISPL
Other Side SISPL
Pastoral Counselor SISPL

...

Pensamiento Cristiano SISPL
Plain Truth SISPL
Presbyterian Journal SISPL
Review of Religion SISPL
Speculum SISPL
Themelios SISPL
Tomorrow's World SISPL
Wesleyan Studies in Religion SISPL
Weslyan Theolcgical Journal SISPL
World Archaeolcgy SISPL
World Vision SISPL

UMPI UNITED METHODIST PERIODICAL INDEX

Accent UMPI
Accent on Youth UMPI
Accion Metodista UMPI
Adult Bible Course UMPI
Adult Bible Studies UMPI
Adult Leader UMPI
Adult Teacher UMPI
Bible Lessons for Adults UMPI
Bible Lessons for Youth UMPI
Bible Teacher for Adults UMPI
Central Christian Advocate UMPI
Christian Action UMPI
Christian Adventure UMPI
Christian Faith in Life-Supplement UMPI
Church School UMPI
Circuet Rider UMPI
Classmate UMPI
Commonlife Bulletin UMPI
Concern UMPI
Epworth Notes UMPI
Explore UMPI
Explore Resource Kit UMPI
Explore Teacher's Guide UMPI
Face to Face UMPI
Five/Six UMPI
Foundation Studies in Christian Faith
Study-Selected Reading UMPI
Hi Times UMPI
Junior Hi Times UMPI
Kindergarten UMPI
Lecciones Cristianas UMPI
Mature Years UMPI
Methodist Story UMPI
Methodist Student UMPI
Methodist Teacher UMPI
Methodist Woman UMPI
Music Ministry UMPI
New Creation UMPI
New Creation Leaders Guide UMPI
New Creation Resource Packet UMPI
Nursery Days UMPI

One/Two UMPI
Planbook for Adults UMPI
Program Quarterly UMPI
Psychology for Living UMPI
Real UMPI
Real Class Guide UMPI
Real Resource Packet UMPI
Religious Book Guide UMPI
Response UMPI
Roundtable UMPI
Series (United Methodist Student) UMPI
Series (United Methodist Teacher) UMPI
Studies in Christian Living UMPI
Sunday Night UMPI
Thesis Theological Cassettes UMPI
Three/Four UMPI
Twelve/Fifteen UMPI
United Methodist Student (Series) UMPI
United Methodist Teacher (Series) UMPI
Wesley Quarterly UMPI
Workers with Youth UMPI
Youth Leader UMPI
Youth Teacher and Counselor UMPI